THE
AGAMEMNON OF AESCHYLUS

A REVISED TEXT

WITH

INTRODUCTION, VERSE TRANSLATION, AND CRITICAL NOTES

BY

J. C. LAWSON, O.B.E., M.A.

*Fellow and Tutor of Pembroke College, Cambridge,
and University Lecturer in Classics*

CAMBRIDGE
AT THE UNIVERSITY PRESS
1932

CAMBRIDGE
UNIVERSITY PRESS

University Printing House, Cambridge CB2 8BS, United Kingdom

Cambridge University Press is part of the University of Cambridge.

It furthers the University's mission by disseminating knowledge in the pursuit of education, learning and research at the highest international levels of excellence.

www.cambridge.org
Information on this title: www.cambridge.org/9781316626115

© Cambridge University Press 1932

First published 1932
First paperback edition 2016

A catalogue record for this publication is available from the British Library

ISBN 978-1-316-62611-5 Paperback

AESCHYLI
AGAMEMNON

CONTENTS

INTRODUCTION

THE PLAY'S THE THING

I<small>F</small> the function of Tragedy be paradoxical, the production of pleasure by the excitation of certain painful emotions, his function who would edit a tragic drama may be conceived and defined in simpler terms. The pity and fear excited by the story may achieve the end in view; vexation and bewilderment produced whether by a corrupt text or by the intrinsic difficulties of Greek idiom are far from pleasurable and detract from such achievement. The editor's task therefore, as I conceive it, is first to present the text, if possible, in the form in which Aeschylus wrote it or, failing that, in such form as would have given unalloyed pleasure to an audience of Aeschylus' contemporaries; and secondly to provide an English rendering faithful in all respects to the thought of the original, conservative of its general form and specific imagery, and sufficiently literal to enable the less proficient scholar to appreciate its construction and idiom. My notes are intended to subserve only these two purposes, by justifying departures from the traditional text or by explaining the emphasis and the *nuance* of a particular word or phrase.

While thus formulating and defining my own task, I would not have it thought that I am by implication criticising adversely the projects which other editors have proposed to themselves and executed. Wecklein's edition of Aeschylus is an indispensable piece of work conceived on wholly different lines. He prints lines which fail both of metre and of meaning; he provides no translation, and no commentary of his own such as might in some measure replace translation. His work was conceived as a collection of the available material for the reconstruction of the text, the variant readings of all MSS., the scholia, and the conjectural emendations of a host of scholars. The result is a monument of invaluable labour, but not a thing of beauty nor an instrument of pleasure.

Then at the other extreme we have such an edition of the

viii INTRODUCTION

Agamemnon as would Headlam's have been if he had lived to
complete it, a work comparable in conception with another un-
completed work, Neil's edition of the *Knights* of Aristophanes.
In these the commentary assumes a larger importance than I
seek to give to mine. It illumines the dark places of the text,
without doubt; but it tends to lavish such wealth of illumination
as may dazzle and distract. The text has become in some measure
a focus of wide erudition and an occasion of scholarly discourse;
an alien pleasure is infused, fortifying, it may be, or diluting, but
certainly varying, the pleasure proper to pure drama.

Intermediate between these extremes in intention and scope
lies Verrall's edition; for his whole interest is in Aeschylus' story
and in the manner in which it is told. But in execution it is an
edition *sui generis* and not comparable with those of other editors
who have set before themselves the same aim,—that of lucid
interpretation and strictly relevant comment. For in analysing
the story Verrall found himself confronted with so wilful and
glaring a discrepancy, as he regarded it, that he argued the whole
plot to have been totally misconceived from Byzantine times
onward. This discrepancy is one of time; the herald and, after
him, Agamemnon are made to arrive within an hour or two of
the sighting of the beacon, whereas the passage from Troy to
Argos, even without a storm to hinder the ship, would necessarily
occupy some days.[1] Verrall builds up on the foundation of this
discrepancy a theory that Aeschylus' audience were familiar with
a version of the story in which Aegisthus, somewhere in the
neighbourhood but not in Argos, was having a watch kept for
Agamemnon's return; that on Agamemnon's arrival off the coast
Aegisthus caused a beacon to be lighted on Mount Arachnaeum as
a signal to Clytemnestra and his partisans in the city; and that
a long-prepared political intrigue, supported largely by the young

---

[1] Verrall, I should note, postulates "several weeks." No one will concede so
large an assumption. εἰ δέ κεν εὐπλοίην δώῃ κλυτὸς ἐννοσίγαιος | ἤματί κε τριτάτῳ Φθίην
ἐρίβωλον ἱκοίμην (*Iliad* ix. 362). Two days to Phthia; not more than four to Argos
even with a storm on one night. Thus Homer: but in the fifth century B.C.
greater speeds were attained. According to Xenophon (*Hell.* II. i. 30) Theo-
pompus of Miletus in 405 B.C. brought the news of the victory of Aegospotami
from the Hellespont to Sparta "on the third day" (τριταῖος).

men in the city who had grown up during the ten years' war, and
suspected but hardly combated by the Elders of the city, then
took its normal course—the murder of the king and the pro-
clamation of Aegisthus as tyrant. Clytemnestra's graphic description of the chain of beacons therefore, so argues Verrall, was
designed only to throw dust in the eyes of the Elders; she knew
that Agamemnon had already reached the coast; they were to
picture him still at Troy,—her next speech elaborates that
picture,—and so believing were to be lulled into a false security,
not knowing that the critical hour was near.

To me the whole structure of this theory appears fantastic,
and its foundation insecure.

First let it be noted that there is no inherent improbability in
the use of beacons for signalling by the route which Clytemnestra
names. The longest stage, from Athos to North Euboea, is about
a hundred miles; and I myself have seen from a boat in the
latitude of N. Euboea the snow on the peak of Athos flushed by
the setting sun. A beacon therefore at night on Athos would be
easily seen in the clearer atmosphere, some thousands of feet above
sea-level, by watchers on the heights of Euboea.

Verrall grants that this would be possible "on a clear night,"
and that seafaring people like the Athenians knew the distances
involved "and their relation to the purpose of a beacon." But,
he argues, they would have known too that the use of the beacons
might "be defeated by clouds at any point in a traject of one
hundred miles." And so, he concludes, "the statement that a
beacon-signal was transmitted in the midst of a storm from Athos
to Euboea stood to the knowledge and habits of Athens then in
much the same relation as the statement that a steamer ran across
the Atlantic in one day would stand to the knowledge and habits
of Liverpool now."[1]

Granted: but no such statement is ever made in the play.
Clytemnestra certainly makes, and the Chorus accept, the assumption that there has been no delay in the transmission of the news
by her chain of beacons, and that the fall of Troy may therefore
have taken place in the night just past. But, when that assump-

[1] Introd. p. xxii (1904 Edit.)

tion is made, no one yet knows that there has been a storm in the
Aegean: that information is brought by the herald afterwards.
We have been led rather by the watchman at the opening to
picture the night as clear, with the stars, which he has conned
so often, visible overhead. Had the night been thick, and had
Clytemnestra's whole account of the beacons been, as Verrall
supposes, a mere fabrication designed to mislead the Chorus,
then indeed her inventive powers would hardly deserve admiration
and the gullibility of the Chorus would be incredible. Verrall, in
trying to fasten upon Clytemnestra a statement which she never
makes, incidentally represents the Chorus as dolts.

But if the assumption that Troy had been taken overnight
presents no difficulty at this stage of the play, what of that
greater discrepancy which manifests itself, according to Verrall,
at a later stage—the shortness of the interval between the sighting
of the beacon and the arrival of the herald? It is time to turn to
the crucial passage (vv. 278–9). The question asked by the
Chorus is

ποίου χρόνου δὲ καὶ πεπόρθηται πόλις;

not πότε ἐπορθήθη, and Clytemnestra's answer is

τῆς νῦν τεκούσης φῶς τόδ᾽ εὐφρόνης λέγω,

not τῇ νῦν τεκούσῃ. With this point of idiom I have dealt in
my note on the passage, and I believe that I am right in rendering
the lines as in my translation:

Cho. Since when in sooth hath Ilium lain despoiled?
Cly. Since that same night, I say, whence sprang this dawn.

Clytemnestra's answer, that is, is conditioned by the knowledge
she possesses; the beacon-message had been received just before
dawn; she can safely therefore answer that Troy has been in
Achaean hands 'since this past night.' And as soon as the next
question was put, and elicited the information that a beacon-signal
was her source of knowledge, it must immediately have been
manifest to the Chorus (and to an Athenian audience) that all
she knew was the fact, and not the precise date, of the fall of Troy:
dates cannot be signalled by bonfires.

Aeschylus then did not mislead his audience at this point; the
message transmitted by beacons during the night was evidence

that Troy had been in the hands of the Argives as from that
night,—but there was no evidence one way or the other as to
whether it had been in their hands from an earlier date. Clytemnestra, it is true, in her excitement assumes quite naturally in
the two speeches which follow that her train of beacons has been
operated successfully and without delay; but this quite obviously is
surmise only. She surmises all the detail of the kindling of the
beacons; she knows only the route. She surmises afterwards all the
happenings in the captured city; she knows nothing of them. She is
here surmising similarly the date; she knows only the fact of Troy's
fall. And what of the Chorus? They accept at first Clytemnestra's
πιστὰ τεκμήρια (v. 352) and her surmises, date and all. "Hail,
Zeus our king, hail, gladdening night, that hast won for our host
great glories,..."—so begins their ode of joy and thanksgiving. But
how does it end? With suggestions (vv. 475—487) that it may be
a false rumour after all; that it would be childish to be too much
elated over a beacon-signal; that a woman is too ready to believe
what she hopes. And immediately thereafter, when the herald is
sighted, the train of thought is still the same: "soon we shall know
whether the beacon-message is true..."—*whether* Troy is fallen,
not *when* it fell.

Yes, the Chorus—and an Athenian audience—knew enough
about the transmission of messages by beacons to be chary of
accepting them till confirmation was received. Delay in transmission was a small matter; there was a graver risk of erroneous
transmission; any one beacon in the whole chain might be kindled
accidentally or mistakenly. Nothing is easier on a dark night
than to mistake a small fire lit by some shepherd at a few miles
distance for a larger fire which you are hoping to see lit at some
greater distance. During the War I used fires on occasion at
night for passing messages in the Aegean, and can answer for
that from my own experience. The Chorus were well justified in
revising their hasty acceptance of Clytemnestra's assurance and
in questioning whether indeed Troy had fallen.

And, once reassured by the herald, what further interest had
they in the beacon-message? If they had given it another thought,
they would have said to themselves, "Obviously it was delayed in

transmission; at this time of year (ἀμφὶ Πλειάδων δύσιν, v. 826)
a continuance of clear and cloudless nights is not to be expected";
and when the herald went on to describe the great storm which
had wrecked the fleet, they would have known that visibility had
in fact been bad. But would they even have given the matter a
thought? The alternating excitements which follow—joy in the
victory achieved, distress at the calamity which had befallen
the returning fleet, joy again at the entry of Agamemnon, dismay
caused by the tension of the scene between him and Clytemnestra,
pity excited by Cassandra and perplexity induced by her prophecies, horror at the final catastrophe—would not these emotions
automatically exclude from their minds the paltry question how
the beacon-message came to be delayed in transmission? Indeed,
had they even wished to investigate the matter, there was no
one whom they could ask; the herald obviously would know no
more about the beacons than they.

I conclude then that there is no glaring discrepancy in the story
such as Verrall believed himself to have exposed, and holding, as
I do, that his whole theory of the plot is built on the sands, I need
not examine further its superstructure. But on the same grounds
on which I reject Verrall's theory I reject also Headlam's counter-
theory that there was a break in the play after the second chorus
(at v. 487) and that an interval lasting some days is there postu-
lated. That chorus ends with expressions of incredulity concerning
the beacon-message, and the speech immediately following (which
Headlam, be it noted, attributes also to the Chorus) continues
in the same vein:

> τάχ᾽ εἰσόμεσθα λαμπάδων...παραλλαγάς,
> εἴτ᾽ οὖν ἀληθεῖς εἴτ᾽ ὀνειράτων δίκην
> τερπνὸν τόδ᾽ ἐλθὸν φῶς ἐφήλωσεν φρένας.

Here is obvious continuity of thought, and I cannot believe that
Aeschylus intended his Chorus to continue their talk after an
interval of some days as if it had never been interrupted. Headlam,
I think, took Verrall's criticism of the plot too seriously. I regard
Verrall's Introduction as an amazing *tour de force* in the perversion
of a simple story which presents no real difficulty and involves no
real discrepancy.

But when I reject the theory developed in Verrall's Introduction I am bound also to reject many of the readings and many of the renderings which he accepts or proposes, as being coloured or, as I regard it, discoloured by his preconceived theory. I will give but two examples out of many available. After verse 1520 the MSS. give the words οὔτ' ἀνελεύθερον οἶμαι θάνατον τῷδε γενέσθαι, which most editors strike out as an interpolation arising from a marginal comment by some rather foolish annotator. Verrall retains it and assigns it to "one of the queen's party," who, "indignant at the repeated accusation of setting up a τυραννίς" (for Verrall extracts that meaning from ἀνελεύθερον κοίταν) "begins to answer the elders on this point, *This man, methinks, is not the victim of despotism, nor—*" but is then interrupted by Clytemnestra, "who is in no mood for such a discussion." The second example shall be from the very end of the play. Verrall's own summary of the plot ends thus: "This is too much for the friends of the king" (i.e. the Chorus). "Stung by their taunts Aegisthus calls on his ruffians to commence a massacre, when the queen, with hypocritical clemency, interposes to prevent an impolitic cruelty which might yet have endangered the success. ' Less,' she says, 'than blood-shed will serve the occasion'(*vv.* 1654–1664). Accordingly the elders are led away to imprisonment; and with this final triumph of Clytemnestra the scene comes to an end." Turn now to the admittedly corrupt lines (1657–8) on which the suggestion of imprisonment is based. Verrall in his text merely reproduces the MSS.:

στείχετε δ' οἱ γέροντες πρὸς δόμους πεπρωμένους τούσδε
πρὶν παθεῖν ἔρξαντες καιρόν· χρῆν τάδ' ὡς ἐπράξαμεν.

And here is his note thereon: "1657–58 are beyond restoration: ἔρξαντα g, h: M probably had ἔρξαντας, as Mr Housman infers, but it is doubtful whether even this ἔρξαντας, or the word which it represents, is from ἔρδω, ῥέζω or from εἴργω. The general sense may be

στείχετ' ἤδη τοὺς γέροντας πρὸς δόμους πεπρωμένους
πρὶν παθεῖν ἔρξοντες· ἀρκεῖν χρῆν τάδ' ὡς ἐπράξαμεν,

'go at once and take them to prison before they come to harm; we should have been content with what was done,' an order addressed to her attendants and spoken as if she would gladly save the elders from their own folly. The expression δόμους πεπρωμένους, *destined dwelling-place*, is perhaps not inapplicable to a prison. All however is uncertain." This, on Verrall's own showing, is weak evidence on which to state that the play ends with the incarceration of the Elders, and weak evidence on which to impute to Clytemnestra 'hypocritical clemency.'

Indeed I judge the presentment of Clytemnestra very differently. From the moment when she speaks the lines (1372–3)

πολλῶν πάροιθεν καιρίως εἰρημένων
τἀναντί' εἰπεῖν οὐκ ἐπαισχυνθήσομαι

up to the end of the play, I can discern no trace of hypocrisy in her character. There is hatred still and vindictiveness—even towards the dead; but there is grandeur and dignity and genuine conviction in her claim to be the minister of Justice. Even the Chorus are shaken in their first condemnation of her as a murderess; δύσμαχα δ' ἐστὶ κρῖναι, they confess (v. 1561); and then, when Aegisthus at length appears, the contrast between him and the queen regains for her in some measure the respect or even admiration of the audience. The very lines which Verrall quotes as evidence of her 'hypocritical clemency' are (whether in the form in which Headlam restores them or in that which I have suggested in preference) the best evidence of her true queenliness:

στείχετ', αἰδοῖοι γέροντες, πρὸς δόμους, Πεπρωμένης,
πρὶν παθεῖν, στέρξαντες οὖρον· χρῆν τάδ' ὡς ἐπράξαμεν.

"Ye reverend signors, get you to your homes;
Tempt not your fate, but go your way resigned
To Destiny, howe'er she blow; we wrought
As she ordained..."

There is nothing here but courtesy and dignity; and it is not until the Elders have filed out, in obedience to her, though still with defiance and abuse of Aegisthus,—it is not till then that she turns to Aegisthus and by a word of quiet contempt for the Elders' 'feeble snarling' pacifies Aegisthus too.

Though then I set before me the same simple object as Verrall, namely the elucidation of the play and nothing more, the execution of my purpose, seeing that I reject *in toto* his theory of the

plot, will inevitably be widely different. And when I approach
the reconstruction of the text, there too I find that my opinion
is directly opposed to his. "Continual study," he writes in his
Preface (p. viii, 1904 edition), "strengthens my conviction on
one not unimportant point in relation to Aeschylus, the substantial
integrity of the text...Although this edition adheres more closely
to the MSS. than its predecessors in modern times, my revision,
were I to revise it now, would tend rather to closer adhesion than
the other way." My own judgement, based also, I may venture
to claim, on long-continued study, is the reverse; I find every
justification for the opinion pronounced by Sidgwick[1]: "quam-
quam enim CCCL iam annos (usque a Turnebo Robortello Victorio)
doctorum labore arte iudicio Aeschyli textus indies fit correctior,
ea tamen vel optimi libri est corruptio, ut permulta hodie restare
sit fatendum quae neque recte tradita neque coniectura adhuc
fuerint sanata." And the verdict of Wilamowitz-Moellendorff is, in
its special bearing upon the *Agamemnon*, of even greater severity :
"ut summam faciamus: Choephoros et Supplices uni deberi Mediceo dudum constat; Agamemnonis et Eumenidum est quidem
altera memoria, sed adeo corrupta, ut exigui usus sit; itaque
Agamemnonis ea pars, quam deficiente Mediceo haec sola tradit,
tam incerto nititur fundamento, ut aperta damna coniciendo
reparari vix possint, alia ne animadvertantur quidem."[2] Indeed
when I bear in mind the fact that these last words of Wilamowitz-
Moellendorff apply to the whole of the *Agamemnon* with the
exception of lines 1–310 and 1067–1159, I feel that there is little
cause for apology even if my estimate of the number of passages
'neque recte tradita neque coniectura adhuc sanata' is, as my
tabula lectionum will show, somewhat higher than Sidgwick's.

It is rather my attempt to restore to readable condition a text
so admittedly corrupt that may appear to savour of the pre-
sumptuous. Had I been invited, say twenty years ago, to produce
a new edition of the *Agamemnon*, I should certainly have hesi-
tated, probably refused. I should have said to myself, "Here is
a play which has been studied, criticised, and edited as thoroughly

---

[1] Sidgwick, *Aeschyli Tragoediae, Praefatio ad init.*
[2] Wilamowitz-Moellendorff, *Aeschyli Tragoediae*, Introd. p. xxii.

as any that is extant. Here in this last century alone are the names of Hermann, Blomfield, Klausen, Enger, Karsten, Schneidewin, Davies, Kennedy, Paley, Wecklein, Weil, Verrall, and Headlam—and how many other equal or lesser luminaries?—closely associated with the criticism and elucidation of this text. What hope can I have of adding to the results of their labours anything of such note or value as will justify a new edition?"

But this volume has not come into being as the outcome of any such invitation. It has rather grown up of its own accord. The *Agamemnon* has always been among my favourite plays. I have lectured on it many times. My criticisms and my notes have accumulated and, I hope, matured. My translation has been written and re-written at intervals during a number of years. If I am bold now in risking comparison with that list of great scholars, I have at any rate not been hasty; and if my conception of an editor's functions is more adventurous than some would approve, it has at any rate been fully considered. Not least among Verrall's merits as a scholar, in my esteem, was the fact that he had the courage of his convictions; and if his convictions provoked a measure of friendly controversy, what of it? Such controversy is not detrimental to classical learning but may θείᾳ τύχῃ be a stimulus.

It is in that spirit that I would commit and commend to the mercies of my critics this experiment.

What then is my conception of an editor's duties in his treatment of the text? In general terms, as I have already said, to present the text, if possible, in the form in which Aeschylus wrote it—all will agree so far—or, failing that, in such form as would have given unalloyed pleasure to an audience of Aeschylus' contemporaries. It is in the execution of the second part of this project that the editor's troubles lie. In an extreme case such as occurs in *vv.* 1324-5, where the MSS. give

$$\text{τοῖς ἐμοῖς τιμαόροις}$$
$$\text{ἐχθροῖς φονεῦσι τοῖς ἐμοῖς τίνειν ὁμοῦ,}$$

even the most conservative of critics may condone the action of an editor who declines to print a meaningless text and supplies in its place something which, if only because it makes sense, is

superior to the reading of the MSS.; nor should it be difficult
in such a case to devise a line which would not have offended an
Athenian audience. But where there is a divergence of view
among scholars, some maintaining that the traditional text is
tenable and others denying it, there at once the editor exposes
himself to attack if he introduce any emendation.

But, apart from this definition of my purpose, let me state a
little more explicitly the position which I take, first as regards
textual criticism in general, and secondly as regards the textual
criticism of the *Agamemnon* in particular.

In the course of some thirty years of teaching I have found
myself gradually more convinced that editors are apt to err on
the side of conservatism. And there are, I think, two very human
reasons for this. First there is our natural disinclination to pit
our personal judgements against the authority of the MSS. except
where there is some quite obvious error, a defect of metre or of
elementary grammar, patent to every reader. An emendation
based on bolder criticism will perhaps be admitted to the text if
a Hermann or a Porson can be named as responsible for it; but
otherwise there is a tendency, I think, τὰ ἀκίνητα μὴ κινεῖν and
to dedicate a greater ingenuity to justifying a dubious text than
would be needed for emending it. Ingenuity in defending the indefensible appears to me to have been the last infirmity of not
a few scholarly minds. And the second reason for this conservative tendency may be sheer familiarity with the traditional text.
Just as a choir chants unperturbedly, "Or ever your pots be
made hot with thorns, so let indignation vex him, even as a
thing that is raw," so some phrase of a Greek chorus to which
we are inured may strike on our ears with so accustomed a sound
that we no longer question its sense. In more than one passage
of the *Agamemnon* it was not until I was faced with the difficulty
of translating it into coherent English that I realised to the full
its obscurity or irrelevance.

Passing next to the particular text with which I am now
concerned, I ask myself first, "How reliable are the manuscripts?"
Here, I assume, the general trend of editors' opinion may be
accepted. Sidgwick, whose text is of a moderately conservative

type, either indicates some loss or corruption, or admits some specific correction, at roughly three hundred and sixty points; and if my own text, which is not conservative, would make the figure about ten per cent. higher, there is still no very substantial difference in our estimate of the manuscripts' reliability. An average of one error, either large or small, in every four or five lines of the play represents the measure of the accumulated inaccuracies of the copyists.

The divergence of our views is concerned rather with the latitude of criticism and emendation which an editor may exercise in dealing with such manuscripts. Sidgwick[1] estimated his duties thus,—"ut...ubi omnes (codices) viderentur errare, optimis coniecturis ita uterer ut certiora modo nec longius a libris aberrantia in textum asciscerem, probabilia in apparatu critico commendarem, cetera quamvis ingeniosa omitterem."

Now I am not criticising here Sidgwick's execution of his task; he allowed himself, I should say, a little more latitude than this quotation would suggest; I am criticising merely the typically conservative policy which he enunciated. For what in effect is the principle advocated? If the words "certiora nec longius a libris aberrantia" mean anything, they mean this,—that the probability of a conjecture is to be tested by the *ductus literarum* only. Firstly, that is, there would be no diagnosis of the malady from which the text in a given passage was suffering: the primary question whether an erroneous reading is due to the incorporation of a gloss or to a misreading of the true text would not be considered. And, secondly, any operation performed would be only of the mildest character: indeed it would amount to little more than such manicure as will restore orthography and such pedicure as will remove superficial deformities of metre. The editor who follows Sidgwick's policy will not account himself a surgeon. Rather he will treat the emendations offered by others as a number of exhibits which he has to classify and to judge by a single criterion; he will classify them as petty, medium, or large, in terms of their deviation from what the scribe erroneously wrote; and having so classified them he will adjudge prizes to the petty, award

[1] *loc. cit.*

(in a footnote) an honourable mention to the medium, and disqualify the large,—with the fantastic result that the place of honour, a place in his text, will be shared by minor corrections and major corruptions. Larger emendations, which, just because the traditional text of a given passage is gravely corrupt, deviate more widely from it, may, it is admitted, be 'quamvis ingeniosa'; syntax, idiom, balance of thought, relevance of dialogue, may clamour for their adoption; but no: if the scribe has made a blunder of the first magnitude, *stet*!

Let me propound an example. At *vv.* 559—562 the MSS. give us:

> εὐναὶ γὰρ ἦσαν δαΐων πρὸς τείχεσιν·
> ἐξ οὐρανοῦ γὰρ κἀπὸ γῆς λειμώνιαι
> δρόσοι κατεψέκαζον, ἔμπεδον σίνος
> ἐσθημάτων, τιθέντες ἔνθηρον τρίχα.

The point with which I am here concerned is the masculine τιθέντες following on the feminine δρόσοι, and I choose this example because it involves a matter not of literary judgement, which may vary, but of grammatical fact, which is constant. "The masculine participle τιθέντες," says Paley, "seems best explained on the view of most commentators, that he (Aeschylus) was thinking of ὄμβροι ἐξ οὐρανοῦ rather than δρόσοι ἀπὸ γῆς," and both Verrall and Headlam concur in this view. Are we to infer that an Athenian audience, on hearing the word τιθέντες, cast back in their minds to ἐξ οὐρανοῦ, while the actor continued to speak his lines, and whispered to themselves or their neighbours ὑπακουστέον τὸ 'ὄμβροι'? I distrust these *subaudienda*. Yet these same editors, or some of them, are offended by ἐξ οὐρανοῦ γάρ. The γάρ, they say, is illogical, and they replace it on Pearson's suggestion by δέ. Why strain at a gnat and swallow a camel? Or why indeed swallow this camel at all? If ἐξ οὐρανοῦ γάρ is illogical in the text, it may still be logical as a gloss, and that gloss may have ousted that which τιθέντες presupposes, the nominative masculine of some substantive. In other words one emendation may cure both defects of the passage, the logical and the grammatical. I suggest therefore that ἐξ οὐρανοῦ γάρ is a gloss which has ousted ὄμβροι δὲ δῖοι, and that δῖοι was the word to which that marginal note was originally affixed.

Suppose then that an editor who accepts the principle stated by Sidgwick is faced here with a choice between writing δὲ in place of γὰρ and ὄμβροι δὲ δῖοι in place of ἐξ οὐρανοῦ γάρ. Which will he adopt? If he be true to his principle he must prefer the smaller change; "a first-class emendation," he will say, "fairly to be classed among 'certiora nec longius a libris aberrantia'; for other instances of the same corruption see Porson on *Med.* 34, 1083": while as regards the bolder suggestion he will murmur perhaps "ingeniosum" (if I may be pardoned in assuming this much of compliment) "sed longius a libris aberrans," and so murmuring will incorporate in his text the minor emendation, and will leave as an example of Aeschylus' peculiar style the participle τιθέντες in disaccord with its subject δρόσοι.

To such a principle then I cannot subscribe; the integrity of the manuscripts does not appear to me such as to counsel so conservative a policy. And in defence of my more radical treatment of many passages which have long presented difficulties and excited suspicion (together with just a few in which I seem to myself to find new cause for suspicion) I will adventure the thesis that the textual criticism of a great masterpiece, given an equal degree of integrity or corruption in the MSS., should theoretically be undertaken with greater assurance than that of some second-rate production.

Socrates, in a famous passage of the *Phaedo* (97 c, d), depicts the delight with which he first heard Anaxagoras' conception of mind as the force which orders all things and is the cause of all things. "I assumed," he says, "that, if it is mind which orders things, it must order them collectively and dispose them severally in whatever is the best way; if therefore a man should wish to ascertain why each thing is produced or perishes or exists in a particular way, all he need discover is in what way it is best for that thing to exist or be affected or act; and that on this reckoning a man had nothing else to do but to enquire, with regard both to mind and to the rest of creation, what was best and finest." Similarly I hold that in this play the master-mind of Aeschylus so dealt with its creations as to order them collectively and dispose them severally in the best possible way; and that the textual critic

(the ideal one, *bien entendu*), if a doubt should arise as to the
authenticity of the text, would have nothing else to do but to
enquire what reading or arrangement was best and finest; whereas,
if he were dealing with an author of lesser genius, he might with
justice say, 'This is inferior work, but not so far below the author's
general level as to provoke suspicion.'

"Nothing else to do"! There is abundant irony in that phrase.
The principle may be admirable, but the application of it by any
other than a very Socrates among critics, how arduous and how
controversial! Or must I first defend the principle itself? Very
briefly perhaps.

When Aeschylus composed the *Agamemnon*, he was in the full
maturity of his power and experience as a playwright. The
conditions of production were such that every phrase of a play
had to be immediately intelligible as it was spoken, or, harder
still, as it was sung, at the first hearing. The audience, whose
general education had been based on Homer and on the early lyric
poets, was in the highest degree sensitive and critical. And finally
that audience having heard this play under those conditions
awarded Aeschylus the prize.

Those are the undisputed facts: what is the inference from
them? This at any rate, I suppose,—that the Athenian audience
did not find the play as they heard it so full of obscurities or
irrelevancies as we find it in its traditional form. But, it may be
argued, this is our fault, not the fault of our text. To that
argument there can of course be no final answer; but for my own
part I do not so disparage the classical learning of the past or of
the present as to hold that phrases which were lucid at the first
hearing to an Athenian audience would at all frequently have
remained a source of perplexity to the generations of scholars who
have studied them at leisure from the time when the first scholia
on them were written down to the present day. When therefore
I find a given passage annotated from the earliest days and sub-
jected to varying explanations and varying emendations by one
critic after another, I incline generally to the opinion that their
chorus of dissatisfaction indicates a corrupt passage, and that
emendation and not explanation is required.

There then is the principle which I adopt, and my justification of it. What of its application? Only the wisdom of Socrates, as I have said, would be entitled to pronounce on that which is absolutely 'best and finest'; the ordinary textual critic must be content to propose that which on mature consideration he deems 'better and finer' than a text which he believes corrupt. But he need not abandon his principles because in practice he fails to live up to them. If 'the best and finest' constitute an ideal objective which he cannot hope to reach, yet 'the better and finer' represents a nearer approach thereto than the bad and ugly. If he cannot hope to determine what Aeschylus must have written, he will do better to print what Aeschylus may or might have written than what he is convinced Aeschylus did not write.

Indeed the application of the principle in its negative aspect—in the sense, that is, in which 'the choice of the better' involves 'the rejection of the worse'—will provoke in many cases little or no controversy. A number of passages of the *Agamemnon* are by universal or almost universal suffrage condemned as corrupt; in others, though some champions of the MS. text are found, yet the very divergence of the interpretations which they offer may, as I have said, be used as an argument that those passages as they now stand would have mystified an Athenian audience too. In all such cases 'the rejection of the worse' will involve me in no censure. The few passages in which I have relied on my own judgement in wishing to eject what previous editors have admitted to the text cannot be reviewed collectively in an introduction but are dealt with individually in my notes.

It is in my notes too and individually that I must deal with the positive emendations which I accept from others or propose myself. But it may be convenient that I should state here how far I have gone in pursuance of my aim and in compliance with the principle which I have advocated. That aim is to present the text in such form as would have given unalloyed pleasure to an audience of Aeschylus' contemporaries,—a text which now too may be read with pleasure and without pause, a clean text, that is, free from obelisks which stigmatize phrases as corrupt and from brackets which intern words as alien and suspect. And the principle which I advocate is, in its negative aspect, that we should not accept as Aeschylean, in a play produced in the maturity of his genius, obscurities and irrelevancies unbecoming a masterpiece, and, in its positive aspect, that we should for the same reason attribute to him only the best and finest, or at any rate the better and the finer estimated to the best of our own very fallible judgements.

Here then is a brief summary of the deviations from the text of the MSS. which this conception of an editor's task has led me to make. I have judged that text faulty in lesser or greater degree at about four hundred points,—a figure a little in excess, as I have said, of Sidgwick's estimate. I have accepted at these points about three hundred emendations proposed by others, and have added to them about a hundred suggestions of my own,—an average exceeding one in every twenty lines,—but very unevenly distributed; for, as regards the iambics at any rate, I consider that the latter part of the play has sustained more textual damage than the earlier part. These emendations of my own include the complete reconstruction of two lines admittedly corrupt (*vv.* 1172 and 1325) in a different sense from that which the *débris* in the MSS. would at first suggest; the excision of lines at three points (after *vv.* 1261, 1274, and 1305) as being inferior variants wrongly incorporated in the text side by side with the genuine version; the insertion of complete, though as it happens short, lines (after *vv.* 794 and 1005) to fill acknowledged gaps; several transpositions, as of *vv.* 968, 1230, 1312–13, and 1649, in addition to the interchange of two speeches of the Chorus (*viz.* 1625–7 and 1643–8) on which I propose to touch later; the attribution to the Greek language of six words not elsewhere found,—ἐγκαταπνεύει (*v.* 105), ἀγελακτόνου (*v.* 718), χραντήριον (*v.* 1092), θράγματα (*v.* 1166), φόνευτρα (*v.* 1325), ἀγκυλοτοίχου (*v.* 1539),—and of two forms equally unknown, ἐπεῦκτο (*v.* 288) and ἀκτήνασα as aorist participle of the rare word ἀκταίνω (*v.* 1230); the vindication of five more words as classical,— λαγίναν (*v.* 119) as the accusative of a substantive λαγίνης known only as a Byzantine by-form of λαγῶς,—ἀόπτοις (*v.* 141) in the active sense of 'sightless,' the word in its passive sense 'unseen' being ascribed by Harpocration and others to Antiphon, —προβουλευτάς (v. 386), another word known otherwise only in Byzantine Greek,—ἐριφύλλους (v. 697), recorded by Hesychius, —and ἄμηνιν (v. 1450) used by Josephus; and the consequent exclusion from the Greek language of the harmless ἀεξιφύλλους (v. 697) and the monstrous προβουλόπαις (v. 386).

These then are my major aberrations, and in my notes will be found the pleas by which I seek to justify them. I must leave it to my critics to judge whether and where I have achieved in any degree my purpose of choosing the best.

Yet I would add just one word. 'The best' has many meanings; there is the best metrically, the best grammatically, the best logically, and the best in the literary or dramatic sense. And the degree of certainty or probability attainable varies widely with these several meanings. Metrically that which does not scan correctly is bad, and that which does scan correctly is good; there we are all agreed, and if by the change of διά into διαί the requisite metre is restored, we all make the correction in complete assurance that it is right. Logically again there are simple cases in which no one would hesitate; if in a dialogue the MSS. should accidentally invert the order of question and answer, we should all agree that answer preceding question is logically bad, and should transpose the lines accordingly; but there will be more debatable cases in which such transposition is a matter less of logical necessity than of literary effect. Grammatically,—for my own part here again I should say that in simple cases we might be certain what was best; βλαβέντα (v. 120) in would-be agreement with λαγίναν γένναν and τιθέντες (v. 562) in would-be agreement with δρόσοι are in my view grammatically bad, and 'the best' seems to me unprocurable by any expedient other than that of finding masculine substantives with which they may agree; but, inasmuch as the existing text in both passages has had its defenders, I must classify the grammatically best as less certain than the metrically best. And finally the best in the literary and dramatic sense,—who shall be qualified to pronounce judgement there? Metre has rules, logic has rules, grammar has rules, but the canons of literary taste and dramatic propriety are hard to formulate and hard to apply. So be it; if τὸ ἄριστον καὶ τὸ βέλτιστον is beyond attainment, the editor can but do his own best.

Yet faint hope does not excuse faint heart; and even where the traditional text has not hitherto fallen under any general suspicion, I have occasionally ventured to suggest that it falls so far short of the best as to require reconstruction.

I select as my example a proposed interchange in position of two short speeches of the Chorus (*vv.* 1625–7 and 1643–8). A transposition will best serve the purpose of illustrating my views for three reasons. First, whereas in cases of ordinary verbal corruption there may be a dozen or more emendations offered from which to choose, in the case of a proposed transposition the issue is simpler; either the existing position of the lines or the proposed new position is presumably right; no third alternative position is likely to be claimed for them. Secondly, any transposition may involve the choice of what is 'best' in more than one sense of that word, and this particular instance does so. Thirdly, no other type of emendation could illustrate so aptly the Socratic principle that the lines under consideration should be ordered collectively and disposed severally in the best possible way.

The passage affected as a whole is that in which occurs the altercation between the Chorus and Aegisthus (*vv.* 1612–1653). In what way then do I claim that the several speeches composing the passage are not ordered collectively for the best? In this: the passage opens with Αἴγισθ᾽, ὑβρίζειν ἐν κακοῖσιν οὐ σέβω, and ends not merely with verbal ὕβρις but with a challenge to fight. I argue therefore that it would be dramatically best for the Chorus, provoked by Aegisthus, to be worked up stage by stage from dignified rebuke at the outset to the fighting mood in which they finish. But what do I find? The most abusive word which they flung at him, γύναι, forms the opening not of their last speech before swords are drawn, but of their second speech, and follows immediately upon their expressed intention of refraining from ὕβρις. On the other hand, if we make the interchange which I propose, we obtain thereby a sequence of speeches on the part of the Chorus which I should characterize thus: (1) Αἴγισθ', ὑβρίζειν..., dignified rebuke, and warning of punishment by the people; (2) τί δὴ τὸν ἄνδρα τόνδ' ἀπὸ ψυχῆς κακῆς οὐκ αὐτὸς ἠνάριζες..., expostulation, and prayer that Orestes may return and take vengeance; (3) ὡς δὴ σύ μοι τύραννος Ἀργείων ἔσει..., indignant protest that one who had lacked the courage to slay Agamemnon with his own hand should think now to usurp his place; (4) γύναι..., the last insult.

And what of the two speeches to be interchanged? Are they disposed severally in the MSS. in the best way?

The first (in the accepted order) runs:

> γύναι, σὺ τοὺς ἥκοντας ἐκ μάχης νέον
> οἰκουρὸς εὐνὴν ἀνδρὸς αἰσχύνων ἅμα
> ἀνδρὶ στρατηγῷ τόνδ' ἐβούλευσας μόρον;

Criticism here is easy. The sentence contains a redundant ungoverned accusative in the first line, so that both grammatically and logically it falls a good deal short of the best. True, some editors accept Wieseler's μένων in place of νέον, and so procure at any rate correct syntax; but μένων τοὺς ἥκοντας, 'while you were waiting for those who have now come,' seems to me a little cumbrous in expression, and in any case an alternative remedy which leaves νέον unaltered may be considered. Let me present the lines with a different punctuation:

> γύναι, σὺ τοὺς ἥκοντας ἐκ μάχης νέον;
> οἰκουρὸς εὐνὴν ἀνδρὸς αἰσχύνων ἅμα
> ἀνδρὶ στρατηγῷ τόνδ' ἐβούλευσας μόρον.

So punctuated they will make good sense as they stand, provided that a verb to complete the meaning of the first line can readily be supplied from the speech of Aegisthus to which the Chorus thus replies. Now there is one, and only one, sentence spoken by Aegisthus which would allow the required verb to be in thought repeated here:

> τὸν δὲ μὴ πειθάνορα
> ζεύξω βαρείαις—οὔτι μὴ σειραφόρον
> κριθῶντα πῶλον....

So he threatens, and it is to that threat, I submit, that the Chorus rejoins:

> γύναι, σὺ τοὺς ἥκοντας ἐκ μάχης νέον;

If so, that which I am maintaining to be logically and grammatically best in the treatment of this line and the two which follow on it is to be attained by the same means as that which I have argued to be dramatically best in the treatment of the whole altercation.

Finally, what fault, if any, do I find in the second of the speeches which I wish to interchange? One obvious fault, which Heimsoeth long ago pointed out: the question with which it opens

$$\text{τί δὴ τὸν ἄνδρα τόνδ' ἀπὸ ψυχῆς κακῆς}$$
$$\text{οὐκ αὐτὸς ἠνάριζες, ἀλλὰ σὺν γυνή...}$$

has already been answered. That answer,

$$\text{τὸ γὰρ δολῶσαι πρὸς γυναικὸς ἦν σαφῶς·}$$
$$\text{ἐγὼ δ' ὕποπτος ἐχθρὸς ἦ παλαιγενής,}$$

is not, to my thinking, itself out of place, for it follows on the taunt

$$\text{δρᾶσαι τόδ' ἔργον οὐκ ἔτλης αὐτοκτόνως.}$$

But, when the answer has once been made, a further question which could only evoke the same answer would seem to be out of place; whereas, if this second speech be set back to the position which I would assign to it, the sequence becomes more natural,—first the question τί δὴ τὸν ἄνδρα..., evoking no direct reply from Aegisthus, but merely bluster and threats; then the substance of the question repeated by the Chorus in the form of a taunt,

$$\text{δρᾶσαι τόδ' ἔργον οὐκ ἔτλης αὐτοκτόνως,}$$

and then thirdly Aegisthus' reply,

$$\text{τὸ γὰρ δολῶσαι πρὸς γυναικὸς ἦν σαφῶς.}$$

I submit therefore that in the treatment of this speech too the transposition suggested will achieve what is logically best, the normal sequence of question and answer.

One point more. Whether we leave the speech beginning γύναι in its traditional place or assign that place to the other speech τί δὴ τὸν ἄνδρα..., the speech of Aegisthus which follows, καὶ ταῦτα τἄπη κλαυμάτων ἀρχηγενῆ..., will, so far as the general trend of this passage is concerned, fit equally well; it is merely an angry and threatening speech. But, if my transposition be

adopted, there will result a literary embellishment of the lines
which otherwise is absent. The speech beginning τί δὴ τὸν ἄνδρα...
ends with the lines

Ὀρέστης ἆρά που βλέπει φάος,
ὅπως κατελθὼν δεῦρο πρευμενεῖ τύχῃ
ἀμφοῖν γένηται τοῖνδε παγκρατὴς φονεύς;

and if Aegisthus then makes answer

καὶ ταῦτα τἄπη κλαυμάτων ἀρχηγενῆ,

there will be no lack of tragic irony in that phrase: the κλαύματα
which he means are those of the Chorus, but, if ταῦτα τἄπη be
fulfilled and Orestes return, the κλαύματα will be Aegisthus'
own. He is the unconscious prophet of his own fate.

If then it appear that alike the dramatic effect of this passage
as a whole and the grammatical, logical, or literary qualities of its
component parts are improved by a single emendation, I cannot
treat these several improvements as fortuitous coincidences, but,
following my principle, must assume that Aeschylus disposed the
speeches in what (*me scilicet iudice*) is the best way; at any rate
let this example suffice as an illustration of the method which
I have adopted in approaching all the textual problems of this
play.

Before passing from the topic of the text I should add that,
in pursuance of my plan of providing a pleasurable text, I have
substituted for the usual *apparatus criticus* at the foot of each
page a *tabula lectionum* occupying a few pages by itself. In editions
of Aeschylus such as those of Wecklein and Wilamowitz-Moellendorff, in which the compilation and comparison of all the minutiae
of manuscript evidence is of the essence of their project, the con-
venience of presenting the variant readings page by page along
with the text properly outweighs any aesthetic considerations;
but none the less the *apparatus criticus* so presented does constitute a disfigurement. The purpose of this edition of a single
play being different, a difference in the method of presentation
too is, I hope, permissible. I am attempting no re-examination of
the actual sources at first hand. I accept Wilamowitz' estimate
of the value and relationships of the several manuscripts and his
confirmation of Elmsley's opinion that all our existing manuscripts

"are transcribed mediately or immediately from the same copy, which appears to have survived alone the general wreck of ancient literature." I judge too that the work of determining, on the evidence of existing variants, what must have been the readings in that common archetype, has been already carried out with some degree of finality. But if, after those documentary sources have been fully explored, there still remain abundant passages in which the existing manuscripts concur in attributing to Aeschylus words or phrases which in the opinion of scholars as a whole are either suspect or obviously corrupt—if, that is, the sole archetype from which they all derive was a document by no means impeccable— then, I think, there is still room for speculative criticism. Such criticism therefore as I can contribute will be based more largely on general linguistic and literary grounds than on divergences in particular manuscripts now existing, and will deal with the early corruptions which are attributable to that archetype and its predecessors more generally than with later vagaries in the transcription of existing manuscripts from that archetype.

In these circumstances I have felt myself free to dispense with a formal *apparatus criticus*. Where a reading preserved in one manuscript only, whether that manuscript be of greater or of lesser worth, is none the less generally accepted, the purpose of this edition will in no way be served by recording the aberrations of other manuscripts; and in the comparatively few instances in which the choice between two or more manuscript readings is less generally agreed, the point at issue can be discussed in my notes. It is rather for those passages in which my actual text tacitly treats the unanimous testimony of the manuscripts as wrong, that such special provision must be made as will enable me to show clearly what readings of the manuscripts have been rejected or modified, to record the emendations which I accept from others or myself propose in their place, and to acknowledge the authorship of these emendations. This purpose can, I think, be adequately served, without encroachment upon the pages devoted to text and translation, by means of a detached *tabula lectionum*.

Of my translation I will say but a few words. The difficulties of providing a rendering which will at once serve as an accurate interpretation of the text and possess withal some fluency and rhythm of its own are immense. The primary requisites of linguistic accuracy are, I assume, fidelity to the thought of the original in point of substance, stress, and sequence, and fidelity to the expression of that thought in point of the imagery employed. This latter requirement need involve no great difficulty. The imagery proper to English poetry is no less bold and varied than that of Greek; and if occasionally the lyrical profusion of Greek allows within the compass of a single sentence such accumulation of diverse imagery as would in English be condemned as confusion, a simple expedient is open to the translator; he may legitimately remodel the expression of thought by resolving a single complex sentence into a number of short and distinct English phrases each containing one of the series of images: the ear which would be offended by the combination of them in one sentence will, I think, if each be presented in a detached phrase, find no offence, but rather pleasure, in the rapidity of their succession. It is the other requirement,—fidelity to the thought of the original in point of substance, stress, and sequence,— which constitutes the greater and the more constant difficulty.

Fidelity here may easily be displaced by servility, reproduction of thought by verbal mimicry. The translator is not concerned with the specific words of the original except in so far as they are the vehicle of thought. He will not, because Greek is polysyllabic, seek out polysyllabic words in our own tongue, but will avail himself of that wealth of monosyllables which is the glory of English. He will not coin and utter strange compound adjectives in all the variety of the Greek models, but will see that such as he mints bear the impress of English idiom and ring true to English ears, while, for the rest, he gives the value of the original in simpler currency. And similarly, I think, he should set no great store on a word-for-word translation. Except in passages of very simple narrative where the words employed are such as must have exact counterparts in the vocabulary of all languages alike, to attempt a strictly verbal rendering is to put the translator's own language to servile employ wherein the free choice of the native phrase is superseded by the necessity of conforming to an alien idiom. The translator's function is not to provide a continuous glossary of the particular words that happen to form the text, verb for verb and substantive for substantive, but to reproduce in terms of one free and living language that which the poet produced in terms of another.

And what is it that the poet, the ποιητής, creates or produces? Not words; the words are the material in which he works,—the pigments with which he paints his picture, the flowers from which he weaves his garland,—but those flowers and pigments are of his choosing only and not of his own making. The produce of his genius is a composition and a fabric, which has for its minimum unit not the word but the phrase; for, if ever he seem to create a new word by fusing two others into one, that compound is only a phrase compressed.

If then the translator is seeking to reproduce that which the poet has produced, he should surely follow the poet's method and build up his translation not word by word but phrase by phrase. If it so happen that the words composing the Aeschylean phrase have English equivalents so exact and withal so mutually harmonious that from them may be composed an adequate phrase in his own tongue, let him count that an ἕρμαιον but not pride himself on the greater fidelity of his rendering; mere verbal resemblance proves nothing but a casual coincidence of vocabulary in the two languages; let him rather rejoice if in reproducing a phrase whose several components are less readily transmutable he achieve by less obvious means an equal fidelity of thought and spirit, and avoid that semblance of fidelity which is only servility,—a literal rendering in which 'the letter killeth.' A live paraphrase is better than a dead parody; and if my translation fail to preserve the happy mean between them, I should prefer it to err on the side of freedom.

But, if some measure of freedom may rightly be used on the linguistic side, it is even more essential in the sphere of metre. Just as the translator will not seek to imitate the construction, or to maintain the order of words, of a highly inflexional and synthetic language in a language of fixed forms and analytic tendency, so too, in the sphere of metre, he should not attempt to reproduce in English verse, which is governed in the main by the ordinary stresses of pronunciation, the metrical intricacies and varieties of a quantitative language in which every syllable has its own proper musical value.

No one, I imagine, would suggest that the iambics of tragic dialogue should be rendered in English by means of Alexandrines, on the ground that these too are *senarii* and subject to a pause comparable with the *caesura* of iambics. Elizabethan drama has settled once and for all the metre proper for this purpose. And in the rendering of Greek lyrics English must claim the same freedom. Any attempt to reproduce the exact metre must be a matter of artifice and convention; for (with all deference to some modern theories) the quantity of English words and of their syllables is not fixed. The most massive of monosyllables may on occasion be used as if quantitatively short; the ear is not offended by "Friends, Romans, countrymen..."; while words like 'verity' or 'melody' which have every claim to be pure tribrachs may, under the influence of metrical stress, do duty as dactyls or even cretics. And there are a multitude of words intermediate between these extremes in which syllabic quantity is wholly indeterminate.

English lacks then that quantitative precision without which the intricacies of Greek metre could not exist. Here and there indeed, where for a time the Greek lyrics are largely, let us say, of some simple trochaic form, the translator may do well to adopt the same rhythm; here and there, as in the opening of the first chorus, where the dactylic element in the metre is designed to give to the lyric narrative some suggestion of the epic, he may find an equivalent in such English metre as will recall the tone of the ballad; but in general he must content himself with such variations of treatment as his own taste suggests.

But, if the modulations of the Greek lyric could not be reproduced even by the greatest poet in the medium of English, yet English possesses in rhyme and in alliteration two instruments of music which may compensate in part for the lesser delicacy of her rhythm. Rhyme, if not too monotonously regular in its incidence but interwoven at varied intervals, produces a musical expectancy; and the satisfaction of that expectancy is musical pleasure. Alliteration, though proper to Greek too and indeed beloved of Aeschylus, is yet, I conceive, (owing to the greater preponderance of consonants in our language) peculiarly suited to English, and the source,—often the unsuspected source,—of much of the pleasure derived from verse which both in its thought and in its metrical structure is of the simplest. But such alliteration must be genuine,—not a garish illusion of the eye as in

> apt alliteration's artful aid,

but true music for the ear, now insistent, now subdued, here wild, there wistful, but always a symphony of pure sound, like

> The moan of doves in immemorial elms
> And murmuring of innumerable bees.

One topic more, and I have finished. It has often been said that a great masterpiece of literature does not belong to one country or to one generation, but is universal in its appeal; and this in some degree is true. But, just as this implies ability on the part of alien after-comers to speak or at least to read the language in which that masterpiece was written, so too does it postulate an understanding of those beliefs which the author assumed as pre-existent in the minds of those to whom first his work was presented.

The philosophical theme, or the very human question,—put it which way you will,—with which Aeschylus was dealing in the *Agamemnon* and the whole *Oresteia*, was the same as the nominal theme of Plato's *Republic*,—'What is justice?' Every actor of importance in the whole drama contends that justice is on his side. Agamemnon, so say the Chorus, consented to the sacrifice of Iphigeneia with the words παυσανέμου γὰρ θυσίας...ἐπιθυμεῖν θέμις. Agamemnon again, after razing to the ground the sanctuaries of the gods of Troy, renders thanks to the gods of Argos for their aid in exacting from Priam's city his just dues—δικαίων ὧν ἐπραξάμην πόλιν Πριάμου. Clytemnestra prays that justice may lead Agamemnon to a home unlooked-for (*v.* 911), and later makes oath in the name of "justice for my child now satisfied..." (*v.* 1431). Aegisthus opens his first speech with "O dawn of justice..." (v. 1577), and ends it with joy that Agamemnon is taken "in the toils of justice." The Chorus time after time revert to the problem of justice (e.g. vv. 250, 383, 772). And in the *Choephoroe* and *Eumenides* Orestes and Electra, Apollo and the Furies and Athena, all harp on the same theme.

Now admittedly this theme is in itself of universal interest. But what of Aeschylus' treatment of it? He does not deal with it, as a philosopher, in the abstract; but as a poet and dramatist he takes as a concrete case the gravest example of injustice or wrong-doing—the taking of human life—aggravated by every circumstance of close family ties between slayer and slain. How shall justice be done on the father who slays his daughter, on the wife who slays her husband, on the son who slays his mother,— how and by whom?

The answer to this more specific question may still be of universal interest, but the same answer will not be given among every people and in every age. The answer of civilised peoples now would be, 'The law must take its course.' But even in Athens in the time of Aeschylus the law did not take its course unless it had been set in motion by the next-of-kin to the murdered man; and in the age which Aeschylus is depicting the whole duty of vengeance rested on the next-of-kin, and there was no embodiment of law to aid him.

What then were the ideas concerning murder and all the sequel of murder which Aeschylus assumed as pre-existent in the minds of the audience who watched his plays, and which equally his younger contemporary Antiphon assumed as pre-existent in the minds of the juries whom he sought to sway?

Were I now editing the whole *Oresteia* it would be proper to deal with this matter at some length and to discuss many passages of the *Choephoroe* and *Eumenides* which cannot be understood by a reader not conversant with the mental attitude of a Greek audience towards murder. But the elucidation of the *Agamemnon* is less affected by the beliefs in question, and it will suffice to present them here in a short summary, referring those who desire the authorities and arguments for my statement to Chapter IV of my *Modern Greek Folklore and Ancient Greek Religion* as supplemented and in some particulars amended by my two articles in the *Classical Review* (May and September 1926) Περὶ ἀλιβάντων.

According then to Greek belief, persons who met with a violent death were liable to become ἀλίβαντες. Their bodies, that is, were withheld from the normal process of decay, and, while presenting a withered and shrivelled appearance, remained whole and intact. This was the most pitiable misfortune which could befall the dead. In this condition their bodies might be reanimated from time to time by their souls; and a murdered man, bent on vengeance, might emerge in bodily form from his grave, in order to hunt down his murderer. Such a *revenant* was named an ἀλάστωρ, a word derived from that verb of which ἀλάομαι is the passive, and meaning a 'pursuer,' or, owing to the connotation of vindictiveness, 'one who seeks vengeance upon' another, one who seeks to vent upon another the μῆνις or 'vindictive anger' (for that word too is almost technical) with which the wrongs he has suffered have inspired him.

But the murdered man was not left to execute his own vengeance unaided. There were beings of divine status, charged with the punishment of murder and the like, and known by a variety of names—ἀλιτήριοι, παλαμναῖοι, προστρόπαιοι,—who might act on behalf of the murdered man and, when so acting, were denoted by the same name, ἀλάστορες. The ghost of Clytemnestra (the nearest approach which Aeschylus dared make to a bodily ἀλάστωρ) complains indeed, when the Furies are found sleeping, that οὐδεὶς ὑπέρ μου δαιμόνων μηνίεται (*Eumen.* 101), but this is true only while the Furies sleep: the Furies themselves are but one species of the genus ἀλάστωρ, and, for all her guilt, they are hunting down Orestes who murdered her. They have the same function as ὁ παλαιὸς δριμὺς ἀλάστωρ Ἀτρέως χαλεποῦ θοινατῆρος (*Agam.* 1501), save that this latter is pursuing with his vengeance not Atreus himself but the succeeding generation.

But, though vengeance for murder might thus be executed either by the murdered man himself or by ghostly agents acting on his behalf, yet the next-of-kin was not on that account exempt from obligations. On the contrary, any remissness on his part in exacting vengeance was liable to be punished by the dead man or those agents. This was the dilemma of Orestes: in the last scene between him and Clytemnestra, ὅρα, she says, φύλαξαι μητρὸς ἐγκότους κύνας (*Choeph.* 924), and Orestes replies τὰς τοῦ πατρὸς δὲ πῶς φύγω, παρεὶς τάδε; and at an earlier point of the same play Orestes has recounted the full tale of penalties which he himself, so Apollo had warned him, was doomed to suffer if he should fail to pursue to the death his father's murderers,—a list of penalties which culminates not with the threat of death only, but with the threat that he, Orestes, too will become an ἀλίβας; for, as I have shown elsewhere, no other significance can attach to the climax of threatenings which is reached in the words κακῶς ταριχευθέντα (*Choeph.* 296). Orestes himself would suffer after death the same dreadful fate as had befallen his murdered father.

So then no real understanding of the *Oresteia* would be possible if the wrong done by the murderer to the murdered were conceived by us in modern fashion to consist in the act of murder only: the consequences of murder whereby the dead man was, so to speak, housed in a grave but cut off from the society alike of the dead and of the living,—those consequences too were no negligible part of the wrong done. And indeed in the *Agamemnon* itself the full grandeur and range of Clytemnestra's hatred cannot be understood without knowing this,—this and one thing more. It was not only a violent death which condemned men to this strange doom after death: lack of burial or the operation of a curse might produce the same result. And in this knowledge not only does Clytemnestra deny to Agamemnon (*v.* 1554) that rite of lamentation which formed an effective part of funeral usage, but in one of the most dramatic scenes of the whole play, that in which she is shown standing over the dead man and exulting in her crime, the climax is not reached until, pursuing now her victim with vindictive execration even beyond death, she cries (*vv.* 1395–8):

> If for his funerals there might be poured
> Such wine as doth beseem,—thus, thus, would I
> Empty o'er him my vials of hate; 'twere just,
> Aye, more than justice. May he take it hence,
> Empoisoned with my curse, that cup which erst
> He filled for me with miseries manifold,
> And with his own lips drain it to the dregs!

An Athenian audience needed no interpreter of that curse.

CATALOGUS CODICUM

Catalogus codicum quorum mentionem uspiam feci Weckleinii verbis descriptorum (nisi quod dinumerationem versuum usitatiorem servavi) iisdemque quibus ille notavit signis notatorum:

M=Codex Mediceus sive Laurentianus plut. xxxii. 9, membranaceus, quem Cobetus saec. x, alii saec. xi scriptum esse iudicant....Quattuordecim foliis amissis interierunt Agam. v. 311–1066, 1160–1673. (*m*=manus secunda.)

a=Codex Marcianus 468 sive xci. 4, olim Bessarionis, saec. xiii vel xiv scriptus.

f=Codex Florentinus sive Laurentianus plut. xxxi. 8, chartaceus, saeculi xiv priore parte scriptus.

g=Codex Venetus sive Marcianus 616 (xci. 5), membranaceus, saeculi xv....Iactura aliquot foliorum interciderunt Agamemnonis v. 46–1094. (Hunc iudicat Wilamowitz-Moellendorff gemellum esse Florentini sed multo deteriorem.)

h=Codex Farnesianus (I. E. 5),...ex recensione et cum scholiis Demetrii Triclinii.

TABULA LECTIONUM

A CODICUM TESTIMONIO DISCREPANTIUM

VERSUS	LECTIONES	AUCTORES	CODICES
Ex catalogo dramatis personarum	omissum est, monente	Stanley,	ΑΓΓΕΛΟΣ
,,	omissum est ante ΚΗΡΥΞ, monente	Stanley,	ΤΑΛΘΥΒΙΟΣ
7.	delendum iudicavit	Pauw	ἀστέρας, ὅταν φθίνωσιν, ἀντολάς τε τῶν
8.	φυλάσσων	nos	φυλάσσω
12.	ἔχων	nos	ἔχω
14.	ἀντίος	nos	ἀνθ' ὕπνου
70.	ante ἀπύρων delevit	Bamberger	οὔτε δακρύων
87.	θυοσκεῖς	Turnebus	θυοσκινεῖς
97.	λέξαι θ'	nos	λέξασ'
101.	ἀγάν' αὖ	nos	ἀγανά
102.	post ἀμύνει delevimus	nos	φροντίδ' ἄπληστον
103.	τὴν θυμοβόρον φρενὶ λύπην	nos	τὴν θυμοφθόρον λύπης φρένα M τὴν θυμοβόρον λύπης φρένα f
105.	ἐκτελεοῦν	nos	ἐκτελέων
	θεὸς ἐγκαταπνεύει	nos	θεόθεν καταπνεύει
106–7.	μολπᾶν τ' ἀλκᾷ	nos	μολπὰν ἀλκὰν (in M olim μολπᾶν)
109.	ἥβας	Ar. Ran. 1285	ἥβαν (in M olim ἡβᾶν)
111.	καὶ χερὶ	Ar. Ran. 1288	δίκας
115.	ἀργᾶς	Thiersch	ἀργίας
119.	γέννας	Beckmann	γένναν
131.	ἄγα	Hermann	ἄτα
133.	τίθησι νεῖκος	nos	στρατωθέν. οἴκῳ
135.	ἐπίφθονον	nos	ἐπίφθονος
141.	δρόσοις ἀόπτοις	nos	δρόσοισιν ἀέλπτοις M (ἀέπτοις af)
	λεόντων	Stanley ex Et. M. p.377,39	ὄντων M: omis. fh
144.	ἵεται	nos	αἰτεῖ
145.	σούσθω	nos	στρουθῶν
165.	τὸ	Pauw	τόδε Maf
168.	ὃς μὲν τοῖς	nos	οὐδ' ὅστις
170.	οὐδὲ λέξεται	H. L. Ahrens	οὐδὲν λέξαι
177.	τὸν	Schütz	τῶ (vel τῷ)
182.	βίαιος	Turnebus	βιαίως
190.	παλιρρόχθοις	H. L. Ahrens	παλιρρόθοις
195.	νεῶν	Pauw	ναῶν
	τε addidit	Porson	
197.	Ἀργολᾶν	nos	Ἀργείων
206.	πιθέσθαι	Turnebus	πείθεσθαι
216.	περιόργῳ σφ'	Bamberger	περιόργως

VERSUS	LECTIONES	AUCTORES	CODICES
222.	βροτούς	Spanheim	βροτοῖς
229.	αἰῶ τε	O. Müller	αἰῶνα
233.	πάντ' ἄθυμον	nos	παντὶ θυμῷ
239.	ἐκ πέδονδε χεύασ'	nos	ἐς πέδον χέουσα
247.	παιᾶνα	Enger	αἰῶνα
251.	δ' (post μέλλον) addidit post μέλλον omiserunt	Elmsley codd. Mh	τὸ δὲ προκλύειν maî
252.	κλύουσι, χαιρέτω	nos	κλύοις· προχαιρέτω
254.	σύνορθρον αὐγαῖς	Wellauer Hermann	σύνορθον M: σύναρθρον fh αὐταῖς
261.	εἴ τι	Auratus	εἴτε
275.	λαλοῖμι	nos	λάβοιμι
282.	ἀγγάρου	Canter ex Etym. M. p. 7	ἀγγέλου
284.	πανὸν	Casaubon ex Athen. (xv. 700 E)	φανὸν
288.	ἐπεῦκτο	nos	πεύκη τὸ
289.	σκοπαῖς	Turnebus	σκοπάς
304.	χρονίζεσθαι	Casaubon	χαρίζεσθαι
307.	κάτοπτον	Canter	κάτοπτρον
308.	ἔστ'...εὖτ'	Hermann	εἶτ'...εἶτ
312.	τοιοίδε τοί μοι	Schütz	τοιοίδ' ἔτοιμοι
322.	ἐγχέας	Canter	ἐκχέας
336.	δ' εὐδαίμονες	Stanley	δυσδαίμονες
338.	εὖ σέβουσι	Scaliger	εὐσεβοῦσι
340.	οὖ τᾶν ἑλόντες ἀνθαλοῖεν	Hermann Auratus	οὐκ ἀνελόντες a: οὐκ ἂν γ' ἑλόντες fh ἂν θάνοιεν a: αὖ θάνοιεν fh
342.	τὰ	codex a	ἀ ceteri
345.	θεοῖς δ' ἄρ' ἀμπλάκητος	Bamberger	θεοῖς δ' ἀναμπλάκητος
346.	ἐγρηγορὸς μήνιμα	Porson nos	ἐγρήγορον τὸ πῆμα
350.	τήνδ'	Hermann	τὴν
353.	αὖ	Paley	εὖ
367.	ἔχουσ', ἀνειπεῖν	nos	ἔχουσ' (corr. ex ἔχουσαν) εἰπεῖν î: ἔχουσιν h
368.	πάρεστιν τοί τόδ'	Hartung Karsten	πάρεστι τοῦτ' î: τοῦτο γ' h
369.	ἔπραξαν	Hermann	ὡς ἔπραξεν
374–5.	ἐγγὺς οὖσα λύμα τῶν	nos	ἐγγόνους ἀτολμήτων
383.	μέγαν	Canter	μεγάλα
386.	προβουλευτὰς	nos	προβουλόπαις
391.	προσβολαῖς	J. Pearson	προβολαῖς
394.	ποτανὸν	Schütz	πτανὸν
395.	θεὶς ἄφερτον	Wilamowitz	ἄφερτον θεὶς î: ἄφερτον ἐνθεὶς h
397.	τῶν	Klausen	τῶνδε
404.	τε καὶ κλόνους λογχίμους	H. L. Ahrens	κλόνους λογχίμους τε καὶ
405.	θ' addidit	Hermann	
412.	σιγᾶς ἀτίμους ἀλοιδόρους	Hermann	σιγᾶς ἄτιμος ἀλοίδορος
413.	ἄστοις ἐφημμένων	nos	ἀδιστος ἀφεμένων
423.	ματᾷ γὰρ εὐχᾶν	nos	μάταν γὰρ, εὖτ' ἂν
429.	Ἕλλανος	Bamberger	Ἑλλάδος
430.	τηξικάρδιος	Auratus (ex gloss. in cod. h)	τλησικάρδιος

VERSUS	LECTIONES	AUCTORES	CODICES
433.	τις addidit	Porson	
448.	διαί	Hermann	διά
457.	δημοκράντου	Porson	δημοκράτου
465.	παλιντυχεῖ	Scaliger	παλιντυχῇ
468.	ὑπερκόπως	Grotius	ὑπερκότως
474.	ἄλλῳ	Headlam	ἄλλων
477.	ἐτήτυμος	Auratus	ἐτητύμως
478.	ἤ τι θεῖον οὖν ἐστὶ ψύθος	nos	ἤ τοι θεῖόν ἐστι μὴ ψύθος
483.	γυναικὸς	Scaliger	ἐν γυναικὸς
485.	ἔρος	Blomfield	ὅρος
489–500.	ΦΤΛΑΚΙ assignavimus	nos	ΚΛΤΤΑΙΜΗΣΤΡΑΙ codices
504.	δεκάτου	Jacob	δεκάτῳ
511.	ἦσθ᾽	Askew	ἦλθες h: ἦλθ᾽ (supra adscripto ες) f.
512.	καὶ παιώνιος	Dobree	καὶ παγώνιος f: κάπαγώνιος h
520.	εἴ που	Auratus	ἦπου
539.	τὸ τεθνάναι	Schneidewin	τεθνᾶναι
544.	πεπληγμένοι	Tyrwhitt	πεπληγμένος
546.	μ᾽ addidit	Scaliger	
547.	στύγος; φράσον	Jacob	στύγος στρατῷ
550.	ὡς	Scaliger	ὧν
552.	ἄν	Auratus	εὖ
557.	ἐξηντλοῦμεν	nos	οὐ λαχόντες
558.	καὶ πλέον προσῆν	Headlam	καὶ προσῆν πλέον
560.	ὄμβροι δὲ δῖοι	nos	ἐξ οὐρανοῦ γὰρ
561.	ἐμπέδως τρίχα	nos	ἔμπεδον σίνος
562.	σίνος	nos	τρίχα
572.	ξυμφορὰς	Blomfield	συμφοραῖς
579.	δόμων...ἀρχαίων	Hartung	δόμοις...ἀρχαῖον
598.	σέ μοι	Wieseler	σ᾽ ἐμοὶ
613–4.	ΚΛΤΤΑΙΜΗΣΤΡΑΙ assignavit	Hermann	ΚΗΡΤΚΙ codices
618.	τε	Hermann	γε
622–35.	ΧΟΡΩΙ assignavit	Stanley	quos versus ΚΛΤΤΑΙΜΗΣΤΡΑΙ codices
622.	τύχοις	Porson	τύχης
624.	ἀνὴρ	Hermann	ἀνὴρ
634.	λέγεις; χειμῶνα	nos	λέγεις χειμῶνα
644.	σεσαγμένον	Schütz	σεσαγμένων
649.	Ἀχαιοῖς...θεῶν	Dobree	Ἀχαιῶν...θεοῖς
660.	ναυτικοῖς τ᾽ ἐρειπίοις	Auratus	ναυτικῶν τ᾽ ἐριπίων
672.	τί μήν	Linwood	τί μή
673.	ταῦτ᾽	Stanley	ταῦτ᾽
675.	μογεῖν	Sonny	μολεῖν
684.	προνοίαισι	Pauw	προνοίαις
689.	ἐλέναυς	Blomfield	ἐλένας
695.	πλατᾶν	Heath	πλάταν
697.	εἰς ἐριφύλλους	nos	εἰς δεξιφύλλους h: ἐπ᾽ ἀξιφύλλους f
701.	ἤνυσεν	Headlam	ἤλασε
702.	ἀτίμωσιν	Canter	ἀτίμως ἵν᾽ f: ἀτίμως h
714.	παμπορθῇ	Seidler	παμπρόσθη
717–8.	λέοντος ἵνιν	Conington	λέοντα σίνιν
718–9.	ἀγελακτόνου τέως	nos	ἀγάλακτον οὕτως
723.	ἔσκ᾽	Casaubon	ἔσχ᾽

VERSUS	LECTIONES	AUCTORES	CODICES
727–8.	ἦθος	Conington	ἔθος
730.	μηλοφόνοισι σὺν	Fix	μηλοφόνοισιν
737.	προσεθρέφθη	Heath	προσετράφη
741.	δ' addidit	Porson	
758.	δυσσεβὲς γὰρ	Pauw	γὰρ δυσσεβὲς
761.	δ' ἄρ'	Auratus	γὰρ
766.	ὅτε	Klausen	ὅταν
767.	φάος τόκου	H. L. Ahrens	νεαρὰ φάους κότον
768.	τὰν	Hermann	τὸν
771.	εἰδομένας	Casaubon	εἰδομέναν
775.	post τίει delevit	H. L. Ahrens	βίον
776.	ἔδεθλα	Auratus	ἐσθλὰ
778.	προσέσυτο	H. L. Ahrens	προσέβα τοῦ
782.	πτολίπορθ'	Blomfield	πολίπορθ'
794–5.	lacunam indicavit	Hermann	
	φθονερὰς κλέπτουσι μερίμνας supplevimus	nos	
800.	σ' addidit	Musgrave	
803.	ἐκ θυσιῶν	H. L. Ahrens et Franke	ἐκούσιον
804.	θρήσκοισι	Karsten et Newman	θνήσκουσι
805–6.	ἔστιν ἐπειπεῖν supplevit	Headlam	
819.	συνθρώσκουσα	nos	συνθνήσκουσα
822.	ἁρπαγὰς	nos	καὶ πάγας
	ὑπερκόπους	Heath	ὑπερκότους
831.	ταὐτὰ	Auratus	ταῦτα
839.	ὁμιλίαις κάτοπτον	nos	ὁμιλίας κάτοπτρον
850.	πῆμ' ἀποστρέψαι νόσου	Porson	πήματος τρέψαι νόσον
863.	κληδόνας	Auratus	ἡδονὰς
868.	τέτρηται	H. L. Ahrens	τέτρωται
870.	τὰν	Wellauer	τ' ἂν
871	delendum iudicavit	Schütz	πολλὴν ἄνωθεν, τὴν κάτω γὰρ οὐ λέγω,
872.	λαβεῖν	Paley	λαβών
876.	ἐνημμένης	Emperius	λελημμένης
878.	πιστωμάτων	Spanheim	πιστευμάτων
890.	κλαίουσι	nos	κλαίουσα
903.	τοί νιν	Schütz	τοίνυν
926.	ποικιλμάτων	nos	τῶν ποικίλων
931.	εἷκε	nos	εἰπὲ
933.	ἔρξειν	Headlam	ἔρδειν
935.	δοκεῖ	Stanley	δοκῇ
942.	τῆσδε	Auratus	τήνδε
943.	κρατεῖς...παρεὶς	Weil et Wecklein	κράτος...πάρες γ'
948.	δωματοφθορεῖν	Schütz	σωματοφθορεῖν
950.	τούμὸν	Emperius	τούτων
954.	αὕτη	Auratus	αὐτὴ
959.	ἰσάργυρον	Salmasius	εἰς ἄργυρον
963.	δ' εἱμάτων	Canter	δειμάτων
965.	μηχανωμένη	Abresch	μηχανωμένης
965–8.	v. 968 post v. 965 collocavimus	nos	
966.	παρούσης	nos	γὰρ οὔσης
967.	σκιάν θ'	nos	σκιὰν

xlii

TABULA LECTIONUM

VERSUS	LECTIONES	AUCTORES	CODICES
969.	σημαίνει (ad aliam tamen interpretationem accommodatum)	Karsten	σημαίνεις
	μολόν (ad aliam tamen interpretationem accommodatum)	Voss	μολών
970.	ἀπ'	Auratus	τἀπ' f: τ' ἀπ' h
972.	ἐπιστρωφωμένου	Victorius	ἐπιστρεφωμένου f: ἐπιστροφωμένου h
982.	ἵξει	Scaliger	ἵξει h: ἵξει f
984.	ξὺν ἐμβολαῖς	Casaubon	ξυνεμβόλοις
985.	ψαμμὶς ἀκτά	H. L. Ahrens	ψαμμίας ἀκάτας
985–6.	περιήχησεν	nos	παρήβησεν
990.	ὅμως	Auratus	ὅπως
991.	Ἐρινύος	Porson	ἐρινύς
995.	οὔτι	Casaubon	οὔτοι
998.	ἐκτὸς ἐμᾶς	nos	ἐξ ἐμᾶς f: ἀπ' ἐμᾶς τοι h
1001.	τεταμένας	nos	τᾶς πολλᾶς
1002.	ἀόριστον	Karsten	ἀκόρεστον
1005–7.	lacunae causa explendae ἱεμένου θρασέως addidimus	nos	
1008.	πρὸ μέν τι	Enger	τὸ μὲν πρὸ
1012.	πημονᾶς	Victorius	πημονὰς
1016.	ἤλασεν	Schütz	ὤλεσεν
1018.	πεσὸν	Auratus	πεσόνθ'
1024.	ἂν ἔπαυσεν	nos	αὖτ' ἔπαυσ'
1041.	πλῆσθαι δουλίας μάξης βίᾳ	nos	τλῆναι δουλείας μάξης βία f: τλῆναι καὶ ζυγῶν θιγεῖν βίᾳ h
1046.	ἕξεις	Auratus	ἔχεις
1048.	ἀλοῦσα	C. G. Haupt	ἂν οὖσα
1054.	πιθοῦ	Blomfield	πείθου
1055.	θυραίᾳ	Casaubon	θυραίαν
	τῇδ'	Musgrave	τήνδε
1056–7.	ἑστίας ἤδη πάρος | ἔστηκε μῆλα πρὸς σφαγὰς μεσομφάλους (πάρος pro πυρὸς Musgrave)	nos	ἑστίας μεσομφάλου | ἔστηκεν ἤδη μῆλα πρὸς σφαγὰς πυρός
1071.	εἴκουσ'	Robortello	ἐκοῦσ'
1078.	ἤδ'	nos	ἡ δ'
1084.	περ ἐν	Schütz	παρ' ἔν
1091.	καὶ ἀρταμάς	Headlam	καρτάναι
1092.	ἀνδροσφαγεῖον	Dobree	ἀνδρὸς σφάγιον
	πέδου χραντήριον (πέδου Porson)	nos	πεδορραντήριον M: πέδον ραντήριον mfh
1094.	ἀνευρήσει	Porson	ἂν εὑρήσῃ
1095.	μαρτυρίοισι	Pauw	μαρτυρίοις
	τοῖσδ' ἐπιπείθομαι	Abresch	τοῖσδε πεπείθομαι
1099.	τούτων	Weil	ἡμὲν
	ματεύομεν	Schütz	μαστεύομεν
1111.	ὀρέγματα	Hermann	ὀρεγόμενα M: ὀρεγμένα fh
1117.	ἀκόρετος	Bothe	ἀκόρεστος
1122.	καιρία	Dindorf	καὶ δορία
1123.	ξυνάνεται	nos	ξυνανύτει
1128.	ἐν addidit	Schütz	
	κύτει	Blomfield	τεύχει
1129.	δολοφόνον	nos	δολοφόνου

VERSUS	LECTIONES	AUCTORES	CODICES
1133.	τέλλεται	Emperius	στέλλεται
	διαί	Hermann	διά
1137.	ἐπεγχύδαν	Headlam	ἐπεγχέασα
1143.	ἀκόρετος	Aldina	ἀκόρεστος
1146.	μόρον ἀηδόνος	Hermann	ἀηδόνος μόρον
1147.	περίβαλον	Blomfield	περεβάλοντο
1150.	θεοφόρους	Hermann	θεοφόρους τ'
1161.	ὄχθας	Casaubon	ὄχθους
1163.	καὶ νεογνὸς	nos	νεογνὸς
	ἂν ἀίων	Karsten	ἀνθρώπων
1164.	δάκει	Hermann	δήγματι
1165.	δυσαλγεῖ	Canter	δυσαγγεῖ
	delendum iudicavit	Schütz	κακὰ (post μινυρὰ)
1166.	θράγματ'	nos	θραύματ' fg: θαύματ' h
1171.	ἔχρων	nos	ἔχειν fg: ἔχει h
1172.	ἐγὼ δ' ἔθ' ὁρμαίνουσα	nos	ἐγὼ δὲ θερμόνους τάχ' ἐμπέδῳ
	τἀμποδὼν ματῶ		βαλῶ
1173.	ἐπεφημίσω	Paley	ἐφημίσω
1174.	κακοφρονῶν	Schütz	κακοφρονεῖν
1181.	ἐσάξειν	Bothe	ἐς ἥξειν
1182.	κλύζειν	Auratus	κλύειν
1194.	κυρῶ	H. L. Ahrens	τηρῶ
1198.	πῆγμα	Auratus	πῆμα
1199.	σε	Auratus	σου
1203–4.	inversum in codicibus		
	ordinem correxit	Hermann	
1207.	ἠλθέτην	Elmsley	ἤλθετον
1211.	ἄνατος	Canter	ἄνακτος
1212.	οὐδέν'	Canter	οὐδὲν
1216.	ταράσσει	nos (ex Hesy-	ταράσσων
		chio)	
	ξυνηγόρου	nos	ἐφημένους (e prox. versu)
1227.	ἔπαρχος	Canter	ἄπαρχος
1228–30.	v. 1230 (ἄτης...τύχῃ)		
	post v. 1227 (νεῶν...		
	ἀναστάτης) collocavi-		
	mus	nos	
1228.	οἷα	Herwerden	οἷα
1229.	κἀκτήνασα (=καὶ ἀκτή-	nos	καὶ κτείνασα
	νασα)		
1231.	τοιάνδε τολμᾷ	nos	τοιάδε τολμᾷ
1235.	ἄρη	Porson	ἀρὰν
1240.	μ' ἐν	Auratus	μὴν
1242.	παιδείων	Schütz	παιδίων
1249.	παρέστη	nos	παρέσται
1251.	ἄγος	Auratus	ἄχος
1252.	σὺ addidimus	nos	η
	παρεκόπης	Hartung	παρεσκοπεῖς f: παρεσκόπης h
1255.	δυσμαθῆ	Stephanus	δυσπαθῆ
1256.	post πῦρ delevimus	nos	ἐπέρχεται δέ μοι
1258.	δίπους	Victorius	δίπλους
1261.	μνῆστιν	nos	μισθὸν (supra adscripto μνείαν f)
1262–3	delevimus	nos	ἐπεύχεται θήγουσα φωτὶ φάσγανον | ἐμῆς ἀγωγῆς ἀντιτίσασθαι φόνον
1267.	πεσόντα· τῇδ'	nos	πεσόντ' · ἀγαθὼ δ'
	ἀμείβομαι	prima manus	ἀμείψομαι
		in cod. f	

VERSUS	LECTIONES	AUCTORES	CODICES
1268.	ἄτης	Stanley	ἄτην
1271.	μέγα	Hermann	μετὰ
1272.	ὅτ᾽ ἔχρων	nos	ὑπ᾽ ἐχθρῶν
1273.	φοιβάς	Spanheim	φοιτὰς
1275.	delevimus	nos	καὶ νῦν ὁ μάντις μάντιν ἐκπράξας ἐμέ
1278.	θερμὸν	Schütz	θερμῷ
	κοπέντος	Headlam	κοπείσης
1284.	post v. 1290 in codicibus scriptum huc revocavit	Hermann	
1286.	κάκοιτος	Wieseler	κάτοικος
1288.	εἷλον	Musgrave	εἷχον
1291.	τάσδ᾽ ἐγὼ	Auratus	τὰς λέγω
1299.	οὗ	nos	οὔ
	χρόνοι πλέῳ	Weil	χρόνῳ πλέω
1305.	σῶν	Auratus	τῶν
1306.	delevimus	nos	τί δ᾽ ἐστὶ χρῆμα; τίς σ᾽ ἀποστρέφει φόβος;
1313-14.	post v. 1326 collocavimus	nos	scilicet ἀλλ᾽ εἰμι...βίος
1313.	τὰν δόμοισιν ὠκύνουσ᾽	nos	κἂν δόμοισι κωκύσουσ᾽
1317.	ἄλλως	Hermann	ἀλλ᾽ ὡς
	νοούσῃ	nos	θανούσῃ
	τότε	Rauchenstein	τόδε
1322.	καὶ πορευθῆναι	nos	ῥῆσιν ἢ θρῆνον
1323.	οἶμον τὸν αὐτῆς	nos	ἐμὸν τὸν αὐτῆς
1325.	ἐλευθέρους φόνευτρ᾽ ἐμοῦ τίνειν πρόμους	nos	ἐχθροῖς φονεῦσι τοῖς ἐμοῖς τίνειν ὁμοῦ
1327-30	ΧΟΡΩΙ assignavit	Weil	
1328.	ἂν πρέψειεν	Boissonade	ἀντρέψειεν
	δυστυχῇ	Victorius	δυστυχῆ
1330.	οὐ	nos	καὶ
1332.	βροτοῖσιν	Pauw	βροτοῖς
1334.	μηκέτ᾽ ἐσέλθῃς	Hermann	μηκέτι δ᾽ εἰσέλθῃς
1338.	ἀποτίσῃ	Sidgwick	ἀποτίσει (cf. v. 1340)
1339.	τοῖς θείνουσι	nos	τοῖσι θανοῦσι
1340.	ἐπικράνῃ	Sidgwick	ἐπικρανεῖ
1341.	ποτ᾽ addidit	E. A. Ahrens	
1347.	αὐτοῖς	nos	ἄν πως
1356.	μελλοῦς	Trypho	μελλούσης
1357.	πέδοι	Hermann	πέδον
1362.	τείνοντες	Canter	κτείνοντες
1364.	κρατεῖ	Casaubon	κράτει
1368.	θυμοῦσθαι	E. A. Ahrens	μυθοῦσθαι
1375.	πημονῆς	Auratus	πημονὴν
	ἀρκύστατ᾽ ἂν	Elmsley	ἀρκύστατον
1378.	νείκης	Heath	νίκης
1381.	ἀμύνεσθαι	Victorius	ἀμύνασθαι
1384.	οἰμωγμάτοιν	Elmsley	οἰμώγμασιν
1392.	γαίει	nos	γᾶν εἰ
1398.	ἐκπίνοι	nos	ἐκπίνει
1408.	ῥυτᾶς	Stanley	ῥυσᾶς
	ὅρμενον	Abresch	ὁρώμενον
1410.	ἀπόπολις	Seidler	ἄπολις
1414.	τότ᾽	Voss	τόδ᾽
1418.	ἀημάτων	Canter	τελημμάτων

TABULA LECTIONUM xlv

VERSUS	LECTIONES	AUCTORES	CODICES
1419.	χρῆν	Porson	χρὴ
1428.	ἐμπρέπειν	Hermann	εὖ πρέπει
1430.	τύμματι	Voss	τύμμα
1431.	ἀκούεθ'	nos	ἀκούεις
1433.	ἄτην τ'	Butler	ἄτην
1434.	ἐμπελάσσεται	nos	ἐλπὶς ἐμπατεῖ
1435.	ἐμῆς	Porson	ἐμὰς
1438.	τῆσδ' ὁ	Kayser	τῆσδε
1443.	ἰσοτριβής	Pauw	ἰσοτριβής
1446.	τῳδ'	Hermann	τοῦδ'
1450.	ἄμηνιν	nos	ἐν ἡμῖν
1453.	πολέα	Haupt	καὶ πολλὰ
1455.	ἰὼ ἰὼ	Blomfield	ἰὼ
	παράνους	Hermann	παρανόμους
1459.	ἐπήκρισεν	nos	ἐπηνθίσω
1468.	ἐμπίτνεις	Canter	ἐμπίπτεις
1469.	διφυίοισι	Hermann	διφυεῖσι
1470.	δ' addidit	Pearson	
1471.	καρδιόδηκτον	Abresch	καρδία δηκτὸν
1472.	post δίκαν delendum iudicavit	Dindorf	μοι
1473.	σταθεῖσ'	Stanley	σταθεὶς
1474.	lacunae causa explendae δίκας supplevimus	nos	
1475.	νῦν	nos	νῦν δ'
1476.	τριπάχυντον	Bamberger	τριπάχυιον
1479.	νείκει	Scaliger	νείρει
1480.	νεόχμ' ὦρτο	nos	νέος ἰχώρ
1481.	οἰκοσινῆ	Wilamowitz-Moellendorff	οἴκοις τοῖσδε
1484.	ἀκόρεστον	Todt	ἀκορέστου
1497.	μὴ δῆτ' αὔχει	nos	αὐχεῖς εἶναι
1498.	ἐνιδεχθῆς	nos	ἐπιλεχθῆς
1511.	δίκαν	Scholefield	δὲ καὶ
	προβαίνων	Canter	προσβαίνων
1521-2	delendos iudicavit	Seidler	οὔτ' ἀνελεύθερον οἶμαι θάνατον τῷδε γενέσθαι
1523.	ὧδε γὰρ αὔτως	nos	οὐδὲ γὰρ οὗτος
1525.	ante ἐμὸν delevimus	nos	ἀλλ'
1527.	ξένα δὴ	nos	ἀνάξια
1535.	θηγάνει	Hermann	θήγει
	βλάβας	nos	βλάβης
1536.	μοίρας	nos	μοῖρα
1539.	ἀγκυλοτοίχου	nos	ἀργυροτοίχου
1545.	ψυχῇ τ'	E. A. Ahrens	ψυχὴν
1547.	ἐπιτύμβιον αἶνον	Voss	ἐπιτύμβιος αἶνος
1551.	μέλημ' ἀλέγειν	Karsten	μέλημα λέγειν
1553.	ἡμεῖς	Paley	κάτθανε
1555.	Ἰφιγένειά νιν	Auratus	Ἰφιγένειαν ἵν'
1559.	χεῖρε	Porson	χεῖρα
1563.	θρόνῳ	Schütz	χρόνῳ
1565.	ἀραῖον	Hermann	ῥᾷον
1566.	πρὸς ἄτᾳ	Blomfield	προσάψαι
1567.	ἐνέβης	Canter	ἐνέβη
1574.	μοι	Canter	μοι δ'
1575-6.	μανίας μελάθρων | ἀλληλοφόνους	Erfurdt	ἀλληλοφόνους | μανίας μελάθρων

VERSUS	LECTIONES	AUCTORES	CODICES
1579.	ἄγη	Auratus	ἄχη
1585.	αὐτοῦ δ'	Elmsley	αὐτοῦ τ'
1595.	ἔκρυπτ'	Casaubon	ἔθρυπτ'
	ἄνευθεν...καθημένους	nos	ἄνωθεν...καθήμενος
1599.	ἀμπίπτει	Canter	ἄν, πίπτει
	σφαγὴν	Auratus	σφαγῆς
1602.	ὀλέσθαι	Tzetzes	ὀλέσθη
1605.	ὄντ' ἐπίδικον	nos	ὄντα μ' ἐπὶ δεκ'
1613.	τόνδ' εἰ φῆς	nos	τόνδ' ἔφης
1624.	παῖσας (ex schol. ad Pind. Pyth. ii)	Hermann	πήσας
1625-7.	hos versus post v. 1642 collocavimus; huc revocavimus vv. 1643-8	nos	
1626.	αἰσχύνων	Keck	αἰσχύνουσ'
1631.	νηπίοις	Jacob	ἠπίοις
1637.	ἦ	Porson	ἤ
1638.	τῶν δὲ	Jacob	τῶνδε
1641.	σκότῳ	Scaliger	κότῳ
1643-8.	(scilicet τί δὴ τὸν ἄνδρα ...φονεύς) post v. 1624 collocavimus; huc revocavimus vv. 1625-7	nos	
1650.	(scilicet εἶα δὴ, φίλοι λοχῖται...) ante v. 1649 (ἀλλ' ἐπεὶ...) collocavimus eundem ΑΙΓΙΣΘΩΙ dedit	nos Stanley	codices ΧΟΡΩΙ
1649	huc transpositum ΧΟΡΩΙ assignavimus	nos	codices ΑΙΓΙΣΘΩΙ
	κού	Auratus	καί
1653.	αἱρούμεθα	Auratus	ἐρούμεθα
1654.	δράσωμεν	Victorius	δράσομεν
1655.	θέρος	Schütz	ὁ ἔρως
1656.	ἄλλης	nos	ἅλις γ'
	ἡματώμεθα	Wilamowitz	ἡματώμεθα
1657.	στείχετ' αἰδοῖοι	H. L. Ahrens	στείχετε δ' οἱ
1657-8.	Πεπρωμένης, ǀ πρὶν παθεῖν, στέρξαντες οὖρον	nos	πεπρωμένους τούσδε ǀ πρὶν παθεῖν ἔρξαντες καιρὸν f: (ἔρξαντα gh)
1659.	δεχοίμεθ'	Martin	γ' ἐχοίμεθ'
1662.	τούσδ' ἐμοὶ	Voss	τούσδε μοι
1663.	δαίμονος	Casaubon	δαίμονας
1664.	ἁμαρτεῖν τὸν	Casaubon	ἁμαρτῆτον
	θ' ὑβρίσαι addidit	Blomfield	
1671.	ὥστε	Scaliger	ὥσπερ
1672.	lacunae causa explendae ἐγὼ addidit (ex schol.)	Auratus	
1673.	lacunae causa explendae σέβας addidimus	nos	

ΤΑ ΤΟΥ ΔΡΑΜΑΤΟΣ ΠΡΟΣΩΠΑ

ΦΥΛΑΞ
ΧΟΡΟΣ
ΚΛΥΤΑΙΜΗΣΤΡΑ
ΚΗΡΥΞ
ΑΓΑΜΕΜΝΩΝ
ΚΑΣΑΝΔΡΑ
ΑΙΓΙΣΘΟΣ

DRAMATIS PERSONAE

WATCHMAN
CHORUS OF ELDERS
CLYTEMNESTRA
HERALD
AGAMEMNON
CASSANDRA
AEGISTHUS

AGAMEMNON

ΑΓΑΜΕΜΝΩΝ

ΦΥΛΑΞ

Θεοὺς μὲν αἰτῶ τῶνδ' ἀπαλλαγὴν πόνων,
φρουρᾶς ἐτείας μῆκος, ἣν κοιμώμενος
στέγαις Ἀτρειδῶν ἄγκαθεν, κυνὸς δίκην,
ἄστρων κάτοιδα νυκτέρων ὁμήγυριν
καὶ τοὺς φέροντας χεῖμα καὶ θέρος βροτοῖς   5
λαμπροὺς δυνάστας ἐμπρέποντας αἰθέρι,
καὶ νῦν φυλάσσων λαμπάδος τὸ σύμβολον,
αὐγὴν πυρὸς φέρουσαν ἐκ Τροίας φάτιν
ἁλώσιμόν τε βάξιν· ὧδε γὰρ κρατεῖ   10
γυναικὸς ἀνδρόβουλον ἐλπίζον κέαρ.
εὖτ' ἂν δὲ νυκτίπλαγκτον ἔνδροσόν τ' ἔχων
εὐνὴν ὀνείροις οὐκ ἐπισκοπουμένην
ἐμήν—φόβος γὰρ ἀντίος παραστατεῖ
τὸ μὴ βεβαίως βλέφαρα συμβαλεῖν ὕπνῳ—   15
ὅταν δ' ἀείδειν ἢ μινύρεσθαι δοκῶ,
ὕπνου τόδ' ἀντίμολπον ἐντέμνων ἄκος,
κλαίω τότ' οἴκου τοῦδε συμφορὰν στένων
οὐχ ὡς τὰ πρόσθ' ἄριστα διαπονουμένου.
νῦν δ' εὐτυχὴς γένοιτ' ἀπαλλαγὴ πόνων   20
εὐαγγέλου φανέντος ὀρφναίου πυρός.

ὦ χαῖρε λαμπτὴρ νυκτός, ἡμερήσιον
φάος πιφαύσκων καὶ χορῶν κατάστασιν
πολλῶν ἐν Ἄργει τῆσδε συμφορᾶς χάριν.
ἰοὺ ἰού.   25
Ἀγαμέμνονος γυναικὶ σημαίνω τορῶς
εὐνῆς ἐπαντείλασαν ὡς τάχος δόμοις
ὀλολυγμὸν εὐφημοῦντα τῇδε λαμπάδι
ἐπορθιάζειν, εἴπερ Ἰλίου πόλις
ἑάλωκεν, ὡς ὁ φρυκτὸς ἀγγέλλων πρέπει·   30
αὐτός τ' ἔγωγε φροίμιον χορεύσομαι.

AGAMEMNON

WATCHMAN.

God send me quit of this my weary post!
This whole year's length, here on the palace-roof,
Kennelled like watch-dog couching muzzle on paws,
Night on night I have conned the starry host
Whose lustrous chieftains blazon in the sky
The seasons' march, while still these eyes require
That signal-flare whose tongues of fire shall cry
Troy taken; so runs the queenly ordinance,
Enforcing woman's hope with man's resolve.
Pacing the night or stretched on rheumy pallet,—
No bed of dreams, I trow, for me, where Fear
Stands staring and withholds my lids from closing—
If ever I would whistle or troll a stave
And brew from melody slumber's antidote,
My song is merged in sorrow for this house,
Whose days of goodly governance are gone.
Oh! come the benison of toil reprieved,
And gladdening message set this gloom ablaze!

(*As he speaks the last words, the first gleam of the beacon shows behind him;
he pauses awhile, and then turning espies it*)

The beacon! ho! the beacon! Night is past,
The day-star risen. Oh! now shall Argos dance
In jubilation o'er our victory.
Ho there! Oho!
Loud ring my summons and arouse from sleep
Our sovereign lady, swift to solemnise
In swelling anthem of triumphant joy
The flaming advent of her messenger
Who cries Troy taken! Aye, and I too will dance

I-2

τὰ δεσποτῶν γὰρ εὖ πεσόντα θήσομαι
τρὶς ἓξ βαλούσης τῆσδέ μοι φρυκτωρίας.
γένοιτο δ᾽ οὖν μολόντος εὐφιλῆ χέρα
ἄνακτος οἴκων τῇδε βαστάσαι χερί. 35
τὰ δ᾽ ἄλλα σιγῶ· βοῦς ἐπὶ γλώσσῃ μέγας
βέβηκεν· οἶκος δ᾽ αὐτός, εἰ φθογγὴν λάβοι,
σαφέστατ᾽ ἂν λέξειεν· ὡς ἑκὼν ἐγὼ
μαθοῦσιν αὐδῶ κοὐ μαθοῦσι λήθομαι.

ΧΟΡΟΣ

δέκατον μὲν ἔτος τόδ᾽ ἐπεὶ Πριάμου 40
μέγας ἀντίδικος
Μενέλαος ἄναξ ἠδ᾽ Ἀγαμέμνων,
διθρόνου Διόθεν καὶ δισκήπτρου
τιμῆς ὀχυρὸν ζεῦγος Ἀτρειδᾶν,
στόλον Ἀργείων χιλιοναύτην 45
τῆσδ᾽ ἀπὸ χώρας
ἦραν, στρατιῶτιν ἀρωγήν,
μέγαν ἐκ θυμοῦ κλάζοντες Ἄρη
τρόπον αἰγυπιῶν, οἵτ᾽ ἐκπατίοις
ἄλγεσι παίδων ὕπατοι λεχέων 50
στροφοδινοῦνται
πτερύγων ἐρετμοῖσιν ἐρεσσόμενοι,
δεμνιοτήρη
πόνον ὀρταλίχων ὀλέσαντες·
ὕπατος δ᾽ ἀΐων ἤ τις Ἀπόλλων 55
ἢ Πὰν ἢ Ζεὺς οἰωνόθροον
γόον ὀξυβόαν τῶνδε μετοίκων
ὑστερόποινον
πέμπει παραβᾶσιν Ἐρινύν.
οὕτω δ᾽ Ἀτρέως παῖδας ὁ κρείσσων 60
ἐπ᾽ Ἀλεξάνδρῳ πέμπει ξένιος
Ζεὺς πολυάνορος ἀμφὶ γυναικὸς
πολλὰ παλαίσματα καὶ γυιοβαρῆ
γόνατος κονίαισιν ἐρειδομένου
διακναιομένης τ᾽ ἐν προτελείοις 65
κάμακος θήσων

A prelude; my lord's luck I'll score as mine;
Yon beaconage has thrown me a royal tierce.
   Soon may he come, and soon his gracious hand
Receive my homage! Old misgivings now
Are hushed; my lips are sealed. Yet might these walls,
Quicken'd to utterance, tell full plain a tale.
Whoso hath ears to hear, to him alone
I'll speak; for others is my memory void.

      (*Enter* The CHORUS of ELDERS)

CHORUS. Ten years have passed since first in the suit
           Of justice on Priam,
   Two brother-princes of Atreus' line,
   Exalted by grace of God and endowed
   With twofold sceptre and twofold throne,
      Agamemnon and Lord Menelaus,
   Led forth from our land on warrior-quest
     Their fleet of a thousand frigates.
   Loud rang their challenge as rings in the wild
   The wail of vultures who circle and stoop
   Disconsolate over a nest despoiled,
        Or sweep the skies
   With stroke of pinion for beat of the oar
   In dolorous quest of the vanished brood
    They tended of old in the eyrie.
   And the wail of the birds wins hearing on high,
   And Apollo may-be or Pan or Zeus
   Gives ear to his vassals' anguished cry
   And sends for vengeance in after-time
    A Fury to smite the offender.
   E'en so for vengeance on Paris were sent
   Lord Atreus' sons by a greater Lord,
   Who watches the troth of host and guest,
    In the cause of a much-wooed woman.
   Full many a struggle did he ordain,
   Where wearied knee is pressed in the dust
   And spears are splintered in first affray,

Δαναοῖσιν Τρωσί θ' ὁμοίως.
ἔστι δ' ὅπη νῦν ἔστι· τελεῖται δ'
ἐς τὸ πεπρωμένον·
οὔθ' ὑποκλαίων οὔθ' ὑπολείβων
ἀπύρων ἱερῶν   70
ὀργὰς ἀτενεῖς παραθέλξει.
ἡμεῖς δ' ἀτίται σαρκὶ παλαιᾷ
τῆς τότ' ἀρωγῆς ὑπολειφθέντες
μίμνομεν ἰσχὺν
ἰσόπαιδα νέμοντες ἐπὶ σκήπτροις.   75
ὅ τε γὰρ νεαρὸς μυελὸς στέρνων
ἐντὸς ἀνάσσων
ἰσόπρεσβυς, Ἄρης δ' οὐκ ἔνι χώρᾳ,
τό θ' ὑπέργηρων φυλλάδος ἤδη
κατακαρφομένης τρίποδας μὲν ὁδοὺς   80
στείχει, παιδὸς δ' οὐδὲν ἀρείων
ὄναρ ἡμερόφαντον ἀλαίνει.

    σὺ δέ, Τυνδάρεω
θύγατερ, βασίλεια Κλυταιμήστρα,
τί χρέος; τί νέον; τί δ' ἐπαισθομένη,   85
τίνος ἀγγελίας
πειθοῖ, περίπεμπτα θυοσκεῖς;
πάντων δὲ θεῶν τῶν ἀστυνόμων,
ὑπάτων, χθονίων,
τῶν τ' οὐρανίων τῶν τ' ἀγοραίων,   90
βωμοὶ δώροισι φλέγονται·
ἄλλη δ' ἄλλοθεν οὐρανομήκης
λαμπὰς ἀνίσχει,
φαρμασσομένη χρίματος ἁγνοῦ
μαλακαῖς ἀδόλοισι παρηγορίαις,   95
πελάνῳ μυχόθεν βασιλείῳ.
τούτων λέξαι θ' ὅ τι καὶ δυνατὸν
καὶ θέμις αἰνεῖν,
παιών τε γενοῦ τῆσδε μερίμνης,
ἢ νῦν τοτὲ μὲν κακόφρων τελέθει,   100
τοτὲ δ' ἐκ θυσιῶν ἀγάν' αὖ φαίνουσ'

For Achaean alike and for Trojan.
Yet, hap what may, that end must come
  Which Fate hath willed;
No tears of remorse, no balm outpoured,
Shall avail to soften the stubborn wrath
  Of a sacrifice unconsumèd.
But we whose bodies are spent and scorned,—
No part was ours in the great campaign,
  But here we abide,
And feeble as children we rest our frames
  On a staff's support.
For e'en as humours that bear their sway
In the childish breast are weak as in Age,—
For the Spirit of War stands not at his post,—
So doth Eld far-spent, when the leaf grows sere,
Crave that third foot to support his steps,
And feeble as childhood he wanders forth
  All astray like a dream in the daylight.

  (*Enter* CLYTEMNESTRA and attendants)

O Tyndarus' child, Clytemnestra, our Queen,
What thing is afoot? What news hast heard?
What tidings move thee to visit each shrine
  With solemn procession and incense?
Each several God who guards our state
From height of heaven or depth of earth,
Far above us or midst our assembly-place,
  Hath altar with gifts a-glowing;
And on every side doth the leaping flame
  Soar skyward, allured
By the soft sweet spell of the unguent pure
  From the royal store of spikenard.
Speak then, O Queen, whatsoe'er thou canst
  And mayest proclaim,
And heal with thy words these brooding cares
That awhile do beset us with boding of ill,
Till anon Hope peeps from the altar-flame

ἐλπὶς ἀμύνει
τὴν θυμοβόρον φρενὶ λύπην.

κύριός εἰμι θροεῖν ὅδιον κράτος αἴσιον ἀνδρῶν   [στρ. α.
ἐκτελεοῦν· ἔτι γὰρ θεὸς ἐγκαταπνεύει   105
πειθώ, μολπᾶν τ᾽
ἀλκᾷ σύμφυτος αἰών·
ὅπως Ἀχαιῶν
δίθρονον κράτος, Ἑλλάδος ἥβας
ξύμφρονα ταγάν,   110
πέμπει σὺν δορὶ καὶ χερὶ πράκτορι
θούριος ὄρνις Τευκρίδ᾽ ἐπ᾽ αἶαν,
οἰωνῶν βασιλεὺς βασιλεῦσι νε-
ῶν ὁ κελαινός, ὅ τ᾽ ἐξόπιν ἀργᾶς,   115
φανέντες ἴκταρ μελάθρων
χερὸς ἐκ δοριπάλτου
παμπρέποις ἐν ἕδραισι,
βοσκόμενοι λαγίναν ἐρικύμονα φέρματι γέννας,
βλαβέντα λοισθίων δρόμων.   120
αἴλινον αἴλινον εἰπέ, τὸ δ᾽ εὖ νικάτω.

κεδνὸς δὲ στρατόμαντις ἰδὼν δύο λήμασι δισσοὺς   [ἀντ. α.
Ἀτρείδας μαχίμους ἐδάη λαγοδαίτας
πομποὺς τ᾽ ἀρχάς·
οὕτω δ᾽ εἶπε τεράζων·   125
ʽΧρόνῳ μὲν ἀγρεῖ
Πριάμου πόλιν ἅδε κέλευθος,
πάντα δὲ πύργων
κτήνη πρόσθε τὰ δημιοπληθῆ
Μοῖρ᾽ ἀλαπάξει πρὸς τὸ βίαιον·   130
οἷον μή τις ἄγα θεόθεν κνεφά-
σῃ προτυπὲν στόμιον μέγα Τροίας.
τίθησι νεῖκος γὰρ ἐπί-
φθονον Ἄρτεμις ἁγνὰ
πτανοῖσιν κυσὶ πατρὸς   136

With a vision of good, and eases again
Each aching heart of his sorrow.

(*Exit* CLYTEMNESTRA *without replying*)

'Tis mine to sing of warriors bold right eager to fulfil
The favouring omen seen beside their road;—
Upon my lips God's grace is still bestowed;
My minstrelsy wanes not with age, but hath her vigour still;—
How once it fell that sovrans twain
With single heart intent on war
Had bird of prowess to their counsellor,
And, sword in hand, th' Achaean train
Sailed for the Trojan shore.
Then were monarchs met with monarchs, lords of air with lords
of sea:
Where the uplifted sword-arm pointeth, plain doth every eye
discern
Quartered nigh the kings' pavilion, peers in martial majesty,
This an eagle robed in sable, that a silver-skirted erne,
And in their pounce, behold, all rent and torn
For their banquet, lies a hare
Big-burdened with a brood unborn,
Arrested while she sought to reach her lair.
Lift thy voice in lilt of sorrow!
Yet with blessing dawn the morrow!

Then came the trusty soldier-seer and lifted searching eyes
And marked the brother-kings in temper twain,
And to his soul the eagles' feast made plain
That issue whereunto should move the princes' bold emprise.
"In time shall Priam's city fall
A prey", quoth he, "to this our chace;
And all her people's wealth without the wall,
Their flocks, their herds, shall Doom withal
Seize and consume apace;
Save it be some God's displeasure, lowering like a tempest-cloud,
Blast this curb of Troy untimely, ere her spirit be subdued.
Holy Artemis is angered, holy Artemis hath vowed
'Gainst her father's wingèd huntsmen heritage of bitter feud,

αὐτότοκον πρὸ λόχου μογερὰν πτάκα θυομένοισι·
στυγεῖ δὲ δεῖπνον αἰετῶν.'
αἴλινον αἴλινον εἰπέ, τὸ δ' εὖ νικάτω.

'τόσον περ εὔφρων ἀ καλά   [μεσῳδ.
  δρόσοις ἀόπτοις   141
μαλερῶν λεόντων
πάντων τ' ἀγρονόμων φιλομάστοις
θηρῶν ὀβρικάλοισι τερπνά,
τούτων ἵεται ξύμβολα κρᾶναι
δεξιὰ μέν,—κατάμομφα δὲ φάσματα σούσθω.   145
ἰήιον δὲ καλέω Παιᾶνα,
μή τινας ἀντιπνόους Δαναοῖς
  χρονίας ἐχενῇδας
  ἀπλοίας τεύξῃ,   150
σπευδομένα θυσίαν ἑτέραν
ἄνομόν τιν', ἄδαιτον,
νεικέων τέκτονα σύμφυτον,
οὐ δεισήνορα. μίμνει γὰρ
φοβερὰ παλίνορτος
οἰκονόμος δολία μνάμων   155
μῆνις τεκνόποινος.'
τοιάδε Κάλχας ξὺν μεγάλοις
ἀγαθοῖς ἀπέκλαγξεν
μόρσιμ' ἀπ' ὀρνίθων ὁδίων
οἴκοις βασιλείοις·
τοῖς δ' ὁμόφωνον
αἴλινον αἴλινον εἰπέ, τὸ δ' εὖ νικάτω.

Ζεύς, ὅστις ποτ' ἐστίν, εἰ τόδ' αὐ-   [στρ. β.
τῷ φίλον κεκλημένῳ,   161
τοῦτό νιν προσεννέπω.
οὐκ ἔχω προσεικάσαι
πάντ' ἐπισταθμώμενος

Who o'er their victim's trembling form decreed,
    For deliverance, a death
        That sparèd not the very seed.
'Accursèd be the eagles' feast', she saith."
    Lift thy voice in lilt of sorrow!
    Yet with blessing dawn the morrow!

"Gracious is she, that Goddess fair, gracious and mild
    Unto the ravening lion's sightless brood;
    The sucklings of all beasts that range the wild
        Have pleasure in her wardenhood;
Yet she craveth now accomplish'd all the eagles did portend,
Be it prosperous of issue—nay, God's mercy now forfend
Threat of evil! Lord Apollo, let thy healing grace prevail
        To stay her hand,
Lest she rouse the winds to hold us, thwarted long, with idle sail,
        And e'en demand
    A sacrifice of other life,—
    No festal victim nor ordained of law,—
        Engrafting in this house a strife
    Wherein its lord be held no more in awe!
Horror haunts the house where lurketh, mindful of her children's
    fate,
Unrelenting Wrath, devising guilefully new deed of hate."
    So rang the prophet's warning words
    When he proclaimed the message sent
    To royal house by roadside birds,
        A woeful cry
    Albeit with joyous promise blent;
    And therewithal harmoniously
        Lift thy voice in lilt of sorrow!
        Yet with blessing dawn the morrow!

    Zeus, whatsoe'er thine essence be,
    If haply, thus invoked, thy heart
    Hath pleasure, thus I call on thee
    Adoring whatsoe'er thou art.
    Nay; other title find I none,
    Measuring all against my need,

πλὴν Διός, εἰ τὸ μάταν   165
ἀπὸ φροντίδος ἄχθος
χρὴ βαλεῖν ἐτητύμως.

ὃς μὲν τοῖς πάροιθεν ἦν μέγας,   [ἀντ. β.
παμμάχῳ θράσει βρύων,
οὐδὲ λέξεται πρὶν ὤν·   170
ὃς δ᾽ ἔπειτ᾽ ἔφυ, τρια-
κτῆρος οἴχεται τυχών.
Ζῆνα δέ τις προφρόνως
ἐπινίκια κλάζων
τεύξεται φρενῶν τὸ πᾶν·   175

τὸν φρονεῖν βροτοὺς ὁδώ-   [στρ. γ.
σαντα, τὸν πάθει μάθος
θέντα κυρίως ἔχειν.
στάζει δ᾽ ἔν θ᾽ ὕπνῳ πρὸ καρδίας
μνησιπήμων πόνος, καὶ παρ᾽ ἄ-   180
κοντας ἦλθε σωφρονεῖν.
δαιμόνων δέ που χάρις βίαιος
σέλμα σεμνὸν ἡμένων.

καὶ τόθ᾽ ἡγεμὼν ὁ πρέ-   [ἀντ. γ.
σβυς νεῶν Ἀχαιικῶν,   185
μάντιν οὔτινα ψέγων,
ἐμπαίοις τύχαισι συμπνέων,
εὖτ᾽ ἀπλοίᾳ κεναγγεῖ βαρύ-
νοντ᾽ Ἀχαιικὸς λεώς,
Χαλκίδος πέραν ἔχων παλιρρό-   190
χθοις ἐν Αὐλίδος τόποις·

Except the name of Zeus alone,
Whereby my burdened soul may be
Enlarged in verity and freed
From all her vain perplexity.

For he whose plenitude of might
Was once acclaimed by men of yore
Supreme o'er all in every fight
Is gone, and shall be named no more;
And he that followed next did yield
To stronger arms; in triple bout
Discomfited, he left the field;
Zeus is the victor; whoso cries
The victor's praise with heart devout,
He shall have wisdom for his prize.

'Twas Zeus who turned men's hearts to see
True understanding, and bestowed
On Sorrow her authority
To guide their feet on Wisdom's road.
E'en in our sleep 'tis manifest:
The anguish of remembered ill
Instilleth prudence in the breast
Till men wax wise against their will.
The Gods enthronèd in their holy place
Use violence, methinks, to give man grace.

So in that hour the prince whose sway
Was sovran o'er the Achaean host,
When tempest-bound their galleys lay
Where Aulis looks on Chalcis' coast
Across those tides that evermore
Swirl to and fro, and now his folk
Were straitened by fast-emptying store,—
Lo! whatsoe'er a prophet spoke
He held for righteousness, and bowed his head
Obedient to the wind that buffeted.

πνοαὶ δ' ἀπὸ Στρυμόνος μολοῦσαι   [στρ. δ.
κακόσχολοι, νήστιδες, δύσορμοι
   βροτῶν ἄλαι,
νεῶν τε καὶ πεισμάτων ἀφειδεῖς,   195
παλιμμήκη χρόνον τιθεῖσαι
τρίβῳ κατέξαινον ἄνθος Ἀργολᾶν·
   ἐπεὶ δὲ καὶ πικροῦ
   χείματος ἄλλο μῆχαρ
   βριθύτερον πρόμοισιν   200
μάντις ἔκλαγξεν προφέρων
Ἄρτεμιν, ὥστε χθόνα βάκτροις
ἐπικρούσαντας Ἀτρείδας
   δάκρυ μὴ κατασχεῖν·

ἄναξ δ' ὁ πρέσβυς τόδ' εἶπε φωνῶν·   [ἀντ. δ.
'Βαρεῖα μὲν κὴρ τὸ μὴ πιθέσθαι,   206
   βαρεῖα δ', εἰ
τέκνον δαΐξω, δόμων ἄγαλμα,
μιαίνων παρθενοσφάγοισι
ῥείθροις πατρῴους χέρας βωμοῦ πέλας.   210
   τί τῶνδ' ἄνευ κακῶν;
   πῶς λιπόναυς γένωμαι
   ξυμμαχίας ἁμαρτών;
παυσανέμου γὰρ θυσίας
παρθενίου θ' αἵματος ὀργᾷ   215
περιόργῳ σφ' ἐπιθυμεῖν
   θέμις. εὖ γὰρ εἴη.'

ἐπεὶ δ' ἀνάγκας ἔδυ λέπαδνον   [στρ. ε.
φρενὸς πνέων δυσσεβῆ τροπαίαν
   ἄναγνον, ἀνίερον, τόθεν   220
τὸ παντότολμον φρονεῖν μετέγνω,—
βροτοὺς θρασύνει γὰρ αἰσχρόμητις
τάλαινα παρακοπὰ πρωτοπήμων,—

For gales that swept amain from Strymon's shore—
Gales that hold in hungry durance, gales that drive in dire distress
Battered ships that fail of mooring wide o'er waters havenless,—
    Had doubled now their wonted stay
    And hour by hour were fretting sore
        That proud array.
    Oh! grievous was the tempest's rage;
    Yet must the chieftains e'en endure
  At Artemis' behest, so cried the sage,
  A grief more bitter for the tempest's cure.
    And they, Lord Atreus' sons renowned,
    When rang that message in their ears,
    Smote with their staves upon the ground
    And stayèd not their tears.

    Then came the elder prince's voice anew:
"Dire the paths of disobedience, dire my destiny withal
If my child, my joy and jewel, slain by deed of mine shall fall
    A victim, where yon altar stands,
    And with a daughter's blood imbrue
        Her father's hands.
    Where all is ill, how can I choose?
    Oh, how can I endure to see
  My ships desert me, how endure to lose
  The comrades of my quest? It may not be.
    'Tis right, their fierce expectant mood,
    Their eager hope to appease the gale
    By sacrifice of virgin blood;
    God grant that good prevail!"

    So when Necessity drew tight
    Her rein, and he no more rebelled,
    When veered his spirit, veered and swelled
    To contumacy and despite,
Till recklessness possessed him utterly,—
For e'er 'tis so; man's heart once set awry
And hardened in desire of froward deed,
'Tis thence that all disaster doth proceed,—

ἔτλα δ᾽ οὖν θυτὴρ γενέ-
σθαι θυγατρός, γυναικοποί-
νων πολέμων ἀρωγὰν   226
καὶ προτέλεια ναῶν.

λιτὰς δὲ καὶ κληδόνας πατρῴους   [ἀντ. ε.
παρ᾽ οὐδὲν αἰῶ τε παρθένειον
ἔθεντο φιλόμαχοι βραβῆς.   230
φράσεν δ᾽ ἀόζοις πατὴρ μετ᾽ εὐχὰν
δίκαν χιμαίρας ὕπερθε βωμοῦ
πέπλοισι περιπετῆ πάντ᾽ ἄθυμον
προνωπῆ λαβεῖν ἀέρ-
δην, στόματός τε καλλιπρῴ-
ρου φυλακὰν κατασχεῖν   236
φθόγγον ἀραῖον οἴκοις

βίᾳ χαλινῶν τ᾽ ἀναύδῳ μένει.   [στρ. ζ.
κρόκου βαφὰς δ᾽ ἐκ πέδονδε χεύασ᾽
ἔβαλλ᾽ ἕκαστον θυτή-   240
ρων ἀπ᾽ ὄμματος βέλει φιλοίκτῳ,
πρέπουσά θ᾽ ὡς ἐν γραφαῖς, προσεννέπειν
θέλουσ᾽, ἐπεὶ πολλάκις
πατρὸς κατ᾽ ἀνδρῶνας εὐτραπέζους
ἔμελψεν, ἁγνᾷ δ᾽ ἀταύρωτος αὐδᾷ πατρὸς   245
φίλου τριτόσπονδον εὔποτμον
παιᾶνα φίλως ἐτίμα.

τὰ δ᾽ ἔνθεν οὔτ᾽ εἶδον οὔτ᾽ ἐννέπω·   [ἀντ. ζ.
τέχναι δὲ Κάλχαντος οὐκ ἄκραντοι.
Δίκα δὲ τοῖς μὲν παθοῦ-   250
σιν μαθεῖν ἐπιρρέπει· τὸ μέλλον δ᾽,
ἐπεὶ γένοιτ᾽ ἂν κλύουσι, χαιρέτω·
ἴσον δὲ τῷ προστένειν.
τορὸν γὰρ ἥξει σύνορθρον αὐγαῖς.
πέλοιτο δ᾽ οὖν τἀπὶ τούτοισιν εὔπραξις, ὡς
θέλει τόδ᾽ ἄγχιστον Ἀπίας   256
γαίας μονόφρουρον ἕρκος.

Oh! then from his own daughter's death he stood no more aloof,
   All for the furtherance of war
   Adventured on a woman's score,
    And in his ships' behoof.

   No prayer, no appeal to fatherhood,
   No pity for a maid unwed,
   Could melt her warrior-judges' mood.
   With prayer of consecration said
Her father bade the serving-men draw nigh
Where huddled in her robes she crouched alone
In uttermost despair, and lift her high,
As 'twere some fatling, o'er the altar-stone,
And, lest her voice denounce his house, conjuring dire redress,
   Her lovely lips he bade be quelled
   With muffling bond, and straitly held
    All mute and murmurless.

But now she rose; her saffron-bordered hood
Slipped to the ground, and from her eyes there went,
Like arrow piercing them that sought her blood,
A glance of anguish; dumbly eloquent,
As in a picture, seemed her piteous soul.
Full oft in other days her voice had thrilled
The guests who thronged her father's festal hall
When, sweet in maiden innocence, she trilled,
In glad obedience to her father's call,
A benediction o'er the flowing bowl.

What passèd next, I saw not, nor can show,
Save that the prophet's lore must be fulfilled.
Yet what avails it? Justice hath not willed
To mete out wisdom ere 'tis earned by woe.
What though men hear what cometh? Doom revealed
Must still befall. Then let the future be!
Foreknowledge were foretaste of misery.
'Twill dawn betimes sure as the break of day.
God send the sequel fair, e'en as doth pray
She who alone is our defence and shield!

LAA   2

Χ|ΟΡΟΣ

ἥκω σεβίζων σόν, Κλυταιμήστρα, κράτος·
δίκη γάρ ἐστι φωτὸς ἀρχηγοῦ τίειν
γυναῖκ' ἐρημωθέντος ἄρσενος θρόνου.   260
σὺ δ' εἴ τι κεδνὸν εἴτε μὴ πεπυσμένη
εὐαγγέλοισιν ἐλπίσιν θυηπολεῖς,
κλύοιμ' ἂν εὔφρων· οὐδὲ σιγώσῃ φθόνος.

ΚΛΥΤΑΙΜΗΣΤΡΑ

εὐάγγελος μέν, ὥσπερ ἡ παροιμία,
ἕως γένοιτο μητρὸς εὐφρόνης πάρα.   265
πεύσει δὲ χάρμα μεῖζον ἐλπίδος κλύειν·
Πριάμου γὰρ ᾑρήκασιν Ἀργεῖοι πόλιν.
ΧΟ. πῶς φής; πέφευγε τοὔπος ἐξ ἀπιστίας.
ΚΛ. Τροίαν Ἀχαιῶν οὖσαν· ἢ τορῶς λέγω;
ΧΟ. χαρά μ' ὑφέρπει δάκρυον ἐκκαλουμένη.   270
ΚΛ. εὖ γὰρ φρονοῦντος ὄμμα σοῦ κατηγορεῖ.
ΧΟ. τί γὰρ τὸ πιστόν; ἔστι τῶνδέ σοι τέκμαρ;
ΚΛ. ἔστιν· τί δ' οὐχί; μὴ δολώσαντος θεοῦ.
ΧΟ. πότερα δ' ὀνείρων φάσματ' εὐπιθῆ σέβεις;
ΚΛ. οὐ δόξαν ἂν λαλοῖμι βριζούσης φρενός.   275
ΧΟ. ἀλλ' ἦ σ' ἐπίανέν τις ἄπτερος φάτις;
ΚΛ. παιδὸς νέας ὣς κάρτ' ἐμωμήσω φρένας.
ΧΟ. ποίου χρόνου δὲ καὶ πεπόρθηται πόλις;
ΚΛ. τῆς νῦν τεκούσης φῶς τόδ' εὐφρόνης λέγω.
ΧΟ. καὶ τίς τόδ' ἐξίκοιτ' ἂν ἀγγέλων τάχος;   280
ΚΛ. Ἥφαιστος,—Ἴδης λαμπρὸν ἐκπέμπων σέλας.
φρυκτὸς δὲ φρυκτὸν δεῦρ' ἀπ' ἀγγάρου πυρὸς
ἔπεμπεν· Ἴδη μὲν πρὸς Ἑρμαῖον λέπας
Λήμνου· μέγαν δὲ πανὸν ἐκ νήσου τρίτον
Ἀθῷον αἶπος Ζηνὸς ἐξεδέξατο,   285
ὑπερτελής τε, πόντον ὥστε νωτίσαι,
ἰσχὺς πορευτοῦ λαμπάδος πρὸς ἡδονὴν
ἐπεῦκτο χρυσοφεγγές, ὥς τις ἥλιος,
σέλας παραγγείλασα Μακίστου σκοπαῖς·
ὁ δ' οὔτι μέλλων οὐδ' ἀφρασμόνως ὕπνῳ   290
νικώμενος παρῆκεν ἀγγέλου μέρος·

(Enter CLYTEMNESTRA*)*

ELDER. My humble duty, Lady, I present;
A kingless throne doth on the queen bestow
Th' inheritance of this my fealty.
Fain would I hear the import of these rites;
Hast thou sure tidings, or no message save
Joy whisper'd by fond hope? Fain would I hear;
Yet shall my patience wait on thy good grace.

CLYT. Though for a night doth heaviness endure,
Bring Morn tidings of gladness!—so men pray;
But thine shall be a joy out-soaring hope:
Th' Achaean hosts have taken Priam's town.

ELDER. Speak it again! Misdoubt hath dimmed my ears.

CLYT. Troy is in Argive hands. Speak I not plain?

ELDER. Dimming mine eyes now with the thrill of joy.

CLYT. That dimness cloudeth not their loyalty.

ELDER. What is thy surety? Hast thou verily proof?

CLYT. Aye, surest proof, so be God cheats me not.

ELDER. Some winsome dream perchance thine oracle?

CLYT. No slumberer's fantasy should set me prattling.

ELDER. Could faery rumour tonic thus thy soul?

CLYT. Am I a child to need thy admonishment?

ELDER. Since when in sooth hath Ilium lain despoiled?

CLYT. Since that same night, I say, whence sprang this dawn.

ELDER. What herald e'er could compass such despatch?

CLYT. Hephaestus,—flashing forth from Ida's crest
To post with swift relay of fiery steeds
From beacon unto beacon. Ida first
To Hermes' crag in Lemnos flung the flame,
To make third station, soaring from the isle,
At Zeus' own sanctuary aloft on Athos;
Where, towering high to bridge the sea's broad span,
The giant courier-blaze made joyful boast
That never sun shot message-beam more bright
With golden glory to Macistus' towers.
Who, faltering not nor merged in lethargy,

2-2

ἑκὰς δὲ φρυκτοῦ φῶς ἐπ᾽ Εὐρίπου ῥοὰς
Μεσσαπίου φύλαξι σημαίνει μολόν.
οἱ δ᾽ ἀντέλαμψαν καὶ παρήγγειλαν πρόσω
γραίας ἐρείκης θωμὸν ἄψαντες πυρί.   295
σθένουσα λαμπὰς δ᾽ οὐδέπω μαυρουμένη,
ὑπερθοροῦσα πεδίον Ἀσωποῦ, δίκην
φαιδρᾶς σελήνης, πρὸς Κιθαιρῶνος λέπας,
ἤγειρεν ἄλλην ἐκδοχὴν πομποῦ πυρός.
φάος δὲ τηλέπομπον οὐκ ἠναίνετο   300
φρουρά, πλέον καίουσα τῶν εἰρημένων·
λίμνην δ᾽ ὑπὲρ Γοργῶπιν ἔσκηψεν φάος,
ὄρος τ᾽ ἐπ᾽ Αἰγίπλαγκτον ἐξικνούμενον
ὤτρυνε θεσμὸν μὴ χρονίζεσθαι πυρός.
πέμπουσι δ᾽ ἀνδαίοντες ἀφθόνῳ μένει   305
φλογὸς μέγαν πώγωνα, καὶ Σαρωνικοῦ
πορθμοῦ κάτοπτον πρῶν᾽ ὑπερβάλλειν πρόσω
φλέγουσαν, ἔστ᾽ ἔσκηψεν, εὖτ᾽ ἀφίκετο
Ἀραχναῖον αἶπος, ἀστυγείτονας σκοπάς·
κἄπειτ᾽ Ἀτρειδῶν ἐς τόδε σκήπτει στέγος   310
φάος τόδ᾽ οὐκ ἄπαππον Ἰδαίου πυρός.
τοιοίδε τοί μοι λαμπαδηφόρων νόμοι,
ἄλλος παρ᾽ ἄλλου διαδοχαῖς πληρούμενοι·
νικᾷ δ᾽ ὁ πρῶτος καὶ τελευταῖος δραμών.
τέκμαρ τοιοῦτο σύμβολόν τε σοὶ λέγω   315
ἀνδρὸς παραγγείλαντος ἐκ Τροίας ἐμοί.
ΧΟ. θεοῖς μὲν αὖθις, ὦ γύναι, προσεύξομαι·
λόγους δ᾽ ἀκοῦσαι τούσδε κἀποθαυμάσαι
διηνεκῶς θέλοιμ᾽ ἂν ὡς λέγεις πάλιν.
ΚΛ. Τροίαν Ἀχαιοὶ τῇδ᾽ ἔχουσ᾽ ἐν ἡμέρᾳ.   320
οἶμαι βοὴν ἄμικτον ἐν πόλει πρέπειν.
ὄξος τ᾽ ἄλειφά τ᾽ ἐγχέας ταὐτῷ κύτει
διχοστατοῦντ᾽ ἂν οὐ φίλως προσεννέποις·
καὶ τῶν ἁλόντων καὶ κρατησάντων δίχα
φθογγὰς ἀκούειν ἔστι συμφορᾶς διπλῆς.   325
οἱ μὲν γὰρ ἀμφὶ σώμασιν πεπτωκότες
ἀνδρῶν κασιγνήτων τε καὶ φυταλμίων
παῖδες γερόντων οὐκέτ᾽ ἐξ ἐλευθέρου
δέρης ἀποιμώζουσι φιλτάτων μόρον·

Fulfilled his part; athwart Euripus' flood
Unto Messapium's sentinels afar
Fled on the signal; they with answering flame
From swiftly-kindled stack of withered heath
Tossed on the story: strong, unquenchable,
O'er the Asopus-prairie leapt the light,
Ruddy as rising moon, eager to wake
High on Cithaeron's crags fresh train of radiance.
There in no churlish wise the watchmen fed
The travelled ray with fuel multiplied,
Whose gleam o'ershot Gorgopis bay, and sprang
To th' heights of Aegiplanctus, challenging
New ministry of fire; that tarried not,
But kindled lavishly a fount of flame
And sent it streaming high, clean to o'erleap
The bluff that frowns on the Saronic strait
And make true landfall where our warder-post
Crowns Arachnaeum's crest; thence to alight
Upon this royal roof, last of his line,
True issue of Mount Ida's beacon-fire.

    So for this pageant marshalled I my team
In ordered sequence of replenishment.
First shall be last, and last be first: the race
Is unto him who first attains his goal.
Such is the warrant of my certitude
To speak a message of my lord from Troy.

ELDER.   Lady, the Gods anon shall have their meed
Of adoration; yet first am I fain
To savour the full wonder of thy tale.

CLYT.   This day the Achaeans hold Troy-town in fee.
Conflicting clamours sound, methinks, her knell.
Dost mark how oil and vinegar consort,
The content of one cup, yet ill-content?
E'en so from vanquished and from victor's throat
Divided cries proclaim their lot diverse.
Here speaketh anguish, where wife, sister, son,
Enfolding fast their fallen, make last moan
From lips that soon captivity shall mute;

τοὺς δ' αὖτε νυκτίπλαγκτος ἐκ μάχης πόνος 330
νήστεις πρὸς ἀρίστοισιν ὧν ἔχει πόλις
τάσσει, πρὸς οὐδὲν ἐν μέρει τεκμήριον,
ἀλλ' ὡς ἕκαστος ἔσπασεν τύχης πάλον.
ἐν αἰχμαλώτοις Τρωικοῖς οἰκήμασιν
ναίουσιν ἤδη, τῶν ὑπαιθρίων πάγων 335
δρόσων τ' ἀπαλλαγέντες, ὡς δ' εὐδαίμονες
ἀφύλακτον εὐδήσουσι πᾶσαν εὐφρόνην.
εἰ δ' εὖ σέβουσι τοὺς πολισσούχους θεοὺς
τοὺς τῆς ἁλούσης γῆς θεῶν θ' ἱδρύματα,
οὔ τἂν ἑλόντες αὖθις ἀνθαλοῖεν ἄν. 340
ἔρως δὲ μή τις πρότερον ἐμπίπτοι στρατῷ
πορθεῖν τὰ μὴ χρή, κέρδεσιν νικωμένους.
δεῖ γὰρ πρὸς οἴκους νοστίμου σωτηρίας,
κάμψαι διαύλου θάτερον κῶλον πάλιν·
θεοῖς δ' ἄρ' ἀμπλάκητος εἰ μόλοι στρατός, 345
ἐγρηγορὸς μήνιμα τῶν ὀλωλότων
γένοιτ' ἄν, εἰ πρόσπαια μὴ τύχοι κακά.
τοιαῦτά τοι γυναικὸς ἐξ ἐμοῦ κλύεις·
τὸ δ' εὖ κρατοίη, μὴ διχορρόπως ἰδεῖν.
πολλῶν γὰρ ἐσθλῶν τήνδ' ὄνησιν εἱλόμην. 350
ΧΟ. γύναι, κατ' ἄνδρα σώφρον' εὐφρόνως λέγεις.
ἐγὼ δ' ἀκούσας πιστά σου τεκμήρια
θεοὺς προσειπεῖν αὖ παρασκευάζομαι·
χάρις γὰρ οὐκ ἄτιμος εἴργασται πόνων.

ὦ Ζεῦ βασιλεῦ καὶ νὺξ φιλία 355
μεγάλων κόσμων κτεάτειρα,
ἥτ' ἐπὶ Τροίας πύργοις ἔβαλες
στεγανὸν δίκτυον, ὡς μήτε μέγαν
μήτ' οὖν νεαρῶν τιν' ὑπερτελέσαι
μέγα δουλείας 360
γάγγαμον, ἄτης παναλώτου.
Δία τοι ξένιον μέγαν αἰδοῦμαι
τὸν τάδε πράξαντ' ἐπ' Ἀλεξάνδρῳ
τείνοντα πάλαι τόξον, ὅπως ἂν
μήτε πρὸ καιροῦ μήθ' ὑπὲρ ἄστρων 365
βέλος ἠλίθιον σκήψειεν.

Yonder the flotsam of the hard-fought night
Stand on no sequence now, but snatch amain
Each casual bounty of the city's stores
To bate their hunger. Lodged in Trojan homes,
Sheltered at last from frost and dew, they dream
Of night-long sleep that needs no sentinel.
And if they reverence now the city's Gods
That guard the captured land, and spare their fanes,
The spoiler shall not in his turn be spoiled.
God grant meanwhile no mastering avarice
Attempt their heart to covet prize forbidden!
For still they need safe home-coming; their course
From turning-post to goal is yet to run.
If they should come in sin and sacrilege,
The anger of the dead perchance might wake,
So be no swifter act of God befall.
Such is the counsel of a woman's tongue.
May right prevail, poised in no dubious scale!
Wide are the blessings compassed in that wish.

ELDER.   Lady, a man's wit moulds thy gracious words;
And I, partaking of thy firm assurance,
Garb now my heart to hymn her gratitude.
The prize achieved hath well repaid the toil.

CHORUS. Hail, Zeus our king, hail, gladdening night,
     That hast won for our host great glories,
That drewest about the towers of Troy
A net so close that nor youth nor strength
Leapt clear of thy toils nor burst thy bonds,
     But are taken in doom all-embracing!
Great Zeus, stern guardian of troth, I extol,
Who wrought the requital, with bow long bent
For vengeance on Paris, in steady intent
That in his due time and true to the mark
     His shaft err not nor miscarry.

"Διὸς πλαγὰν ἔχουσ'," ἀνειπεῖν·   [στρ. α.
πάρεστίν τοι τόδ' ἐξιχνεῦσαι.
ἔπραξαν ὡς ἔκρανεν. οὐκ ἔφα τις
θεοὺς βροτῶν ἀξιοῦσθαι μέλειν   370
    ὅσοις ἀθίκτων χάρις
    πατοῖθ'· ὁ δ' οὐκ εὐσεβής.
πέφανται δ' ἐγγὺς οὖσα λύμα
    τῶν Ἄρη πνεόντων   375
    μεῖζον ἢ δικαίως,
φλεόντων δωμάτων ὑπέρφευ
ὑπὲρ τὸ βέλτιστον. ἔστω δ' ἀπήμαντον ὥστ' ἀπαρκεῖν
    εὖ πραπίδων λαχόντα.   380
οὐ γὰρ ἔστιν ἔπαλξις
πλούτου πρὸς κόρον ἀνδρὶ
λακτίσαντι μέγαν Δίκας
βωμὸν εἰς ἀφάνειαν.   384

βιᾶται δ' ἁ τάλαινα πειθώ,   [ἀντ. α.
προβουλευτὰς ἄφερτος ἄτας·
ἄκος δὲ πᾶν μάταιον. οὐκ ἐκρύφθη,
πρέπει δέ, φῶς αἰνολαμπές, σίνος·
    κακοῦ δὲ χαλκοῦ τρόπον   390
    τρίβῳ τε καὶ προσβολαῖς
μελαμπαγὴς πέλει δικαιω-
θείς, ἐπεὶ διώκει
    παῖς ποτανὸν ὄρνιν,
πόλει πρόστριμμα θεὶς ἄφερτον.   395
λιτᾶν δ' ἀκούει μὲν οὔτις θεῶν·
    τὸν δ' ἐπίστροφον τῶν
    φῶτ' ἄδικον καθαιρεῖ.
οἷος καὶ Πάρις ἐλθὼν
ἐς δόμον τὸν Ἀτρειδᾶν   400
ᾔσχυνε ξενίαν τράπε-
ζαν κλοπαῖσι γυναικός.

'Tis Zeus whose hand hath dealt the blow.
Proclaim it loud! 'tis plain to trace;
   They fared as he decreed.
It hath been said the Gods deign not to heed
When under mortals' feet the mystic grace
   Of hallowed things is trampled low.
      Oh! utterance profane!
Plain to behold stands Ruin at their side
   Who breathe defiance and transgress
   The boundaries of righteousness,
   Trusting in riches multiplied
     That work their masters' bane.
Oh! let the prudent soul be satisfied
To pass a sheltered life untouched of pain!
   The rich in weary-wanton plight
   Hath no defence wherein to trust
   When once he hath dethronèd Right
   And trod her counsels in the dust.

   Temptation mockingly prepares
   The doom that Sin shall ratify,
     And giveth him no rest;
No cure avails; a lurid glint declares
The lurking bane; as doth the touchstone try
   Base metal, so doth justice test
     The soul of blemished grain.
Like to a child chasing a bird, he goes
   Unheeding in his froward quest,
   Unheeding of his city's woes;
   Stained with his guilt and sore oppressed
     She cries to Heav'n in vain.
Whoso with sin consort, to sin consent,
And share withal the sinner's chastisement.
   'Twas on such wise that Paris came
   And feasted at the Atreidae's board,
   And lured a woman from her lord,
   And brought dishonour on his name.

λιποῦσα δ᾽ ἀστοῖσιν ἀσπίστοράς   [στρ. β.
τε καὶ κλόνους λογχίμους
ναυβάτας θ᾽ ὁπλισμούς,   405
ἄγουσά τ᾽ ἀντίφερνον Ἰλίῳ φθορὰν
βέβακεν ῥίμφα διὰ πυλᾶν
ἄτλητα τλᾶσα· πολλὰ δ᾽ ἔστενον
τόδ᾽ ἐννέποντες δόμων προφῆται·
'ἰὼ ἰὼ δῶμα, δῶμα καὶ πρόμοι,   410
ἰὼ λέχος καὶ στίβοι φιλάνορες.
πάρεστι σιγὰς ἀτίμους ἀλοιδόρους
ἄστοις ἐφημμένων ἰδεῖν.
πόθῳ δ᾽ ὑπερποντίας
φάσμα δόξει δόμων ἀνάσσειν.   415
εὐμόρφων δὲ κολοσσῶν
ἔχθεται χάρις ἀνδρί·
ὀμμάτων δ᾽ ἐν ἀχηνίαις
ἔρρει πᾶσ᾽ Ἀφροδίτα.   419

ὀνειρόφαντοι δὲ πενθήμονες   [ἀντ. β.
πάρεισι δόξαι φέρου-
σαι χάριν ματαίαν.
ματᾷ γὰρ εὐχᾶν ἐσθλά τις δοκῶν ὁρᾶν·
παραλλάξασα διὰ χερῶν
βέβακεν ὄψις οὐ μεθύστερον   425
πτεροῖς ὀπαδοῖς ὕπνου κελεύθοις.'
τὰ μὲν κατ᾽ οἴκους ἐφ᾽ ἑστίας ἄχη
τάδ᾽ ἐστὶ καὶ τῶνδ᾽ ὑπερβατώτερα.
τὸ πᾶν δ᾽ ἀφ᾽ Ἕλλανος αἴας συνορμένοις
πένθεια τηξικάρδιος   430
δόμων ἑκάστου πρέπει.
πολλὰ γοῦν θιγγάνει πρὸς ἧπαρ·
οὓς μὲν γάρ τις ἔπεμψεν
οἶδεν, ἀντὶ δὲ φωτῶν
τεύχη καὶ σποδὸς εἰς ἑκά-   435
στου δόμους ἀφικνεῖται.

Unto her townsmen she bequeathed
The clanging shield, the sword unsheathed,
   And ships for war equipped;
And with destruction for the dower
She bare to Troy, in fatal hour
   Light-footed forth she tripped.
Then cried the palace-sages in dismay:
"Woe, woe to these halls! Woe, woe to their king!
Woe for the bed of love wherein she lay!
   Oh piteous sight, mid open shame,
   In silence, with no word of blame,
When joys are vanished, still thereto to cling!
Over the seas is she his soul adored,
And leaves these halls a phantom for their lord.
   The shapely marble hath no grace
   To ease his heart; those eyes that shone
   Enchant for him no more her face,
   And love's allurement all is gone.

"Though slumber bring to dreaming eyes
Her sorrow-gotten phantasies,
   All vain is their delight;
Foiled hope ensues on vision bright,
When slipping through thine arms anon
   'Tis swept away and gone
And numbered with the fleeting things of night."
These sorrows, and surpassing these, press close
About the hearth within our royal hall;
   But in the homes of each and all
   Who in their multitude uprose
And from their country's coasts went forth to fight,
Is mourning meet, and hearts that melt to tears;
Full many are their kinsmen's griefs and fears.
   Whom each sent forth to war, he knows;
   But that which now returneth home
   No human token doth disclose;
   'Tis urns and ashes that are come.

ὁ χρυσαμοιβὸς δ' Ἄρης σωμάτων [στρ. γ.
καὶ ταλαντοῦχος ἐν μάχῃ δορὸς
πυρωθὲν ἐξ Ἰλίου 440
φίλοισι πέμπει βαρὺ
ψῆγμα δυσδάκρυτον ἀν-
τήνορος σποδοῦ γεμί-
ζων λέβητας εὐθέτου.
στένουσι δ' εὖ λέγοντες ἄν- 445
δρα τὸν μὲν ὡς μάχης ἴδρις,
τὸν δ' ἐν φοναῖς καλῶς πεσόντ'—
"ἀλλοτρίας διαὶ γυναικός,"
τάδε σῖγά τις βαΰζει·
φθονερὸν δ' ὑπ' ἄλγος ἕρπει 450
προδίκοις Ἀτρείδαις.
οἱ δ' αὐτοῦ περὶ τεῖχος
θήκας Ἰλιάδος γᾶς
εὔμορφοι κατέχουσιν· ἐχ-
θρὰ δ' ἔχοντας ἔκρυψεν. 455

βαρεῖα δ' ἀστῶν φάτις ξὺν κότῳ· [ἀντ. γ.
δημοκράντου δ' ἀρᾶς τίνει χρέος.
μένει δ' ἀκοῦσαί τί μου
μέριμνα νυκτηρεφές. 460
τῶν πολυκτόνων γὰρ οὐκ
ἄσκοποι θεοί. κελαι-
ναὶ δ' Ἐρινύες χρόνῳ
τυχηρὸν ὄντ' ἄνευ δίκας
παλιντυχεῖ τριβᾷ βίου 465
τιθεῖσ' ἀμαυρόν, ἐν δ' ἀί-
στοις τελέθοντος οὔτις ἀλκά.
τὸ δ' ὑπερκόπως κλύειν εὖ
βαρύ· βάλλεται γὰρ ὄσσοις
Διόθεν κεραυνός. 470
κρίνω δ' ἄφθονον ὄλβον·
μήτ' εἴην πτολιπόρθης
μήτ' οὖν αὐτὸς ἁλοὺς ὑπ' ἄλλῳ βίον κατίδοιμι.

Ares, who doth deem men's bodies things of barter, bought and
    sold,
Weighing them in the scales of battle, trading in exchange his
    gold,
        Doth send from Troy, unto their kin consigned,
          His gold-dust in the fire refined,
        An heavy and a lamentable hoard,
Ashes, to pay the price of men, in caskets deftly stored.
        And 'mid their dirges they give praise and tell
        Of this man's excellence in mortal strife
        And how that other nobly fought and fell—
          "At pleasure of another's wife",
        Their souls do mutter; though their grief be mute,
        With bitterness they judge their princes' suit.
        And some there be whose comeliness
        No pyre did mar; they sought to spoil
        The land of Troy, and now possess
        A coverlet of alien soil.

Ill doth bode the voice of rumour, clamorous with sullen ire;
Curse pronounced in solemn conclave hath not potency more dire.
        I wait and listen in expectant mood
          To learn some deed yet veiled in night.
        The Gods wink not at them who shed much blood.
The black Avengers are not foiled; Fortune disjoined from Right
        Abides not long, but crumbles hour by hour,
        Stricken to nothingness by wasting blight,
        Stricken beyond all grace of saving power.
        And Fame preëminent withal
        Hath peril; hurled by hand divine doth fall
        A thunderbolt to blind the proud man's sight.
        True happiness provokes, I trow,
        No envy; be it mine to see
        A life of quietude, and know
        Nor conquest nor captivity.

    (*During the singing of this chorus a number of citizens have entered
      in twos and threes and approached the palace*)

πυρὸς δ' ὑπ' εὐαγγέλου   [ἐπῳδ.
πόλιν διήκει θοὰ   476
βάξις· εἰ δ' ἐτήτυμος,
τίς οἶδεν, ἤ τι θεῖον οὖν ἐστὶ ψύθος;
τίς ὧδε παιδνὸς ἤ φρενῶν κεκομμένος,
φλογὸς παραγγέλμασιν   480
νέοις πυρωθέντα καρδίαν ἔπειτ'
ἀλλαγᾷ λόγου καμεῖν;
γυναικὸς αἰχμᾷ πρέπει
πρὸ τοῦ φανέντος χάριν ξυναινέσαι.
πιθανὸς ἄγαν ὁ θῆλυς ἔρος ἐπινέμεται   485
ταχύπορος· ἀλλὰ ταχύμορον
γυναικογήρυτον ὄλλυται κλέος.

ΦΥΛΑΞ

τάχ' εἰσόμεσθα λαμπάδων φαεσφόρων
φρυκτωριῶν τε καὶ πυρὸς παραλλαγάς,   490
εἴτ' οὖν ἀληθεῖς εἴτ' ὀνειράτων δίκην
τερπνὸν τόδ' ἐλθὸν φῶς ἐφήλωσεν φρένας.
κήρυκ' ἀπ' ἀκτῆς τόνδ' ὁρῶ κατάσκιον
κλάδοις ἐλαίας· μαρτυρεῖ δέ μοι κάσις
πηλοῦ ξύνουρος διψία κόνις τάδε,   495
ὡς οὔτ' ἄναυδος οὔτε σοι δαίων φλόγα
ὕλης ὀρείας σημανεῖ καπνῷ πυρός,
ἀλλ' ἤ τὸ χαίρειν μᾶλλον ἐκβάξει λέγων,—
τὸν ἀντίον δὲ τοῖσδ' ἀποστέργω λόγον·
εὖ γὰρ πρὸς εὖ φανεῖσι προσθήκη πέλοι.   500

ΧΟΡΟΣ

ὅστις τάδ' ἄλλως τῇδ' ἐπεύχεται πόλει,
αὐτὸς φρενῶν καρποῖτο τὴν ἁμαρτίαν.

ΚΗΡΥΞ

ἰὼ πατρῷον οὖδας Ἀργείας χθονός,
δεκάτου σε φέγγει τῷδ' ἀφικόμην ἔτους,
πολλῶν ῥαγεισῶν ἐλπίδων, μιᾶς τυχών.   505

Sped by flame of goodly tiding,
Through the town hath run fleet rumour,
Whether truth or God's misguiding
Who shall say? As child confiding,
Or of sore-distempered humour,
    Must his spirit be
Whom beacon-message sets aglow,
Till other rumour, quick to grow,
    Turns joy to misery.
'Tis verily a woman's bent,
Ere proof be shown, to yield assent
Unto the hope she cherisheth;
    Quickly kindling with desire
    Woman's faith, like forest-fire,
    By no boundaries is pent;
    Quickly dwindling too and spent
The voice of woman's crying perisheth.

WATCHMAN.

Soon shall we know whether the radiant trail
Of beacon-posts that sped their serial fire
Spake truth, or like the glamour of a dream
Inveigled our fond hearts. A herald comes,—
See yonder shore-ward,—laurel-crowned; and mark
How mire and dust in close fraternity
Declare his expedition. No dumb sign,
No smoke of kindled faggots, now is here,
But speech shall either multiply our joy—
Nay, God forfend the other issue! Good,
Good as the token, be the certitude!

ELDER. May he who is not partner to thy prayer
Be first to reap malignity's reward!

(*Enter* HERALD)

HERALD. O Argos, Argos, my country, my home,
The ten-year exile sees thy light again,
Salving from all the wreckage this one hope.

οὐ γάρ ποτ᾽ ηὔχουν τῇδ᾽ ἐν Ἀργείᾳ χθονὶ
θανὼν μεθέξειν φιλτάτου τάφου μέρος.
νῦν χαῖρε μὲν χθών, χαῖρε δ᾽ ἡλίου φάος,
ὕπατός τε χώρας Ζεύς, ὁ Πύθιός τ᾽ ἄναξ,
τόξοις ἰάπτων μηκέτ᾽ εἰς ἡμᾶς βέλη·   510
ἅλις παρὰ Σκάμανδρον ἦσθ᾽ ἀνάρσιος·
νῦν δ᾽ αὖτε σωτὴρ ἴσθι καὶ παιώνιος,
ἄναξ Ἄπολλον. τούς τ᾽ ἀγωνίους θεοὺς
πάντας προσαυδῶ, τόν τ᾽ ἐμὸν τιμάορον
Ἑρμῆν, φίλον κήρυκα, κηρύκων σέβας,   515
ἥρως τε τοὺς πέμψαντας, εὐμενεῖς πάλιν
στρατὸν δέχεσθαι τὸν λελειμμένον δορός.
ἰὼ μέλαθρα βασιλέων, φίλαι στέγαι,
σεμνοί τε θᾶκοι, δαίμονές τ᾽ ἀντήλιοι,
εἴ που πάλαι, φαιδροῖσι τοισίδ᾽ ὄμμασι   520
δέξασθε κόσμῳ βασιλέα πολλῷ χρόνῳ.
ἥκει γὰρ ὑμῖν φῶς ἐν εὐφρόνῃ φέρων
καὶ τοῖσδ᾽ ἅπασι κοινὸν Ἀγαμέμνων ἄναξ.

ἀλλ᾽ εὖ νιν ἀσπασασθε, καὶ γὰρ οὖν πρέπει,
Τροίαν κατασκάψαντα τοῦ δικηφόρου   525
Διὸς μακέλλῃ, τῇ κατείργασται πέδον.
βωμοὶ δ᾽ ἄιστοι καὶ θεῶν ἱδρύματα,
καὶ σπέρμα πάσης ἐξαπόλλυται χθονός.
τοιόνδε Τροίᾳ περιβαλὼν ζευκτήριον
ἄναξ Ἀτρείδης πρέσβυς εὐδαίμων ἀνὴρ   530
ἥκει, τίεσθαι δ᾽ ἀξιώτατος βροτῶν
τῶν νῦν· Πάρις γὰρ οὔτε συντελὴς πόλις
ἐξεύχεται τὸ δρᾶμα τοῦ πάθους πλέον.
ὀφλὼν γὰρ ἁρπαγῆς τε καὶ κλοπῆς δίκην
τοῦ ῥυσίου θ᾽ ἥμαρτε καὶ πανώλεθρον   535
αὐτόχθονον πατρῷον ἔθρισεν δόμον·
διπλᾶ δ᾽ ἔτισαν Πριαμίδαι θἀμάρτια.

ΧΟ. κῆρυξ Ἀχαιῶν χαῖρε τῶν ἀπὸ στρατοῦ.
ΚΗ. χαίρω· τὸ τεθνάναι δ᾽ οὐκέτ᾽ ἀντερῶ θεοῖς.

Ne'er thought I e'en in death to make my own
One plot of Argive ground. To thee, dear land,
I pay my homage, and to the sun o'erhead,
And Zeus most sovereign, and the Pythian prince,—
So bend he now no more his bow against us!
Scamander's banks beheld thy bitterness;
Repent thee now, and stretch thy hand to heal,
My lord Apollo! You too I acclaim,
Gods presidential one and all, and most
Mine own upholder, Hermes, prince of heralds,
And Heroes who did guide our going-out,—
Invoking you to greet with smile of grace
War's remnant. Oh! lift up your heads, ye gates,
Ye royal halls, and thrones of majesty!
Awake, ye Gods who watch the dawn, and light
Your lustrous eyes as ne'er before, to bless
The king who cometh to his own at last!
To you he bringeth day for darkness,—aye,
And to the heart of all this loyal throng.

(*Turning to* The chorus)

Greet and acclaim him then, as well ye may,
Who plied the pick of Justice, in God's cause,
To waste Troy's terrain and uproot her walls.
Razed are her altars, gone her sanctuaries,
Her every fruitful pleasaunce falls to ruin.
Right heavy is his yoke, who comes God-sped,
Our sovereign lord, first-born of Atreus' blood,
Most worshipful in all the wide-flung world.
Paris nor his confederate folk shall vaunt
Reprisal ill commensurate with wrong:
Convict of rapine, he hath lost his prey,
And 'mid the harvest of his sin hath strown
Ancestral home and realm; at twofold rate
Have Priam's sons rendered the toll of guilt.

ELDER. Forerunner of our hosts, we bid thee joy.
HERALD. And joy is mine; come death, I'll not rebel.

LAA

ΧΟ. ἔρως πατρῴας τῆσδε γῆς σ᾽ ἐγύμνασεν.   540
ΚΗ. ὥστ᾽ ἐνδακρύειν γ᾽ ὄμμασιν χαρᾶς ὕπο.
ΧΟ. τερπνῆς ἄρ᾽ ἦτε τῆσδ᾽ ἐπήβολοι νόσου.
ΚΗ. πῶς δή; διδαχθεὶς τοῦδε δεσπόσω λόγου.
ΧΟ. τῶν ἀντερώντων ἱμέρῳ πεπληγμένοι.
ΚΗ. ποθεῖν ποθοῦντα τήνδε γῆν στρατὸν λέγεις.   545
ΧΟ. ὡς πόλλ᾽ ἀμαυρᾶς ἐκ φρενός μ᾽ ἀναστένειν.
ΚΗ. πόθεν τὸ δύσφρον τοῦτ᾽ ἐπῆν στύγος; φράσον.
ΧΟ. πάλαι τὸ σιγᾶν φάρμακον βλάβης ἔχω.
ΚΗ. καὶ πῶς; ἀπόντων κοιράνων ἔτρεις τινάς;
ΧΟ. ὡς νῦν τὸ σὸν δή, καὶ θανεῖν πολλὴ χάρις.   550
ΚΗ. εὖ γὰρ πέπρακται. ταῦτα δ᾽ ἐν πολλῷ χρόνῳ
    τὰ μέν τις ἂν λέξειεν εὐπετῶς ἔχειν,
    τὰ δ᾽ αὖτε κἀπίμομφα. τίς δὲ πλὴν θεῶν
    ἅπαντ᾽ ἀπήμων τὸν δι᾽ αἰῶνος χρόνον;
    μόχθους γὰρ εἰ λέγοιμι καὶ δυσαυλίας,   555
    σπαρνὰς παρήξεις καὶ κακοστρώτους,—τί δ᾽ οὐ
    στένοντες ἐξηντλοῦμεν ἤματος μέρος;
    τὰ δ᾽ αὖτε χέρσῳ καὶ πλέον προσῆν στύγος·
    εὐναὶ γὰρ ἦσαν δαΐων πρὸς τείχεσιν·
    ὄμβροι δὲ δῖοι κἀπὸ γῆς λειμώνιαι   560
    δρόσοι κατεψέκαζον ἐμπέδως τρίχα,
    ἐσθημάτων τιθέντες ἔνθηρον σίνος.
    χειμῶνα δ᾽ εἰ λέγοι τις οἰωνοκτόνον,
    οἷον παρεῖχ᾽ ἄφερτον Ἰδαία χιών,
    ἢ θάλπος, εὖτε πόντος ἐν μεσημβριναῖς   565
    κοίταις ἀκύμων νηνέμοις εὕδοι πεσών—
    τί ταῦτα πενθεῖν δεῖ; παροίχεται πόνος·
    παροίχεται δέ, τοῖσι μὲν τεθνηκόσιν
    τὸ μήποτ᾽ αὖθις μηδ᾽ ἀναστῆναι μέλειν.
    τί τοὺς ἀναλωθέντας ἐν ψήφῳ λέγειν,   570
    τὸν ζῶντα δ᾽ ἀλγεῖν χρὴ τύχης παλιγκότου;
    καὶ πολλὰ χαίρειν ξυμφορὰς καταξιῶ.
    ἡμῖν δὲ τοῖς λοιποῖσιν Ἀργείων στρατοῦ
    νικᾷ τὸ κέρδος, πῆμα δ᾽ οὐκ ἀντιρρέπει·
    ὡς κομπάσαι τῷδ᾽ εἰκὸς ἡλίου φάει   575
    ὑπὲρ θαλάσσης καὶ χθονὸς ποτωμένοις·
    ‘Τροίαν ἑλόντες δήποτ᾽ Ἀργείων στόλος
    θεοῖς λάφυρα ταῦτα τοῖς καθ᾽ Ἑλλάδα

ELDER. Yearning for home, methinks, did irk thee sore.

HERALD. Yea, so that joy floods now my eyes with tears.

ELDER. Not wholly bane then was your malady.

HERALD. How so? Expound; I master not thy meaning.

ELDER. That mutual was this malady of longing.

HERALD. Ah yes! 'twixt you at home and us at war.

ELDER. Full many a sigh broke from my darkling soul.

HERALD. Whence sprang such sore disquietude, I pray thee?

ELDER. Silence hath long been my phylactery.

HERALD. How now? Our princes gone, you stood in fear?

ELDER. And now released, like thee can smile at death.

HERALD. Success doth warrant thee. The whole long train
        Had much of prosperous cadence, if withal
        Some cause of cavil. Yet who save the Gods
        Could pass the plenitude of life unscathed?
        The tale of hardship and of crowded deck,
        Scarce harbourage and hasty bivouac,—
        With groaning we endured that daily part.
        Then too on shore was misery multiplied:
        Entrenched we lay close by the enemy's wall,
        And rains of heaven and meadow-mist bedewed
        Incessantly our roofless heads, and wrought
        A murrain on our raiment. Then the cold
        Of wintry winds swooping from Ida's snows,
        That killed the very birds! and heat again,
        The high-noon heat, when spent and breathless lay
        The sea asleep! Yet wherefore now repine?
        Past is our pain; past for the dead, who lie
        With nevermore a care to wake and rise.
        Why number wastage, or why, living, grieve
        O'er fortune's stings? Foregone is best forgot.
        For us, the remnant of the Argive host,
        Our gain outweighs all counterpoise of woe.
        Upborne like eagles over sea and land,
        We'll bid the all-seeing Sun attest our boast:
        "These fruits of conquest from long-leaguered Troy
        Unto the glory of the Gods of Greece
        And for th' enrichment of their age-old shrines

36   AESCHYLUS

δόμων ἐπασσάλευσαν ἀρχαίων γάνος.·
τοιαῦτα χρὴ κλύοντας εὐλογεῖν πόλιν   580
καὶ τοὺς στρατηγούς· καὶ χάρις τιμήσεται
Διὸς τόδ᾽ ἐκπράξασα. πάντ᾽ ἔχεις λόγον.
ΧΟ. νικώμενος λόγοισιν οὐκ ἀναίνομαι·
ἀεὶ γὰρ ἡβᾷ τοῖς γέρουσιν εὖ μαθεῖν.
δόμοις δὲ ταῦτα καὶ Κλυταιμήστρᾳ μέλειν   585
εἰκὸς μάλιστα, σὺν δὲ πλουτίζειν ἐμέ.

ΚΛΥΤΑΙΜΗΣΤΡΑ

ἀνωλόλυξα μὲν πάλαι χαρᾶς ὕπο,
ὅτ᾽ ἦλθ᾽ ὁ πρῶτος νύχιος ἄγγελος πυρὸς
φράζων ἅλωσιν Ἰλίου τ᾽ ἀνάστασιν.
καί τίς μ᾽ ἐνίπτων εἶπε, ‘ φρυκτωρῶν δία 590
πεισθεῖσα Τροίαν νῦν πεπορθῆσθαι δοκεῖς;
ἢ κάρτα πρὸς γυναικὸς αἴρεσθαι κέαρ.᾽
λόγοις τοιούτοις πλαγκτὸς οὖσ᾽ ἐφαινόμην.
ὅμως δ᾽ ἔθυον, καὶ γυναικείῳ νόμῳ
ὀλολυγμὸν ἄλλος ἄλλοθεν κατὰ πτόλιν   595
ἔλασκον εὐφημοῦντες ἐν θεῶν ἕδραις
θυηφάγον κοιμῶντες εὐώδη φλόγα.
καὶ νῦν τὰ μάσσω μὲν τί δεῖ σέ μοι λέγειν;
ἄνακτος αὐτοῦ πάντα πεύσομαι λόγον.
ὅπως δ᾽ ἄριστα τὸν ἐμὸν αἰδοῖον πόσιν   600
σπεύσω πάλιν μολόντα δέξασθαι—τί γὰρ
γυναικὶ τούτου φέγγος ἥδιον δρακεῖν,
ἀπὸ στρατείας ἀνδρὶ σώσαντος θεοῦ
πύλας ἀνοῖξαι;—ταῦτ᾽ ἀπάγγειλον πόσει·
ἥκειν ὅπως τάχιστ᾽ ἐράσμιον πόλει·   605
γυναῖκα πιστὴν δ᾽ ἐν δόμοις εὕροι μολὼν
οἵανπερ οὖν ἔλειπε, δωμάτων κύνα
ἐσθλὴν ἐκείνῳ, πολεμίαν τοῖς δύσφροσιν,
καὶ τἄλλ᾽ ὁμοίαν πάντα, σημαντήριον
οὐδὲν διαφθείρασαν ἐν μήκει χρόνου.   610
οὐδ᾽ οἶδα τέρψιν οὐδ᾽ ἐπίψογον φάτιν
ἄλλου πρὸς ἀνδρὸς μᾶλλον ἢ χαλκοῦ βαφάς.

By Argos' armies now are consecrate".
Whoso hath ears to hear, let him acclaim
Our country and her captains, by God's hand,
To whom be glory, raised to this renown!
My tale is told.

ELDER.   Thou vanquishest my doubts; gladly I yield;
Old age apprised of good feels youth renewed.
Albeit thy tale doth nearest touch this house
And Clytemnestra, I too have my meed.

       (*Enter* CLYTEMNESTRA with attendants)

CLYT.   Exultantly I dared uplift my cry
When the first courier flaming in the night
Came telling of Troy taken and devastate.
And some spake chiding, "Dwells such eloquence
In beacons that thou deemest now her doom
Achieved? Oh! lightly soars a woman's heart!"
Errant of wit they argued me, but I
Stayed not from sacrifice; the city rang
With carillons of women's joy, and choirs
Of gratitude at every shrine appeased
The hungry altars with sweet-vaporous spice.
And now what need of narrative from thee?
My King shall be his own interpreter.
But, that I tarry not in welcoming
My lord revered,—for sure no brighter ray
Of comfort breaks upon a woman's eyes
Than when the gates are thrown wide to receive
Her warrior husband by God's grace restored,—
Go, bear this message: bid him make good speed—
His city yearns for him—in hope to find
A loyal wife, home-keeping as of yore,
A watch-dog true to him, fierce to his foes,
In all unalterable, reverencing
Each sealèd aumbry all these long-drawn years.
No other man hath e'er acquainted me
With pleasure or reproach; my steel is true.

τοιόσδ᾽ ὁ κόμπος, τῆς ἀληθείας γέμων,
οὐκ αἰσχρὸς ὡς γυναικὶ γενναίᾳ λακεῖν.

ΧΟ. αὕτη μὲν οὕτως εἶπε,—μανθάνοντί σοι   615
τοροῖσιν ἑρμηνεῦσιν εὐπρεπῶς λόγον.
σὺ δ᾽ εἰπέ, κῆρυξ, Μενέλεων δὲ πεύθομαι,
εἰ νόστιμός τε καὶ σεσωσμένος πάλιν
ἥξει σὺν ὑμῖν, τῆσδε γῆς φίλον κράτος.

ΚΗ. οὐκ ἔσθ᾽ ὅπως λέξαιμι τὰ ψευδῆ καλὰ   620
ἐς τὸν πολὺν φίλοισι καρποῦσθαι χρόνον.

ΧΟ. πῶς δῆτ᾽ ἂν εἰπὼν κεδνὰ τἀληθῆ τύχοις;
σχισθέντα δ᾽ οὐκ εὔκρυπτα γίγνεται τάδε.

ΚΗ. ἀνὴρ ἄφαντος ἐξ Ἀχαιικοῦ στρατοῦ,
αὐτός τε καὶ τὸ πλοῖον. οὐ ψευδῆ λέγω.   625

ΧΟ. πότερον ἀναχθεὶς ἐμφανῶς ἐξ Ἰλίου,
ἢ χεῖμα, κοινὸν ἄχθος, ἥρπασε στρατοῦ;

ΚΗ. ἔκυρσας ὥστε τοξότης ἄκρος σκοποῦ·
μακρὸν δὲ πῆμα συντόμως ἐφημίσω.

ΧΟ. πότερα γὰρ αὐτοῦ ζῶντος ἢ τεθνηκότος   630
φάτις πρὸς ἄλλων ναυτίλων ἐκλῄζετο;

ΚΗ. οὐκ οἶδεν οὐδεὶς ὥστ᾽ ἀπαγγεῖλαι τορῶς,
πλὴν τοῦ τρέφοντος Ἡλίου χθονὸς φύσιν.

ΧΟ. πῶς γὰρ λέγεις; χειμῶνα ναυτικῷ στρατῷ
ἐλθεῖν τελευτῆσαί τε δαιμόνων κότῳ;   635

ΚΗ. εὔφημον ἦμαρ οὐ πρέπει κακαγγέλῳ
γλώσσῃ μιαίνειν· χωρὶς ἡ τιμὴ θεῶν.
ὅταν δ᾽ ἀπευκτὰ πήματ᾽ ἄγγελος πόλει
στυγνῷ προσώπῳ πτωσίμου στρατοῦ φέρῃ,
πόλει μὲν ἕλκος ἓν τὸ δήμιον τυχεῖν,   640
πολλοὺς δὲ πολλῶν ἐξαγισθέντας δόμων
ἄνδρας διπλῇ μάστιγι, τὴν Ἄρης φιλεῖ,
δίλογχον ἄτην, φοινίαν ξυνωρίδα,—
τοιῶνδε μέν τοι πημάτων σεσαγμένον
πρέπει λέγειν παιᾶνα τόνδ᾽ Ἐρινύων.   645
σωτηρίων δὲ πραγμάτων εὐάγγελον
ἥκοντα πρὸς χαίρουσαν εὐεστοῖ πόλιν,—
πῶς κεδνὰ τοῖς κακοῖσι συμμίξω, λέγων
χειμῶν᾽ Ἀχαιοῖς οὐκ ἀμήνιτον θεῶν;

Such honest protest shames not queenly pride.

(*Exit* CLYTEMNESTRA)

ELDER.   A brave speech, herald,—or a brave pretence
If thine ear profit of enlightenment.
But speak thyself, and tell me of Menelaus :
Shall we behold with you our gracious prince
Restored in safety to the land that loves him?

HERALD. To feign good tidings would ill serve my friends;
No lasting profit cometh of deceit.

ELDER.   Would that thy tale might couple truth with joy !
Not long can their disseverance be hid.

HERALD. Know then that he is vanished from our host,
He and his ship withal. I'll not dissemble.

ELDER.   Sailed he alone and openly from Troy,
Or fell some storm that scattered the whole fleet?

HERALD. Thine arrow hath sped true and found his butt;
Those few words compassed large calamity.

ELDER.   How ran the reckoning 'mid the other crews?
Rumoured they him as living or as dead?

HERALD. Knowledge had none, to render sure report,
None save the Sun who hath th' whole world in ward.

ELDER.   How sayest thou of this tempest? Dost impute
Onset and issue to some God's despite?

HERALD. A day of grace, unto God's praise reserved,
Should no disastrous tongue contaminate.
The messenger whose mien of rue proclaims
Th' abhorrèd plight of armies bruised and broken,
Where humbled city-pride and several sorrow
Of stricken homesteads o'er their outcast dead
Are plaited in one lash that Ares plies,
Or form a forkèd goad to pierce twin wounds,—
When such, I say, the pack of pain he bears,
Well may he sound the Furies' clarion.
But when he brings glad news of peace achieved
Unto a city joyous in her weal,—
Oh! how can I mix foul with fair, or paint
A tempest clamouring of angered Gods?

ξυνώμοσαν γάρ, ὄντες ἔχθιστοι τὸ πρίν,   650
πῦρ καὶ θάλασσα, καὶ τὰ πίστ' ἐδειξάτην
φθείροντε τὸν δύστηνον Ἀργείων στρατόν.
ἐν νυκτὶ δυσκύμαντα δ' ὠρώρει κακά.
ναῦς γὰρ πρὸς ἀλλήλαισι Θρῄκιαι πνοαὶ
ἤρεικον· αἱ δὲ κεροτυπούμεναι βίᾳ   655
χειμῶνι τυφῶ σὺν ζάλῃ τ' ὀμβροκτύπῳ
ᾤχοντ' ἄφαντοι, ποιμένος κακοῦ στρόβῳ.
ἐπεὶ δ' ἀνῆλθε λαμπρὸν ἡλίου φάος,
ὁρῶμεν ἀνθοῦν πέλαγος Αἰγαῖον νεκροῖς
ἀνδρῶν Ἀχαιῶν ναυτικοῖς τ' ἐρειπίοις.   660
ἡμᾶς γε μὲν δὴ ναῦν τ' ἀκήρατον σκάφος
ἤτοι τις ἐξέκλεψεν ἢ 'ξῃτήσατο
θεός τις, οὐκ ἄνθρωπος, οἴακος θιγών.
Τύχη δὲ σωτὴρ ναῦν θέλουσ' ἐφέζετο,
ὡς μήτ' ἐν ὅρμῳ κύματος ζάλην ἔχειν   665
μήτ' ἐξοκεῖλαι πρὸς κραταίλεων χθόνα.
ἔπειτα δ' Ἅιδην πόντιον πεφευγότες,
λευκὸν κατ' ἦμαρ, οὐ πεποιθότες τύχῃ,
ἐβουκολοῦμεν φροντίσιν νέον πάθος
στρατοῦ καμόντος καὶ κακῶς σποδουμένου.   670
καὶ νῦν ἐκείνων εἴ τις ἐστὶν ἐμπνέων,
λέγουσιν ἡμᾶς ὡς ὀλωλότας· τί μήν;
ἡμεῖς τ' ἐκείνους ταῦτ' ἔχειν δοξάζομεν.
γένοιτο δ' ὡς ἄριστα. Μενέλεων γὰρ οὖν
πρῶτόν τε καὶ μάλιστα προσδόκα μογεῖν.   675
εἰ δ' οὖν τις ἀκτὶς ἡλίου νιν ἱστορεῖ
καὶ ζῶντα καὶ βλέποντα, μηχαναῖς Διός,
οὔπω θέλοντος ἐξαναλῶσαι γένος,
ἐλπίς τις αὐτὸν πρὸς δόμους ἥξειν πάλιν.
τοσαῦτ' ἀκούσας ἴσθι τἀληθῆ κλύων.   680

ΧΟ. τίς ποτ' ὠνόμαζεν ὧδ'   [στρ. α.
ἐς τὸ πᾶν ἐτητύμως—
μή τις ὅντιν' οὐχ ὁρῶ-
μεν προνοίαισι τοῦ πεπρωμένου
γλῶσσαν ἐν τύχᾳ νέμων—   685
τὰν δορίγαμβρον ἀμφινει-
κῆ θ' Ἑλέναν; ἐπεὶ πρεπόντως

Those fiercest foes aforetime, fire and flood,
Made covenant and proved their fealty
In havoc of the hapless Argive host
'Mid storm and night. Gales from the Thracian main
Drave ship on ship, till buffeted and breached
By foam-capped billow and sleet-laden blast,
Ill-shepherded like sheep that reach no fold,
They foundered. And when day brake bright, behold,
The broad Aegean dappled with our dead
And flotsam wreckage of our argosies!
Us truly, with our hull still whole, some God
Whose hand had sleight or plea had potency—
For ne'er had man prevailed—did steer to haven.
And at our stem rode Fortune fain to save us
From surge of breakers at our anchorage
Or shock of grounding on a granite shore.
So then enlarged from black tempestuous death,
That whole white day, scarce crediting our lot,
Our souls were pasture for th' adversity
That cruelly crushed anew our stricken ranks.
And now if any of them still breathe, they'll speak
Of us as dead, doubtless, as we of them.
God grant th' event belie us! Menelaus
Thou must for all esteem in sorry straits;
Yet if some ray o' the sun doth search him out
And quicken still his sight, hope doth remain
That Zeus, not suffering yet the sheer o'erthrow
O' the royal race, shall compass his home-coming.
Lo! I have spoken, and thou know'st the truth.

(*Exit* HERALD)

CHORUS.   Who bestowed this name so true—
            One perchance beyond our sight
           Who her destiny foreknew
            And could guide his lips aright—
         On Helen, whom the spear should woo
            And war should be her dower?

ἑλέναυς, ἕλανδρος, ἑλέπτολις,
  ἐκ τῶν ἀβροτίμων   690
προκαλυμμάτων ἔπλευσε
ζεφύρου γίγαντος αὔρᾳ,
πολύανδροί τε φεράσπιδες
κυναγοὶ κατ᾽ ἴχνος πλατᾶν ἄφαντον   695
κελσάντων Σιμόεντος
ἀκτὰς εἰς ἐριφύλλους
δι᾽ ἔριν αἱματόεσσαν.

Ἰλίῳ δὲ κῆδος ὀρθ-   [ἀντ. α.
ώνυμον τελεσσίφρων   700
μῆνις ἤνυσεν, τραπέ-
ζας ἀτίμωσιν ὑστέρῳ χρόνῳ
καὶ ξυνεστίου Διὸς
πρασσομένα τὸ νυμφότι-
μον μέλος ἐκφάτως τίοντας,   706
ὑμέναιον, ὃς τότ᾽ ἐπέρρεπεν
  γαμβροῖσιν ἀείδειν.
μεταμανθάνουσα δ᾽ ὕμνον
Πριάμου πόλις γεραιὰ   710
πολύθρηνον μέγα που στένει
κικλήσκουσα Πάριν τὸν αἰνόλεκτρον,
παμπορθῆ πολύθρηνον
αἰῶν᾽ ἀμφὶ πολιτᾶν   715
μέλεον αἷμ᾽ ἀνατλᾶσα.

ἔθρεψεν δὲ λέοντος ἲ-   [στρ. β.
νιν δόμοις ἀγελακτόνου
τέως ἀνὴρ φιλόμαστον,
ἐν βιότου προτελείοις   720
ἄμερον, εὐφιλόπαιδα,
καὶ γεραροῖς ἐπίχαρτον.
πολέα δ᾽ ἔσκ᾽ ἐν ἀγκάλαις
νεοτρόφου τέκνου δίκαν,
φαιδρωπὸς ποτὶ χεῖρα σαί-   725
νων τε γαστρὸς ἀνάγκαις.

For truly Hell encompasseth
Ships, men, and cities, from the hour
She left her silken-curtained bower
Wafted by giant Zephyr's breath,
And forth a multitude must sail
Of huntsmen with their shields bedight
Along her oarsmen's vanished trail
To beach their barques at Simois' leafy bight,
    In quest of strife and death.

    By the bond of plighted love
    Vengeful Destiny hath bound
    Ilium's folk in loveless plight;
    Slowly though her purpose move,
Due recompense at last is found
      To punish that despite
Of friendship's sacred hearth and board
Wherewith their voices erst outpoured
Glad carol for that wedding-night;
Their city now, so old and worn,
Learns a new strain of doleful lilt;
Not Paris' love, but Paris' guilt,
Is now her theme; for she hath borne
Distress and desolation, and doth mourn
      Her children slain in fight.

    There lived an herdsman who awhile
    In his own homestead kept and reared
A whelp of lions who made his kine their prey;
    A whelp that in life's dawning day
Was gentle and to children quick endeared
    And from the old men drew a smile;
    Oft in his arms 'twas wont to rest,
    Even as new-born infant lies,
    And watched his hand with sparkling eyes
      Or fawned when hunger pressed.

χρονισθεὶς δ᾽ ἀπέδειξεν ἠ-   [ἀντ. β.
θος τὸ πρὸς τοκέων· χάριν
γὰρ τροφεῦσιν ἀμείβων
μηλοφόνοισι σὺν ἄταις   730
δαῖτ᾽ ἀκέλευστος ἔτευξεν·
αἵματι δ᾽ οἶκος ἐφύρθη,
ἄμαχον ἄλγος οἰκέταις
μέγα σίνος πολύκτονον.
ἐκ θεοῦ δ᾽ ἱερεύς τις ἄ-   735
τας δόμοις προσεθρέφθη.

πάραυτα δ᾽ ἐλθεῖν ἐς Ἰλίου πόλιν   [στρ. γ.
λέγοιμ᾽ ἂν φρόνημα μὲν
νηνέμου γαλάνας,   740
ἀκασκαῖον δ᾽ ἄγαλμα πλούτου,
μαλθακὸν ὀμμάτων βέλος,
δηξίθυμον ἔρωτος ἄνθος.
παρακλίνασ᾽ ἐπέκρανεν
δὲ γάμου πικρὰς τελευτάς,   745
δύσεδρος καὶ δυσόμιλος
συμένα Πριαμίδαισιν,
πομπᾷ Διὸς ξενίου,
νυμφόκλαυτος Ἐρινύς.

παλαίφατος δ᾽ ἐν βροτοῖς γέρων λόγος   [ἀντ. γ.
τέτυκται, μέγαν τελε-   751
σθέντα φωτὸς ὄλβον
τεκνοῦσθαι μηδ᾽ ἄπαιδα θνήσκειν,
ἐκ δ᾽ ἀγαθᾶς τύχας γένει   755
βλαστάνειν ἀκόρεστον οἰζύν.
δίχα δ᾽ ἄλλων μονόφρων εἰμί. τὸ δυσσεβὲς γὰρ ἔργον
μετὰ μὲν πλείονα τίκτει,
σφετέρᾳ δ᾽ εἰκότα γέννᾳ·   760
οἴκων δ᾽ ἄρ᾽ εὐθυδίκων
καλλίπαις πότμος αἰεί.

But ripening time anon displayed
  The temper of his parent-stock;
For lo! his debt of nurture he repaid
  With cruel carnage of the flock
And feast unbidden; and the house was soiled
  With blood, and hearts were desolate
  O'er wealth so wantonly despoiled;
  Sent by some God, methinks, did come
  The servant of malignant fate
    Once cherished in that home.

So at the first o'er Ilium's folk there spread
  A spirit of unruffled calm,
  And wealth was decked with dainty charm,
  And, 'mid soft glances keenly sped,
  Did blossom love for hearts' undoing.
But soon it was another path she trod:
  To bitter end was brought her wooing;
  Gone were the days of ease and rest;
    The wrath of God
Made her a very fiend, sent forth to sweep
    Like raging pest
O'er all the city of that faithless guest,
  Till brides that smiled were fain to weep.

A rede of immemorial days is rife
  That, once full-grown, Prosperity
  Hath seed, and ne'er shall barren be;
  Good hap, 'tis said, gives birth and life
  To miseries that cark and fret.
But I aloof hold solitary creed;
  I deem not Weal doth e'er beget
  An alien afterbrood of Woe;
    'Tis Sin doth breed
That dismal issue, and their type doth show
    A lineage true:
Their houses who the path of right pursue
  Are ever blessèd in their seed.

φιλεῖ δὲ τίκτειν ὕβρις   [στρ. δ.
μὲν παλαιὰ νεά-
ζουσαν ἐν κακοῖς βροτῶν   765
ὕβριν τότ᾽ ἢ τόθ᾽, ὅτε τὸ κύριον μόλῃ
φάος τόκου,
δαίμονά τε τὰν ἄμαχον ἀπόλεμον,
ἀνίερον θράσος, μελαί-
νας μελάθροισιν Ἄτας,   770
εἰδομένας τοκεῦσιν.

Δίκα δὲ λάμπει μὲν ἐν   [ἀντ. δ.
δυσκάπνοις δώμασιν,
τὸν δ᾽ ἐναίσιμον τίει.   775
τὰ χρυσόπαστα δ᾽ ἔδεθλα σὺν πίνῳ χερῶν
παλιντρόποις
ὄμμασι λιποῦσ᾽, ὅσια προσέσυτο,
δύναμιν οὐ σέβουσα πλού-
του παράσημον αἴνῳ·   780
πᾶν δ᾽ ἐπὶ τέρμα νωμᾷ.

ἄγε δή, βασιλεῦ, Τροίας πτολίπορθ᾽,
Ἀτρέως γένεθλον,
πῶς σε προσείπω; πῶς σε σεβίζω   785
μήθ᾽ ὑπεράρας μήθ᾽ ὑποκάμψας
καιρὸν χάριτος;
πολλοὶ δὲ βροτῶν τὸ δοκεῖν εἶναι
προτίουσι δίκην παραβάντες.
τῷ δυσπραγοῦντι δ᾽ ἐπιστενάχειν   790
πᾶς τις ἕτοιμος· δῆγμα δὲ λύπης
οὐδὲν ἐφ᾽ ἧπαρ προσικνεῖται·
καὶ ξυγχαίρουσιν ὁμοιοπρεπεῖς,
ἀγέλαστα πρόσωπα βιαζόμενοι,
φθονερὰς κλέπτουσι μερίμνας.
ὅστις δ᾽ ἀγαθὸς προβατογνώμων,   795
οὐκ ἔστι λαθεῖν ὄμματα φωτὸς
τὰ δοκοῦντ᾽ εὔφρονος ἐκ διανοίας
ὑδαρεῖ σαίνειν φιλότητι.
σὺ δέ μοι τότε μὲν στέλλων στρατιὰν
Ἑλένης ἕνεκ᾽, οὐ γάρ σ᾽ ἐπικεύσω,   800

Lo! ancient Pride doth procreate,
In men of froward heart to grow,
New-gotten Pride, or soon or late,
When for her birth hath come the destined hour,
And Pride's twin spirit of resistless power,
Defiance, who of holy things makes mock,
Black fiends who whelm the race in utter woe,
    True scions of their parent-stock.

But Justice sheds a radiance clear
'Neath smoke-encrusted cottage-roof
And holdeth righteous dealing dear.
From golden-ceilèd halls that shelter sin
And hands defiled she turns, with eyes aloof,
And seeks the pure; riches she laughs to scorn,—
Still counterfeit for all the applause they win,—
    And guideth all things to her bourne.

(*Enter* AGAMEMNON with retinue)

Lord King, who hast laid Troy's citadel low,
        Atreus' true scion,
How greet thee aright? How honour thy name,
Yet neither o'ercarry nor turn too short
        Of the homage meet?
Full many a man who has transgressed right
    Preferreth the praise of dissemblers;
Right ready to moan are all men's lips
O'er others' misfortune, the while their hearts
    Feel never a touch of sorrow;
Or anon they make false visage of joy,
With lips constrained to a mirthless smile,
    In hope to dissemble their envy.
But whoso discerneth his flock aright
Shall ne'er be deceived by the fawning mien
Of a man that feigneth a loyal heart
    Though his love be as weak as water.
And thou erstwhile, when in Helen's quest
Thine host was launched, I will e'en confess,

κάρτ' ἀπομούσως ἦσθα γεγραμμένος,
οὐδ' εὖ πραπίδων οἴακα νέμων,
θράσος ἐκ θυσιῶν
ἀνδράσι θρήσκοισι κομίζων.
νῦν δ' οὐκ ἀπ' ἄκρας φρενὸς οὐδ' ἀφίλως   805
ἔστιν ἐπειπεῖν
" εὔφρων πόνος εὖ τελέσασιν."
γνώσει δὲ χρόνῳ διαπευθόμενος
τόν τε δικαίως καὶ τὸν ἀκαίρως
πόλιν οἰκουροῦντα πολιτῶν.

ΑΓΑΜΕΜΝΩΝ

πρῶτον μὲν Ἄργος καὶ θεοὺς ἐγχωρίους   810
δίκη προσειπεῖν, τοὺς ἐμοὶ μεταιτίους
νόστου δικαίων θ' ὧν ἐπραξάμην πόλιν
Πριάμου· δίκας γὰρ οὐκ ἀπὸ γλώσσης θεοὶ
κλύοντες ἀνδροθνῆτας Ἰλίου φθορὰς
εἰς αἱματηρὸν τεῦχος οὐ διχορρόπως   815
ψήφους ἔθεντο· τῷ δ' ἐναντίῳ κύτει
ἐλπὶς προσῄει χειρὸς οὐ πληρουμένῳ.
καπνῷ δ' ἁλοῦσα νῦν ἔτ' εὔσημος πόλις.
ἄτης θύελλαι ζῶσι· συνθρώσκουσα δὲ
σποδὸς προπέμπει πίονας πλούτου πνοάς.   820
τούτων θεοῖσι χρὴ πολύμνηστον χάριν
τίνειν, ἐπείπερ ἁρπαγὰς ὑπερκόπους
ἐπραξάμεσθα καὶ γυναικὸς οὕνεκα
πόλιν διημάθυνεν Ἀργεῖον δάκος,
ἵππου νεοσσός, ἀσπιδοστρόφος λεώς,   825
πήδημ' ὀρούσας ἀμφὶ Πλειάδων δύσιν·
ὑπερθορὼν δὲ πύργον ὠμηστὴς λέων
ἄδην ἔλειξεν αἵματος τυραννικοῦ.
θεοῖς μὲν ἐξέτεινα φροίμιον τόδε·
τὰ δ' ἐς τὸ σὸν φρόνημα, μέμνημαι κλύων,   830
καὶ φημὶ ταὐτὰ καὶ συνήγορόν μ' ἔχεις.
παύροις γὰρ ἀνδρῶν ἐστι συγγενὲς τόδε,
φίλον τὸν εὐτυχοῦντ' ἄνευ φθόνου σέβειν.
δύσφρων γὰρ ἰὸς καρδίαν προσήμενος

Wast limned in a guise I sore misliked,
With no deft hand at the helm of thy mind,
Essaying to rouse, by the shedding of blood,
   Fresh heart in thy awe-ridden comrades.
But now in all gladness of soul I'll cry
   "Fair issue reward fair labour!"
And time shall tutor thy mind to discern
'Twixt them that have usèd aright or amiss
   Their stewardship over thy city.

AGAM. To Argos first be rendered my address
And to the Gods of Argos, my consorts
In quest and in exaction of my dues
From Priam's realm. Those high justiciaries
Who scan th' unspoken mind denouncèd death
For Troy's manhood, and cast unwavering votes
I' th' crimson urn,—whose crystal fellow breathed
Vain overtures to empty-handed Hope.
Pennons of smoke still signal Ilium's fall;
Still riots Ruin's storm, and swirling ash
Escorts the fragrance blown from smouldering bowers.
For these achievements to the Gods be paid
Rich tribute of remembrance! for rich toll
Of rapine have we now reclaimed, who erst
Were robbed, and in reprisal for one woman
A citadel lies trampled into dust.
An Argive steed did foal a monstrous brood,
A living armament, that crouched and sprang
What time the Pleiads sank, and like a lion
Hungry of flesh o'erleapt Troy's battlements
And lapped the life-blood of her potentates.
   Be this the prelude ere I pay the Gods
My full thank-offerings! Now to thee I say,
Thy heart hath spoken, and doth stir in me
Mem'ries that give thine utt'rance their consent.
Right rare is he whose native temper yields
Unenvying homage to his prospered friend;
Some taint of malice poisons oft the heart,

ἄχθος διπλοίζει τῷ πεπαμένῳ νόσον·   835
τοῖς τ' αὐτὸς αὑτοῦ πήμασιν βαρύνεται
καὶ τὸν θυραῖον ὄλβον εἰσορῶν στένει.
εἰδὼς λέγοιμ' ἄν, εὖ γὰρ ἐξεπίσταμαι
ὁμιλίαις κάτοπτον, εἴδωλον σκιᾶς
δοκοῦντας εἶναι κάρτα πρευμενεῖς ἐμοί.   840
μόνος δ' Ὀδυσσεύς, ὅσπερ οὐχ ἑκὼν ἔπλει,
ζευχθεὶς ἕτοιμος ἦν ἐμοὶ σειραφόρος,—
εἴτ' οὖν θανόντος εἴτε καὶ ζῶντος πέρι
λέγω. τὰ δ' ἄλλα πρὸς πόλιν τε καὶ θεοὺς
κοινοὺς ἀγῶνας θέντες ἐν πανηγύρει   845
βουλευσόμεσθα. καὶ τὸ μὲν καλῶς ἔχον
ὅπως χρονίζον εὖ μενεῖ βουλευτέον·
ὅτῳ δὲ καὶ δεῖ φαρμάκων παιωνίων,
ἤτοι κέαντες ἢ τεμόντες εὐφρόνως
πειρασόμεσθα πῆμ' ἀποστρέψαι νόσου.   850
νῦν δ' ἐς μέλαθρα καὶ δόμους ἐφεστίους
ἐλθὼν θεοῖσι πρῶτα δεξιώσομαι,
οἵπερ πρόσω πέμψαντες ἤγαγον πάλιν.
νίκη δ' ἐπείπερ ἔσπετ', ἐμπέδως μένοι.
ΚΛ. ἄνδρες πολῖται, πρέσβος Ἀργείων τόδε,   855
οὐκ αἰσχυνοῦμαι τοὺς φιλάνορας τρόπους
λέξαι πρὸς ὑμᾶς· ἐν χρόνῳ δ' ἀποφθίνει
τὸ τάρβος ἀνθρώποισιν. οὐκ ἄλλων πάρα
μαθοῦσ', ἐμαυτῆς δύσφορον λέξω βίον
τοσόνδ' ὅσονπερ οὗτος ἦν ὑπ' Ἰλίῳ.   860
τὸ μὲν γυναῖκα πρῶτον ἄρσενος δίχα
ἧσθαι δόμοις ἔρημον ἔκπαγλον κακόν,
πολλὰς κλύουσαν κληδόνας παλιγκότους·
καὶ τὸν μὲν ἥκειν, τὸν δ' ἐπεσφέρειν κακοῦ
κάκιον ἄλλο πῆμα, λάσκοντας δόμοις.   865
καὶ τραυμάτων μὲν εἰ τόσων ἐτύγχανεν
ἀνὴρ ὅδ', ὡς πρὸς οἶκον ὠχετεύετο
φάτις, τέτρηται δικτύου πλέω λέγειν.
εἰ δ' ἦν τεθνηκώς, ὡς ἐπλήθυον λόγοι,
τρισώματός τἂν Γηρυὼν ὁ δεύτερος   870
χθονὸς τρίμοιρον χλαῖναν ἐξηύχει λαβεῖν,

And loads the sufferer with a double pack:
He chafes beneath his own peculiar woe,
And scans with jealous eye his neighbour's weal.
I speak of that I know; companionship
Hath been a mirror whose experiment
Hath shown me oft a shape but shadow-deep
In such as published most their loyalty.
Only Odysseus, whilom loth to sail,
Once harnessed with me, laboured with taut trace;
And he perchance is dead.
　　　　　　　　For what remains
Of import to our city and her Gods,
In open conclave of th' assembled folk
We will anon take counsel, and devise
How what is wholesome may continue whole;
And whereso canker haply needeth cure,
There knife or fire, compassionately cruel,
Shall seek to turn the mischief from his goal.
But first will I re-enter these my halls
And at the hearth give greeting to the Gods
That prospered mine outgoing and brought me home.
What war hath won may peace perpetuate!

CLYT. Elders of Argos, I shall feel no shame
To avow before your face a woman's love;
Long waiting wears such modesties away.
I need no prompter: none save I can tell
The burden of my life, while still my lord
Tarried at Troy. Her solitude, who sits
In home unhusbanded, is pain supreme;
Reports malign are multiplied; one comes,
And, ere his tale be told, another cries
Tidings more cruel. An there befell my lord
Such fabled woundings as were floated home
On rivulets of rumour, never net
Was riddled more; or had he died as oft
As he was numbered dead, a Geryon he,
Who now might boast three covertures of earth

ἅπαξ ἑκάστῳ κατθανὼν μορφώματι.
τοιῶνδ᾽ ἕκατι κληδόνων παλιγκότων
πολλὰς ἄνωθεν ἀρτάνας ἐμῆς δέρης   875
ἔλυσαν ἄλλοι πρὸς βίαν ἐνημμένης.

ἐκ τῶνδέ τοι παῖς ἐνθάδ᾽ οὐ παραστατεῖ,
ἐμῶν τε καὶ σῶν κύριος πιστωμάτων,
ὡς χρῆν, Ὀρέστης· μηδὲ θαυμάσῃς τόδε.
τρέφει γὰρ αὐτὸν εὐμενὴς δορύξενος   880
Στρόφιος ὁ Φωκεύς, ἀμφίλεκτα πήματα
ἐμοὶ προφωνῶν, τόν θ᾽ ὑπ᾽ Ἰλίῳ σέθεν
κίνδυνον, εἴ τε δημόθρους ἀναρχία
βουλὴν καταρρίψειεν, ὥστε σύγγονον
βροτοῖσι τὸν πεσόντα λακτίσαι πλέον.   885
τοιάδε μέντοι σκῆψις οὐ δόλον φέρει.

ἔμοιγε μὲν δὴ κλαυμάτων ἐπίσσυτοι
πηγαὶ κατεσβήκασιν, οὐδ᾽ ἔνι σταγών.
ἐν ὀψικοίτοις δ᾽ ὄμμασιν βλάβας ἔχω
τὰς ἀμφί σοι κλαίουσι λαμπτηρουχίας   890
ἀτημελήτους αἰέν. ἐν δ᾽ ὀνείρασιν
λεπταῖς ὑπαὶ κώνωπος ἐξηγειρόμην
ῥιπαῖσι θωύσσοντος, ἀμφί σοι πάθη
ὁρῶσα πλείω τοῦ ξυνεύδοντος χρόνου.
νῦν, ταῦτα πάντα τλᾶσ᾽, ἀπενθήτῳ φρενὶ   895
λέγοιμ᾽ ἂν ἄνδρα τόνδε τῶν σταθμῶν κύνα,
σωτῆρα ναὸς πρότονον, ὑψηλῆς στέγης
στῦλον ποδήρη, μονογενὲς τέκνον πατρὶ
καὶ γῆν φανεῖσαν ναυτίλοις παρ᾽ ἐλπίδα,
κάλλιστον ἦμαρ εἰσιδεῖν ἐκ χείματος,   900
ὁδοιπόρῳ διψῶντι πηγαῖον ῥέος·
τερπνὸν δὲ τἀναγκαῖον ἐκφυγεῖν ἅπαν.
τοιοῖσδέ τοί νιν ἀξιῶ προσφθέγμασιν.
φθόνος δ᾽ ἀπέστω· πολλὰ γὰρ τὰ πρὶν κακὰ
ἠνειχόμεσθα. νῦν δέ μοι, φίλον κάρα,   905
ἔκβαιν᾽ ἀπήνης τῆσδε, μὴ χαμαὶ τιθεὶς
τὸν σὸν πόδ᾽, ὦναξ, Ἰλίου πορθήτορα.

For his three bodies severally slain.
Thus rumour did torment me, counselling
Oftwhile the knotted noose about my neck
That other hands did loose in my despite.
    'Tis for this cause that with me standeth not
The living token of love's fealty
'Twixt thee and me, as had beseemèd him,
Our son, Orestes; let not this amaze thee.
A true and knightly friend doth shelter him,
Strophius the Phocian, urgent to forearm
'Gainst twin calamities,—thy jeopardy
'Neath Ilium's walls, and here sage counsel whelm'd
By baseborn clamour of seditious throats
And feet that haste to trample on the fallen.
Plain cause is here; 'tis no dissembler's plea.
    For me, the springs that fed my sorrow's flow
Have spent their every drop and turned to drought;
Mine eyes are worn with vigils, when they wept
The unheeded beacons, or, awaked from dreams
By the light tremor of a gnat's shrill wings,
Saw still such press of ills besetting thee
As ne'er my span of slumber had embraced.
And now, her sufferings o'er, my soul reprieved
Haileth her saviour: not more safe the fold
Whose watch-dog wakes, the ship whose forestay
            stands,
The roof whose pillar springs from spreading base,
The house no longer childless, mariners
Who long adrift descry unlooked-for land
Or sunlight after storm, spent wayfarers
Who spy 'mid desert tracts a bubbling spring.
What gladness matches such deliverance?
Be his then every title of acclaim!
Intrude not envy! 'Tis but recompense
Of tribulations manifold endured.
Step from thy chariot, prithee, dear my lord,
Yet set not on bare earth that royal foot
Whereunder Troy fell prostrate. Haste ye, women,

δμωαί, τί μέλλεθ', αἷς ἐπέσταλται τέλος
πέδον κελεύθου στρωννύναι πετάσμασιν;
εὐθὺς γενέσθω πορφυρόστρωτος πόρος   910
ἐς δῶμ' ἄελπτον ὡς ἂν ἡγῆται Δίκη.
τὰ δ' ἄλλα φροντὶς οὐχ ὕπνῳ νικωμένη
θήσει δικαίως σὺν θεοῖς εἱμαρμένα.

ΑΓ.   Λήδας γένεθλον, δωμάτων ἐμῶν φύλαξ,
      ἀπουσίᾳ μὲν εἶπας εἰκότως ἐμῇ·   915
      μακρὰν γὰρ ἐξέτεινας· ἀλλ' ἐναισίμως
      αἰνεῖν, παρ' ἄλλων χρὴ τόδ' ἔρχεσθαι γέρας·
      καὶ τἆλλα μὴ γυναικὸς ἐν τρόποις ἐμὲ
      ἄβρυνε, μηδὲ βαρβάρου φωτὸς δίκην
      χαμαιπετὲς βόαμα προσχάνῃς ἐμοί,   920
      μηδ' εἵμασι στρώσασ' ἐπίφθονον πόρον
      τίθει· θεούς τοι τοῖσδε τιμαλφεῖν χρεών·
      ἐν ποικίλοις δὲ θνητὸν ὄντα κάλλεσιν
      βαίνειν ἐμοὶ μὲν οὐδαμῶς ἄνευ φόβου.
      λέγω κατ' ἄνδρα, μὴ θεόν, σέβειν ἐμέ.   925
      χωρὶς ποδοψήστρων τε καὶ ποικιλμάτων
      κληδὼν ἀυτεῖ· καὶ τὸ μὴ κακῶς φρονεῖν
      θεοῦ μέγιστον δῶρον. ὀλβίσαι δὲ χρὴ
      βίον τελευτήσαντ' ἐν εὐεστοῖ φίλῃ.
      εἰ πάντα δ' ὡς πράσσοιμ' ἄν, εὐθαρσὴς ἐγώ.   930
ΚΛ.   καὶ μὴν τόδ' εἶκε μὴ παρὰ γνώμην ἐμοί.
ΑΓ.   γνώμην μὲν ἴσθι μὴ διαφθεροῦντ' ἐμέ.
ΚΛ.   ηὔξω θεοῖς δείσας ἂν ὧδ' ἔρξειν τάδε.
ΑΓ.   εἴπερ τις, εἰδώς γ' εὖ τόδ' ἐξεῖπον τέλος.
ΚΛ.   τί δ' ἂν δοκεῖ σοι Πρίαμος, εἰ τάδ' ἤνυσεν;   935
ΑΓ.   ἐν ποικίλοις ἂν κάρτα μοι βῆναι δοκεῖ.
ΚΛ.   μή νυν τὸν ἀνθρώπειον αἰδεσθῇς ψόγον.
ΑΓ.   φήμη γε μέντοι δημόθρους μέγα σθένει.
ΚΛ.   ὁ δ' ἀφθόνητός γ' οὐκ ἐπίζηλος πέλει.
ΑΓ.   οὔτοι γυναικός ἐστιν ἱμείρειν μάχης.   940
ΚΛ.   τοῖς δ' ὀλβίοις γε καὶ τὸ νικᾶσθαι πρέπει.
ΑΓ.   ἦ καὶ σὺ νίκην τῆσδε δήριος τίεις;
ΚΛ.   πιθοῦ· κρατεῖς μέντοι παρεὶς ἑκὼν ἐμοί.

Perform your portioned offices, and spread
With woven splendour the triumphal path,
That by encrimson'd road the king may pass
Guided by Justice to an home undreamed.
All else, God helping, shall my wakeful care
Justly direct toward Heav'n's appointed end.

AGAM.   Daughter of Leda, guardian of my home,
Mine absence hath been long, and thine address
Measured it not amiss; but praise bestowed
Beseemingly should flow from other lips.
Think not withal to entreat me delicately
On woman's wise, nor borrow in mine honour
Their alien use who noise, on bended knee,
Barbaric open-throated wonderment.
Make not this path with purple tissue strewn
A thing of envy. Such honours belong
To Gods alone; for mortal man to tread
Fabric of cunning beauties 'neath his foot,—
Such pride is in my conscience perilous.
I bid thee reverence me as man, not God;
Remote from druggets and refulgent gear
Is true renown; and to be sober-minded
Is God's best gift. Call no life blest until
It closeth still in bliss. Oh! might I act
Alway as now, an heart serene is mine.

CLYT.   Yield just in this, and disappoint me not.
AGAM.   What I appoint, that will I not annul.
CLYT.   Some vow, 'twould seem, is here, some panic-vow.
AGAM.   Not so: 'tis judgement given advisedly.
CLYT.   What think'st thou Priam had done in like success?
AGAM.   He would have trod, I trow, th' empurpled path.
CLYT.   Then heed not thou the cavillings of men.
AGAM.   Yet what the people bruit hath urgency.
CLYT.   Aye, but where none doth envy, none admires.
AGAM.   Sure 'tis no woman's part to covet strife.
CLYT.   But vanquishment doth well beseem the mighty.
AGAM.   Dost prize a victory in such strife as this?
CLYT.   Nay, yield of thine own grace; 'twere no defeat.

ΑΓ. ἀλλ' εἰ δοκεῖ σοι ταῦθ', ὑπαί τις ἀρβύλας
λύοι τάχος, πρόδουλον ἔμβασιν ποδός.   945
καὶ τοῖσδέ μ' ἐμβαίνονθ' ἀλουργέσιν θεῶν
μή τις πρόσωθεν ὄμματος βάλοι φθόνος.
πολλὴ γὰρ αἰδὼς δωματοφθορεῖν ποσὶν
φθείροντα πλοῦτον ἀργυρωνήτους θ' ὑφάς.
τοὐμὸν μὲν οὕτω· τὴν ξένην δὲ πρευμενῶς   950
τήνδ' ἐσκόμιζε· τὸν κρατοῦντα μαλθακῶς
θεὸς πρόσωθεν εὐμενῶς προσδέρκεται.
ἑκὼν γὰρ οὐδεὶς δουλίῳ χρῆται ζυγῷ·
αὕτη δὲ πολλῶν χρημάτων ἐξαίρετον
ἄνθος, στρατοῦ δώρημ', ἐμοὶ ξυνέσπετο.   955
ἐπεὶ δ' ἀκούειν σοῦ κατέστραμμαι τάδε,
εἶμ' ἐς δόμων μέλαθρα πορφύρας πατῶν.

ΚΛ. ἔστιν θάλασσα—τίς δέ νιν κατασβέσει;—
τρέφουσα πολλῆς πορφύρας ἰσάργυρον
κηκῖδα παγκαίνιστον, εἱμάτων βαφάς·   960
οἶκος δ' ὑπάρχει. τῶνδε σὺν θεοῖς, ἄναξ,
ἔχειν πένεσθαι δ' οὐκ ἐπίσταται δόμος.
πολλῶν πατησμὸν δ' εἱμάτων ἂν ηὐξάμην,
δόμοισι προυνεχθέντος ἐν χρηστηρίοις
ψυχῆς κόμιστρα τῆσδε μηχανωμένῃ.   965
καὶ σοῦ μολόντος δωματῖτιν ἑστίαν—
ῥίζης παρούσης φυλλὰς ἵκετ' ἐς δόμους,
σκιάν θ' ὑπερτείνασα σειρίου κυνὸς
θάλπος μὲν ἐν χειμῶνι σημαίνει μολόν,
ὅταν δὲ τεύχῃ Ζεὺς ἀπ' ὄμφακος πικρᾶς   970
οἶνον, τότ' ἤδη ψῦχος ἐν δόμοις πέλει,
ἀνδρὸς τελείου δῶμ' ἐπιστρωφωμένου.

Ζεῦ Ζεῦ τέλειε, τὰς ἐμὰς εὐχὰς τέλει·
μέλοι δέ τοι σοὶ τῶνπερ ἂν μέλλῃς τελεῖν.

AGAM.   Nay, an thou so dost will,—haste, loose, I say,
These shoon that serve the motions of my feet,
And as I tread these splendours, may no God
Turn from afar on me a jealous eye!
'Tis no light scruple that my feet should waste
Vesture of price and treasured tapestry.
Nay, let it pass! This damsel at my side
Receive thou kindly: mercy tempering might
Moveth high heaven to benign regard.
Not e'en the meanest stoops a willing neck
To slavery's yoke; and her the host did deem
The flower most exquisite of all our spoil
And proffered as my prize, to grace my train.
Now will I tread, submissive to thy word,
This crimson pathway to my royal halls.

CLYT.   Shall the sea fail? Shall any drain her deeps
Or staunch the vintage of her precious dyes
And stay her bounty from replenishing
Our present plenty? See, my lord, the wealth
That God hath giv'n! Thy palace doth not brook
To stand possessed, and stoop to penury.
Ten thousand robes, if some respondent shrine
Had counsellèd such instrument, would I
Have vowed to trampling, while I sought thy life.
And now that thou art come to hearth and home,—
Where is the root, there do the tendrils weave,
Ere yet the dog-star blaze, a bower of shade,
First token of warmth in winter; and anon,
When comes the miracle of ripening grape
And mellow wine, cool is that home whereto,
Like mantling vine, its master's presence brings
Both shelter and fulfilment.
                    O Lord God,
In whom all fullness lies, fulfil my prayer!
Bestir thy might to consummate thy will!

        (*Exit* CLYTEMNESTRA)

ΧΟ. τίπτε μοι τόδ' ἐμπέδως   [στρ. α.
    δεῖμα προστατήριον   976
    καρδίας τερασκόπου ποτᾶται,
    μαντιπολεῖ δ' ἀκέλευστος ἄμισθος ἀοιδά,
    οὐδ' ἀποπτύσαι δίκαν   980
    δυσκρίτων ὀνειράτων
    θάρσος εὐπιθὲς ἵζει
    φρενὸς φίλον θρόνον; χρόνος δ' ἐπεὶ
    πρυμνησίων ξὺν ἐμβολαῖς
    ψαμμὶς ἀκτὰ περιή-   985
    χησεν, εὖθ' ὑπ' Ἴλιον
    ὦρτο ναυβάτας στρατός.

    πεύθομαι δ' ἀπ' ὀμμάτων   [ἀντ. α.
    νόστον, αὐτόμαρτυς ὤν·
    τὸν δ' ἄνευ λύρας ὅμως ὑμνῳδεῖ   990
    θρῆνον Ἐρινύος αὐτοδίδακτος ἔσωθεν
    θυμός, οὐ τὸ πᾶν ἔχων
    ἐλπίδος φίλον θράσος.
    σπλάγχνα δ' οὔτι ματάζει,   995
    πρὸς ἐνδίκοις φρεσὶν τελεσφόροις
    δίναις κυκλούμενον κέαρ.
    εὔχομαι δ' ἐκτὸς ἐμᾶς
    ἐλπίδος ψύθη πεσεῖν
    ἐς τὸ μὴ τελεσφόρον.   1000

    μάλα γέ τοι τεταμένας   [στρ. β.
    ὑγιείας ἀόριστον
    τέρμα· νόσος γὰρ
    γείτων ὁμότοιχος ἐρείδει.

CHORUS.   Why, oh why, thus hauntingly
        Doth horror hovering ever nigh
  Beset my soul with presages of doom?
    Why sounds this voice of mystic tone
    Where welcome or reward is none?
    Why doth no gallant confidence
  Take post within my breast, and drive them hence
      Like phantoms of the gloom?
  Time rolleth on; long years are past and o'er
    Since mooring-ropes were hove and stowed
  And shouts re-echoed down the sandy shore
       Where lately rode
    The ships that bare our host to war.

    Yea, mine eyes bear witness too;
    My king is come; 'tis true, 'tis true;
  But still that mystic music troubles me.
    Self-tutored doth my soul intone
    A lamentation all her own;
    She broods o'er wrath to come, and quails;
  Her hope is gone, and all her courage fails.
    'Tis no vain phantasy.
  My heart is not deceived; each pulse is fraught
    With fuller certitude of pain.
  Yet still I pray that all her timorous thought
      Be proven vain,
    And all her boding come to naught.

    Health beyond the wholesome mean
    Hath no safe containing bound;
    Sickness haunts the abutting ground,
    Jealous of the wall between.

καὶ πότμος εὐθυπορῶν   1005
ἱεμένου θρασέως
ἀνδρὸς ἔπαισεν ἄφαντον ἔρμα.
καὶ πρὸ μέν τι χρημάτων
κτησίων ὄκνος βαλὼν
σφενδόνας ἀπ᾽ εὐμέτρου,—   1010
οὐκ ἔδυ πρόπας δόμος
πημονᾶς γέμων ἄγαν,
οὐδ᾽ ἐπόντισε σκάφος.
πολλά τοι δόσις ἐκ Διὸς ἀμ-
φιλαφής τε, καὶ ἐξ ἀλόκων ἐπετειᾶν   1015
νῆστιν ἤλασεν νόσον.

τὸ δ᾽ ἐπὶ γᾶν πεσὸν ἅπαξ   [ἀντ. β.
θανάσιμον πρόπαρ ἀνδρὸς
μέλαν αἷμα τίς ἂν   1020
πάλιν ἀγκαλέσαιτ᾽ ἐπαείδων;
οὐδὲ τὸν ὀρθοδαῆ
τῶν φθιμένων ἀνάγειν
Ζεὺς ἂν ἔπαυσεν ἐπ᾽ εὐλαβείᾳ.
εἰ δὲ μὴ τεταγμένα   1025
μοῖρα μοῖραν ἐκ θεῶν
εἶργε μὴ πλέον φέρειν,
προφθάσασα καρδία
γλῶσσαν ἂν τάδ᾽ ἐξέχει·
νῦν δ᾽ ὑπὸ σκότῳ βρέμει   1030
θυμαλγής τε καὶ οὐδὲν ἐπελ-
πομένα ποτὲ καίριον ἐκτολυπεύσειν
ζωπυρουμένας φρενός.

ΚΛΥΤΑΙΜΗΣΤΡΑ
εἴσω κομίζου καὶ σύ, Κασάνδραν λέγω·   1035
ἐπεί σ᾽ ἔθηκε Ζεὺς ἀμηνίτως δόμοις
κοινωνὸν εἶναι χερνίβων, πολλῶν μετὰ
δούλων σταθεῖσαν κτησίου βωμοῦ πέλας

Steering straight, with favouring skies,
Oft some overbold emprise
Striketh on a rock unseen.
Yet if cautious hands anon
Make of costly merchandise
Well-apportioned jettison,
Clear of the reef the barque will rise;
The nuisant flow is lessened presently,
　　And still she rides the sea.
All is not lost. Behold, God's bounty is broad-spread;
　　He bids the furrows year by year
　　　　Provide our bread,
　That pestilence and famine draw not near.

But, if at thy feet there well
Life-blood that thy hand hath spilt,
When that spreading stain of guilt
Hath incarnadined the ground,
There is no revoking spell.
'Twas for this that Zeus did quell
One whose wizardry had found
Charms to bring the dead again.
Knew I not the Gods ordain
One appointed law to set
Limit unto other law,
Now would my soul outstrip my tongue, and let
　　Her anguish overflow;
Yet still she sees no light; she doth but moan in woe;
　Her thoughts are like a tangled skein;
　　　Some knot or flaw
　Doth foil her; and her fevered hopes are vain.

　　　　(*Enter* CLYTEMNESTRA)

CLYT.　Get thee within these gates, thou too, Cassandra;
　　Seeing God's mercy hath appointed thee
　　To take thy station 'mid our serving-throng,
　　To lave thee in our waters, and to stand
　　Anigh the altar where thy masters worship,

ἔκβαιν᾽ ἀπήνης τῆσδε, μηδ᾽ ὑπερφρόνει.
καὶ παῖδα γάρ τοι φασὶν Ἀλκμήνης ποτὲ   1040
πραθέντα πλῆσθαι δουλίας μάζης βίᾳ.
εἰ δ᾽ οὖν ἀνάγκη τῆσδ᾽ ἐπιρρέποι τύχης,
ἀρχαιοπλούτων δεσποτῶν πολλὴ χάρις.
οἳ δ᾽ οὔποτ᾽ ἐλπίσαντες ἤμησαν καλῶς,
ὠμοί τε δούλοις πάντα καὶ παρὰ στάθμην.   1045
ἕξεις παρ᾽ ἡμῶν οἷάπερ νομίζεται.
ΧΟ. σοί τοι λέγουσα παύεται σαφῆ λόγον.
ἐντὸς δ᾽ ἁλοῦσα μορσίμων ἀγρευμάτων
πείθοι᾽ ἄν, εἰ πείθοι᾽· ἀπειθοίης δ᾽ ἴσως.
ΚΛ. ἀλλ᾽ εἴπερ ἐστὶ μὴ χελιδόνος δίκην   1050
ἀγνῶτα φωνὴν βάρβαρον κεκτημένη,
ἔσω φρενῶν λέγουσα πείθω νιν λόγῳ.
ΧΟ. ἕπου. τὰ λῷστα τῶν παρεστώτων λέγει.
πιθοῦ λιποῦσα τόνδ᾽ ἁμαξήρη θρόνον.
ΚΛ. οὔτοι θυραίᾳ τῇδ᾽ ἐμοὶ σχολὴ πάρα   1055
τρίβειν· τὰ μὲν γὰρ ἑστίας ἤδη πάρος
ἕστηκε μῆλα πρὸς σφαγὰς μεσομφάλους,
ὡς οὔποτ᾽ ἐλπίσασι τήνδ᾽ ἕξειν χάριν·
σὺ δ᾽—εἴ τι δράσεις τῶνδε, μὴ σχολὴν τίθει,
εἰ δ᾽ ἀξυνήμων οὖσα μὴ δέχει λόγον,   1060
σὺ δ᾽ ἀντὶ φωνῆς φράζε καρβάνῳ χερί.
ΧΟ. ἑρμηνέως ἔοικεν ἡ ξένη τοροῦ
δεῖσθαι· τρόπος δὲ θηρὸς ὡς νεαιρέτου.
ΚΛ. ἦ μαίνεταί γε καὶ κακῶν κλύει φρενῶν,
ἥτις λιποῦσα μὲν πόλιν νεαίρετον   1065
ἥκει, χαλινὸν δ᾽ οὐκ ἐπίσταται φέρειν,
πρὶν αἱματηρὸν ἐξαφρίζεσθαι μένος.
οὐ μὴν πλέω ῥίψασ᾽ ἀτιμασθήσομαι.
ΧΟ. ἐγὼ δ᾽, ἐποικτείρω γάρ, οὐ θυμώσομαι.
ἴθ᾽, ὦ τάλαινα, τόνδ᾽ ἐρημώσασ᾽ ὄχον,   1070
εἴκουσ᾽ ἀνάγκῃ τῇδε καίνισον ζυγόν.

Come, get thee from yon wain; abate thy pride.
'Tis told how e'en Alcmene's son was sold
To servitude, and took perforce his fill
Of villain husks. Yet if e'er fortune veer
From freedom to constraint, 'tis no small grace
To serve where wealth is ancient heritage.
They that have garnered riches unforeseen
Are rudely masterful and hold no mean.
From us thou'lt have what custom doth provide.

ELDER.   Her speech is clear; she pauseth for thine answer.
Seeing the toils of fate have closed about thee,
Haply thou'lt choose to yield,—haply refuse.

CLYT.   Nay, except swallow-like she have for speech
Equivocal and alien twitterings,
Her wit might take the tenor of my bidding.

ELDER.   Follow her in; accept the lesser ill;
Come, get thee from this chariot, and obey.

CLYT.   No time have I for lingering thus abroad.
Already by the hearth do victims stand
Whose blood, shed at our midmost shrine, shall pay
Our gratitude for graces we ne'er hoped.
But thou—bestir thee, if thou wilt bear part,
Or, if thine understanding miss my words,
Let tongue depute to hand her foreign task.

ELDER.   Methinks there wanteth an interpreter
To pierce the stranger-lady's mind; she shows
The mood of some wild creature newly caught.

CLYT.   A mood of madness and of frowardness!
If carried hither from her conquered town
She'll brook no bridle nor obey until
Her stubbornness be spent in spume and blood!
No more I'll squander where I meet but scorn.

(*Exit* CLYTEMNESTRA)

ELDER.   But I am pitiful, and will not be wroth.
Come, hapless lady, quit yon wain, and learn
To yield thy neck to destiny's new yoke.

ΚΑΣΑΝΔΡΑ

    ὀτοτοτοτοῖ πόποι δᾶ.   [στρ. α.
    ὤπολλον ὤπολλον.

ΧΟ. τί ταῦτ᾽ ἀνωτότυξας ἀμφὶ Λοξίου;
     οὐ γὰρ τοιοῦτος ὥστε θρηνητοῦ τυχεῖν.   1075

ΚΑ. ὀτοτοτοτοῖ πόποι δᾶ.   [ἀντ. α.
     ὤπολλον ὤπολλον.

ΧΟ. ἥδ᾽ αὖτε δυσφημοῦσα τὸν θεὸν καλεῖ
     οὐδὲν προσήκοντ᾽ ἐν γόοις παραστατεῖν.

ΚΑ. Ἄπολλον Ἄπολλον   [στρ. β.
     ἀγυιᾶτ᾽ ἀπόλλων ἐμός.   1081
     ἀπώλεσας γὰρ οὐ μόλις τὸ δεύτερον.

ΧΟ. χρήσειν ἔοικεν ἀμφὶ τῶν αὑτῆς κακῶν.
     μένει τὸ θεῖον δουλίᾳ περ ἐν φρενί.

ΚΑ. Ἄπολλον Ἄπολλον   [ἀντ. β.
     ἀγυιᾶτ᾽ ἀπόλλων ἐμός.   1086
     ἆ ποῖ ποτ᾽ ἤγαγές με; πρὸς ποίαν στέγην;

ΧΟ. πρὸς τὴν Ἀτρειδῶν· εἰ σὺ μὴ τόδ᾽ ἐννοεῖς,
     ἐγὼ λέγω σοι· καὶ τάδ᾽ οὐκ ἐρεῖς ψύθη.

ΚΑ. μισόθεον μὲν οὖν, πολλὰ συνίστορα   [στρ. γ.
     αὐτόφονα κακὰ καὶ ἀρταμάς,   1091
     ἀνδροσφαγεῖον καὶ πέδου χραντήριον.

ΧΟ. ἔοικεν εὔρις ἡ ξένη κυνὸς δίκην
     εἶναι, ματεύει δ᾽ ὧν ἀνευρήσει φόνον.

ΚΑ. μαρτυρίοισι γὰρ τοῖσδ᾽ ἐπιπείθομαι·   [ἀντ. γ.
     κλαιόμενα τάδε βρέφη σφαγάς,   1096
     ὀπτάς τε σάρκας πρὸς πατρὸς βεβρωμένας.

ΧΟ. ἦμεν κλέος σου μαντικὸν πεπυσμένοι·
     τούτων προφήτας δ᾽ οὔτινας ματεύομεν.

ΚΑ. ἰὼ πόποι, τί ποτε μήδεται;   [στρ. δ.
     τί τόδε νέον ἄχος μέγα   1101
     μέγ᾽ ἐν δόμοισι τοῖσδε μήδεται κακὸν
     ἄφερτον φίλοισιν,
     δυσίατον; ἀλκὰ δ᾽
     ἑκὰς ἀποστατεῖ.

CAS.   Woe, ah woe! ah misery me!
            Apollo, Lord Apollo!

ELDER.   Why cry thus miserably on Loxias' name?
            He is not one to heed a mourner's voice.

CAS.   Woe, ah woe! ah misery me!
            Apollo, Lord Apollo!

ELDER.   Again her dismal cry profanes his name
            Who hath no part nor place in lamentations.

CAS.   Apollo, Lord Apollo!
            My guide and my destroyer!
            This time hast thou destroyed me utterly.

ELDER.   Methinks God's voice still guides her captive soul
            To be the prophet of her own distress.

CAS.   Apollo, Lord Apollo!
            My guide and my destroyer!
            Where hast thou guided me? To what grim dwelling?

ELDER.   Th' Atreidae's dwelling; an thou know'st this not,
            I tell thee, and thou shalt not find me false.

CAS.   Nay, to a godless house,
             Privy to secrets dark
            Of murdered kinsfolk and limb rent from limb
            And butchered men and blood-bespattered floor.

ELDER.   Keen-scented seemeth she as hound for blood;
            She maketh quest and shall not fail of quarry.

CAS.   Clearer the tokens grow;
             Proof of my faith is here.
            Hark to the deathwail, see yon slaughtered babes
            Whose father feasted on their roasted flesh.

ELDER.   Thy fame in prophecy had reached our ears,
            Yet need we now none to expound this saying.

CAS.   Oh God! what thing is plotted here?
            What stroke of malice strange and drear
            'Gainst them that have their home beneath this roof?
            Such as no valour may endure!
            Such as no skill may hope to cure!
              And succour stands aloof.

ΧΟ. τούτων ἄιδρίς εἰμι τῶν μαντευμάτων.　1105
　　ἐκεῖνα δ' ἔγνων· πᾶσα γὰρ πόλις βοᾷ.

ΚΑ.　ἰὼ τάλαινα, τόδε γὰρ τελεῖς;　[ἀντ. δ.
　　τὸν ὁμοδέμνιον πόσιν
　　λουτροῖσι φαιδρύνασα—πῶς φράσω τέλος;
　　　τάχος γὰρ τόδ' ἔσται·　1110
　　προτείνει δὲ χεὶρ ἐκ
　　χερὸς ὀρέγματα.

ΧΟ. οὔπω ξυνῆκα· νῦν γὰρ ἐξ αἰνιγμάτων
　　ἐπαργέμοισι θεσφάτοις ἀμηχανῶ.

ΚΑ.　ἒ ἔ, παπαῖ παπαῖ,　[στρ. ε.
　　τί τόδε φαίνεται;
　　ἢ δίκτυόν τί γ' Ἅιδου.　1115
　　ἀλλ' ἄρκυς ἡ ξύνευνος, ἡ ξυναιτία
　　φόνου. στάσις δ' ἀκόρετος γένει
　　κατολολυξάτω
　　θύματος λευσίμου.

ΧΟ. ποίαν Ἐρινὺν τήνδε δώμασιν κέλει
　　ἐπορθιάζειν; οὔ με φαιδρύνει λόγος.　1120
　　ἐπὶ δὲ καρδίαν ἔδραμε κροκοβαφὴς
　　σταγών, ἅτε καιρία πτώσιμος
　　ξυνάνεται βίου δύντος αὐγαῖς,
　　ταχεῖα δ' ἄτα πέλει.

ΚΑ.　ἆ ἄ, ἰδοὺ ἰδού·　[ἀντ. ε.
　　ἄπεχε τῆς βοὸς
　　τὸν ταῦρον· ἐν πέπλοισι　1126
　　μελαγκέρῳ λαβοῦσα μηχανήματι
　　τύπτει· πίτνει δ' ἐν ἐνύδρῳ κύτει.
　　δολοφόνον λέβη-
　　τος τύχαν σοι λέγω.

ELDER. These oracles of thine surpass my ken;
        The first I grasped; with them the city rings.
CAS.   Oh hardened soul! oh purpose dread!
        Thy lord, the partner of thy bed,
    To lave and cheer, and then—ah! how unfold
        The end? Soon, soon shall all be plain.
        Hand over hand advanced doth gain
            Ever a closer hold.
ELDER. Still am I baffled; though thy riddles cease,
        Thy dim-lit prophecies perplex me sore.
CAS.   Oh horrible, thrice horrible!
            What draweth now to view?
        A net? Aye, such as Hell might cast!
    Nay, 'tis no net: 'tis arms which once embraced,
            And now conspire to kill.
        Rise, ye avenging company,
        Ravage anew this house ye hate!
            Let shrieks of glee
        And crashing rocks record your victim's fate!
ELDER. What clamorous Fury dost thou now invoke
        Against this house? Thy cry dismayeth me.
CHORUS.   My heart doth pulse, my cheek is blenched,
        As in some hour of mortal stroke
        When ebbs the blood unceasingly
            With every breath,
        Until life's westering sun is quenched
            In sudden death.
CAS.   Look! look! Save him! Shall bull be gored
            By his own mate? See, see,
        Those tangled folds that trammel him!
    Those instant horns! That black device of death
        That pierces through and through!
        Where late the limpid waters stood
        In lustral bowl, spreads now the stain
            Of welling blood
    Where prone he lies most traitorously slain.

ΧΟ. οὐ κομπάσαιμ᾽ ἂν θεσφάτων γνώμων ἄκρος
εἶναι, κακῷ δέ τῳ προσεικάζω τάδε.   1131
ἀπὸ δὲ θεσφάτων τίς ἀγαθὰ φάτις
βροτοῖς τέλλεται; κακῶν γὰρ διαὶ
πολυεπεῖς τέχναι θεσπιῳδὸν
φόβον φέρουσιν μαθεῖν.   1135

ΚΑ. ἰὼ ἰὼ ταλαίνας κακόποτμοι τύχαι·   [στρ. ζ.
τὸ γὰρ ἐμὸν θροῶ πάθος ἐπεγχύδαν.
ποῖ δή με δεῦρο τὴν τάλαιναν ἤγαγες;
οὐδέν ποτ᾽ εἰ μὴ ξυνθανουμένην. τί γάρ;
ΧΟ. φρενομανής τις εἶ θεοφόρητος, ἀμ-   1140
φὶ δ᾽ αὑτᾶς θροεῖς
νόμον ἄνομον, οἷά τις ξουθὰ
ἀκόρετος βοᾶς, φεῦ, ταλαίναις φρεσὶν
Ἴτυν Ἴτυν στένουσ᾽ ἀμφιθαλῆ κακοῖς
ἀηδὼν βίον.   1145

ΚΑ. ἰὼ ἰὼ λιγείας μόρον ἀηδόνος·   [ἀντ. ζ.
περίβαλον γάρ οἱ πτεροφόρον δέμας
θεοὶ γλυκύν τ᾽ αἰῶνα κλαυμάτων ἄτερ·
ἐμοὶ δὲ μίμνει σχισμὸς ἀμφήκει δορί.
ΧΟ. πόθεν ἐπισσύτους θεοφόρους ἔχεις   1150
ματαίους δύας,
τὰ δ᾽ ἐπίφοβα δυσφάτῳ κλαγγᾷ
μελοτυπεῖς ὁμοῦ τ᾽ ὀρθίοις ἐν νόμοις;
πόθεν ὅρους ἔχεις θεσπεσίας ὁδοῦ
κακορρήμονας;   1155

ΚΑ. ἰὼ γάμοι γάμοι Πάριδος ὀλέθριοι φίλων.   [στρ. η.
ἰὼ Σκαμάνδρου πάτριον ποτόν.
τότε μὲν ἀμφὶ σὰς ἀιόνας τάλαιν᾽
ἠνυτόμαν τροφαῖς·
νῦν δ᾽ ἀμφὶ Κωκυτόν τε κἀχερουσίους   1160
ὄχθας ἔοικα θεσπιῳδήσειν τάχα.
ΧΟ. τί τόδε τορὸν ἄγαν ἔπος ἐφημίσω;
καὶ νεογνὸς ἂν ἀίων μάθοι.
πέπληγμαι δ᾽ ὑπαὶ δάκει φοινίῳ
δυσαλγεῖ τύχᾳ μινυρὰ θρεομένας,
θράγματ᾽ ἐμοὶ κλύειν.   1166

ELDER.   No master-skill I'll boast, and need no skill
          To mark the shadow of sore trouble here.
CHORUS.   Yet when did omen hint no ill,
             Or pledge of good inspire the seer?
             His artistry of tongue would naught
                   Alone avail;
             'Tis threat of woe that e'er has taught
                   Man's heart to quail.
CAS.   Ah! hapless me! my misery,
             My plaint, fill full the cup of doom.
             Oh! whither hast thou led poor me?
          Or what my portion save to share a tomb?
CHORUS. Thy stricken soul methinks some Spirit sways
             Thus over thine own self to sing
                A tune of dismal tone,
          Like the brown nightingale that maketh moan
             In wistfulness unwearying
          For 'Itys' 'Itys' all her sorrow-laden days.
CAS.   Oh songstress of strange destiny!
             To thee, in feathered form arrayed,
             God gave sweet life and tearless eye:
          For me is whetted now the poignard-blade.
CHORUS. Whence spring these wild tempestuous ecstasies
             Tormenting thee with fruitless throe?
                These sobs of fear untold
             Mingled anon with presage clear and bold?
             What power inspireth thee to know
          The path that thus evokes thine inauspicious cries?
CAS.   Woe to thee, Paris, who didst woo and win
             Destruction for thy kith and kin!
          Woe for the stream our fathers drank! Ah me!
          Beside thy marge, Scamander, did I roam;
             My childish heart was stayed on thee.
          But now Cocytus' stream shall be my home
          And Acheron's shore receive my prophecy.
CHORUS. What moves thee to this utterance all too plain?
             A child might understand untaught.
             Responsive to thy piteous strain
          My heart is riven and rent and utterly distraught.

ΚΑ. ἰὼ πόνοι πόνοι πόλεος ὀλομένας τὸ πᾶν.   [ἀντ. η.
ἰὼ πρόπυργοι θυσίαι πατρὸς
πολυκανεῖς βοτῶν ποιονόμων· ἄκος δ᾽
οὐδὲν ἐπήρκεσαν   1170
τὸ μὴ πόλιν μὲν ὥσπερ οὖν ἔχρων παθεῖν,
ἐγὼ δ᾽ ἔθ᾽ ὁρμαίνουσα τἀμποδὼν ματῶ.

ΧΟ. ἑπόμενα προτέροις τάδ᾽ ἐπεφημίσω,
καί τίς σε κακοφρονῶν τίθη-
σι δαίμων ὑπερβαρὴς ἐμπίτνων   1175
μελίζειν πάθη γοερὰ θανατοφόρα·
τέρμα δ᾽ ἀμηχανῶ.

ΚΑ. καὶ μὴν ὁ χρησμὸς οὐκέτ᾽ ἐκ καλυμμάτων
ἔσται δεδορκὼς νεογάμου νύμφης δίκην·
λαμπρὸς δ᾽ ἔοικεν ἡλίου πρὸς ἀντολὰς   1180
πνέων ἐσάξειν, ὥστε κύματος δίκην
κλύζειν πρὸς αὐγὰς τοῦδε πήματος πολὺ
μεῖζον· φρενώσω δ᾽ οὐκέτ᾽ ἐξ αἰνιγμάτων.
καὶ μαρτυρεῖτε συνδρόμως ἴχνος κακῶν
ῥινηλατούσῃ τῶν πάλαι πεπραγμένων.   1185
τὴν γὰρ στέγην τήνδ᾽ οὔποτ᾽ ἐκλείπει χορὸς
σύμφθογγος οὐκ εὔφωνος· οὐ γὰρ εὖ λέγει.
καὶ μὴν πεπωκώς γ᾽, ὡς θρασύνεσθαι πλέον,
βρότειον αἷμα κῶμος ἐν δόμοις μένει,
δύσπεμπτος ἔξω, συγγόνων Ἐρινύων.   1190
ὑμνοῦσι δ᾽ ὕμνον δώμασιν προσήμεναι
πρώταρχον ἄτην· ἐν μέρει δ᾽ ἀπέπτυσαν
εὐνὰς ἀδελφοῦ τῷ πατοῦντι δυσμενεῖς.
ἥμαρτον, ἢ κυρῶ τι τοξότης τις ὥς;
ἢ ψευδόμαντίς εἰμι θυροκόπος φλέδων;   1195
ἐκμαρτύρησον προυμόσας τό μ᾽ εἰδέναι
λόγῳ παλαιὰς τῶνδ᾽ ἁμαρτίας δόμων.

ΧΟ. καὶ πῶς ἂν ὅρκος, πῆγμα γενναίως παγέν,
παιώνιος γένοιτο; θαυμάζω δέ σε

CAS.   Woe for my country strick'n with blow on blow
        That wrought her utter overthrow!
    Woe for the wealth of rich-fed fatlings slain
    In hope to save my father's citadel!
        Naught it availed that victims fell;
    My country fared as I foretold, and lo!
    Still o'er confronting doom I brood in vain.

CHORUS. To wail doth wail succeed in sequence true;
        Sure some malicious sprite doth urge
        Thy burdened soul to chant a dirge
  That pointeth deathward; but the end is hid from view.

CAS.   No longer shall my prescient muse be veiled
    And dim her vision like a bride new-wed,
    But, clear as breeze that freshens toward the dawn,
    In black array athwart the orient light
    Shall roll billow on billow, woe on woe,
    Vaster and ever vaster. Nay, no more
    Will I instruct ye by dark parables.
    Witness ye now, follow my track, and see
    How true I scent the trail of olden crime.
        Ne'er from this house departs a choir that chants
    In unison of tune its ill-toned lay.
    Drunken to recklessness with human blood
    The rout of revellers bides within this house
    And none may banish her familiar Furies.
    Holding her gates in siege, they hymn aloud
    The primal bane of souls infatuate
    Estranged from wisdom and allured to sin,
    Or spit abhorrence of those brothers matched
    In feud o'er loathly ravishment repaid
    With cruelties malign. Err I herein,
    Or shoot an arrow that doth not miscarry?
    Deemest thou me false prophet, vagrant babbler?
    Give me thine oath now and attest my knowledge
    Of all the fabled sinnings of this house.

ELDER. Ah! would such oath, a pledge in honour giv'n,
    Had power to heal! Yet marvel I that thou,

πόντου πέραν τραφεῖσαν ἀλλόθρουν πόλιν   1200
κυρεῖν λέγουσαν, ὥσπερ εἰ παρεστάτεις.
ΚΑ. μάντις μ' Ἀπόλλων τῷδ' ἐπέστησεν τέλει.
ΧΟ. μῶν καὶ θεός περ ἱμέρῳ πεπληγμένος;
ΚΑ. προτοῦ μὲν αἰδὼς ἦν ἐμοὶ λέγειν τάδε.
ΧΟ. ἁβρύνεται γὰρ πᾶς τις εὖ πράσσων πλέον.   1205
ΚΑ. ἀλλ' ἦν παλαιστὴς κάρτ' ἐμοὶ πνέων χάριν.
ΧΟ. ἦ καὶ τέκνων εἰς ἔργον ἠλθέτην νόμῳ;
ΚΑ. ξυναινέσασα Λοξίαν ἐψευσάμην.
ΧΟ. ἤδη τέχναισιν ἐνθέοις ᾑρημένη;
ΚΑ. ἤδη πολίταις πάντ' ἐθέσπιζον πάθη.   1210
ΧΟ. πῶς δῆτ' ἄνατος ἦσθα Λοξίου κότῳ;
ΚΑ. ἔπειθον οὐδέν' οὐδέν, ὡς τάδ' ἤμπλακον.
ΧΟ. ἡμῖν γε μὲν δὴ πιστὰ θεσπίζειν δοκεῖς.

ΚΑ. ἰοὺ ἰού, ὢ ὢ κακά.
    ὑπ' αὖ με δεινὸς ὀρθομαντείας πόνος   1215
    στροβεῖ ταράσσει φροιμίοις ξυνηγόρου.
    ὁρᾶτε τούσδε τοὺς δόμοις ἐφημένους
    νέους, ὀνείρων προσφερεῖς μορφώμασι;
    παῖδες θανόντες ὡσπερεὶ πρὸς τῶν φίλων,
    χεῖρας κρεῶν πλήθοντες οἰκείας βορᾶς,   1220
    σὺν ἐντέροις τε σπλάγχν', ἐποίκτιστον γέμος,
    πρέπουσ' ἔχοντες, ὧν πατὴρ ἐγεύσατο.
    ἐκ τῶνδε ποινάς φημι βουλεύειν τινὰ
    λέοντ' ἄναλκιν ἐν λέχει στρωφώμενον
    οἰκουρόν, οἴμοι, τῷ μολόντι δεσπότῃ   1225
    ἐμῷ· φέρειν γὰρ χρὴ τὸ δούλιον ζυγόν.
    νεῶν τ' ἔπαρχος Ἰλίου τ' ἀναστάτης
    ἄτης λαθραίου τεύξεται κακῇ τύχῃ.
    οὐκ οἶδεν οἷα γλῶσσα μισητῆς κυνός·
    λέξασα κἀκτείνασα φαιδρόνους δίκην
    τοιάνδε τολμᾷ· θῆλυς ἄρσενος φονεὺς   1231

Bred far beyond the sea, canst tell the story
Of this strange land, as 'twere thine own abode.

CAS. Apollo's self ordained me to this office.

ELDER. Could human love so stir his heart divine?

CAS. Of old I had been shamèd so to avow.

ELDER. Soft living aye doth crave a daintier speech.

CAS. In sooth he did beset me with fierce wooing.

ELDER. And kindled thee to thought of motherhood?

CAS. My troth was giv'n, but I did fail of tryst.

ELDER. Albeit thy mystic dower had made thee his?

CAS. Albeit my folk did name me now inspired.

ELDER. Befell thee then no scathe from Loxias' ire?

CAS. My sin had wage; thenceforth all named me false.

ELDER. Not we; to us thy prophecies ring true.

CAS. Ah! ah! avaunt, ye horrors!
The prelude hath its sequel; once again
My spirit quakes in travail of the truth.
See ye them yonder, hovering at the gates,
Those babe-like phantoms? Children they might be,—
Butchered by such as should have cherished them;
Their hands are laden with flesh; aye, plain it shows,
That piteous load they bear; 'tis their own flesh
Hewn even as for sacrifice, and served
To their own sire. Lo! these do cry for vengeance,
And one there is, I tell ye,—no true lion
But recreant, couching him in sheltered lair
Beside his mate,—who plots, oh! dastardly,
Against my lord new-come unto his home,—
Aye, mine—for I perforce must bear the yoke.
And he who captained Grecian argosies,
He who laid Ilium low, shall meet withal
A fiend that lurketh here to his undoing.
Nought knoweth he the whoredoms of her heart
Or with what gist her smiling lips extolled
Justice—that justice which she now adventures
Lifting a woman's hand to slay her master.

ἔστιν. τί νιν καλοῦσα δυσφιλὲς δάκος
τύχοιμ᾽ ἄν; ἀμφίσβαιναν; ἢ Σκύλλαν τινὰ
οἰκοῦσαν ἐν πέτραισι, ναυτίλων βλάβην;
θύουσαν ᾅδου μητέρ᾽ ἄσπονδόν τ᾽ ἄρη   1235
φίλοις πνέουσαν; ὡς δ᾽ ἐπωλολύξατο
ἡ παντότολμος, ὥσπερ ἐν μάχης τροπῇ,
δοκεῖ δὲ χαίρειν νοστίμῳ σωτηρίᾳ.
    καὶ τῶνδ᾽ ὅμοιον εἴ τι μὴ πείθω· τί γάρ;
τὸ μέλλον ἥξει. καὶ σύ μ᾽ ἐν τάχει παρὼν   1240
ἄγαν γ᾽ ἀληθόμαντιν οἰκτείρας ἐρεῖς.

ΧΟ. τὴν μὲν Θυέστου δαῖτα παιδείων κρεῶν
ξυνῆκα καὶ πέφρικα, καὶ φόβος μ᾽ ἔχει
κλύοντ᾽ ἀληθῶς οὐδὲν ἐξῃκασμένα.
τὰ δ᾽ ἄλλ᾽ ἀκούσας ἐκ δρόμου πεσὼν τρέχω.   1245
ΚΑ. Ἀγαμέμνονός σέ φημ᾽ ἐπόψεσθαι μόρον.
ΧΟ. εὔφημον, ὦ τάλαινα, κοίμησον στόμα.
ΚΑ. ἀλλ᾽ οὔτι παιὼν τῷδ᾽ ἐπιστατεῖ λόγῳ.
ΧΟ. οὔκ, εἰ παρέστη γ᾽· ἀλλὰ μὴ γένοιτό πως.
ΚΑ. σὺ μὲν κατεύχει, τοῖς δ᾽ ἀποκτείνειν μέλει.   1250
ΧΟ. τίνος πρὸς ἀνδρὸς τοῦτ᾽ ἄγος πορσύνεται;
ΚΑ. ἦ κάρτ᾽ ἄρ᾽ ἂν σὺ παρεκόπης χρησμῶν ἐμῶν.
ΧΟ. τοῦ γὰρ τελοῦντος οὐ ξυνῆκα μηχανήν.
ΚΑ. καὶ μὴν ἄγαν γ᾽ Ἕλλην᾽ ἐπίσταμαι φάτιν.
ΧΟ. καὶ γὰρ τὰ πυθόκραντα· δυσμαθῆ δ᾽ ὅμως.   1255

ΚΑ. παπαῖ, οἷον τὸ πῦρ.
ὀτοτοῖ, Λύκει᾽ Ἄπολλον, οἳ ἐγὼ ἐγώ.
αὕτη δίπους λέαινα συγκοιμωμένη
λύκῳ, λέοντος εὐγενοῦς ἀπουσίᾳ,
κτενεῖ με τὴν τάλαιναν· ὡς δὲ φάρμακον   1260
τεύχουσα κἀμοῦ μνῆστιν ἐνθήσει κότῳ.
    τί δῆτ᾽ ἐμαυτῆς καταγέλωτ᾽ ἔχω τάδε,
καὶ σκῆπτρα καὶ μαντεῖα περὶ δέρῃ στέφη;   1265
σὲ μὲν πρὸ μοίρας τῆς ἐμῆς διαφθερῶ.

What noisome monster shall I name, and she
Shall not surpass it? Hath viper more venom?
More cruelty that ogress of the rocks
Who takes for prey the shattered mariner?
The witch who rides the whirlwind hath a heart
More lightly won to truce and tenderness.
Exultantly, defiantly, her cry
Rang, as when foemen break, the while she feigned
Gladness o'er perils past and home regained.

    And now what matter an ye list or doubt?
What must be, shall be; soon thine eyes shall see,
And tears of pity tell, how true I spake.

ELDER. Plain didst thou limn Thyestes that devoured
His children's flesh; my spirit quaked to hear
The abhorrent truth veiled by no fantasy:
All else did baffle me; I missed my road
And marked not whereunto the sequel pointed.

CAS. To Agamemnon's death; thyself shalt see it.

ELDER. Hush thee! let not ill words estrange thy God!

CAS. Deem him not Saviour; 'tis the Seer who speaks.

ELDER. True, if thy words were his. Yet Heav'n forfend it!

CAS. While thou dost pray, they plot their deathly deed.

ELDER. What man is he that wills such wickedness?

CAS. Oh, wide must have my prophecy miscarried!

ELDER. I see not how his will might find a way.

CAS. Yet know I, all too well, this Grecian tongue.

ELDER. A Grecian oracle doth still perplex.

CAS. Ah! ah! this flame that burns me!
Spare me, my Lord Apollo, pity me!
Yon lioness, who hath a wolf for mate
In absence of her lion-hearted lord,—
Her ruthless hand will slay me. Yes, me too;
The cordial of her vengeance will be spiced
With her remembrance of thy prophetess.

    Why should I wear this livery of men's scorn,
Staff in my hand or wreath about my neck?
Thee I'll requite ere comes mine own undoing.

(*She snaps her staff in two; then tearing the wreath from her neck continues*)

ἴτ᾽ ἐς φθόρον πεσόντα· τῇδ᾽ ἀμείβομαι·
ἄλλην τιν᾽ ἄτης ἀντ᾽ ἐμοῦ πλουτίζετε.

ἰδοὺ δ᾽ Ἀπόλλων αὐτὸς ἐκδύων ἐμὲ
χρηστηρίαν ἐσθῆτ᾽· ἐποπτεύσας δέ με　　　　　　1270
κἀν τοῖσδε κόσμοις καταγελωμένην μέγα
φίλων ὅτ᾽ ἔχρων οὐ διχορρόπως μάτην—
καλουμένη δὲ φοιβάς, ὡς ἀγύρτρια
πτωχὸς τάλαινα λιμοθνὴς ἠνεσχόμην—　　　　　1274
ἀπήγαγ᾽ ἐς τοιάσδε θανασίμους τύχας·
βωμοῦ πατρῴου δ᾽ ἀντ᾽ ἐπίξηνον μένει,
θερμὸν κοπέντος φοινίῳ προσφάγματι.

οὐ μὴν ἄτιμοί γ᾽ ἐκ θεῶν τεθνήξομεν.
ἥξει γὰρ ἡμῶν ἄλλος αὖ τιμάορος,　　　　　　1280
μητροκτόνον φίτυμα, ποινάτωρ πατρός·
φυγὰς δ᾽ ἀλήτης τῆσδε γῆς ἀπόξενος
κάτεισιν, ἄτας τάσδε θριγκώσων φίλοις·
ὀμώμοται γὰρ ὅρκος ἐκ θεῶν μέγας,
ἄξειν νιν ὑπτίασμα κειμένου πατρός.　　　　　1285

τί δῆτ᾽ ἐγὼ κάκοιτος ὧδ᾽ ἀναστένω;
ἐπεὶ τὸ πρῶτον εἶδον Ἰλίου πόλιν
πράξασαν ὡς ἔπραξεν, οἳ δ᾽ εἷλον πόλιν
οὕτως ἀπαλλάσσουσιν ἐν θεῶν κρίσει,
ἰοῦσα πράξω· τλήσομαι τὸ κατθανεῖν.　　　　　1290

Ἅιδου πύλας δὲ τάσδ᾽ ἐγὼ προσεννέπω·
ἐπεύχομαι δὲ καιρίας πληγῆς τυχεῖν,
ὡς ἀσφάδαστος, αἱμάτων εὐθνησίμων
ἀπορρυέντων, ὄμμα συμβάλω τόδε.

Begone, ye gauds! Here is my retribution.
Lie in the dust abased like me and broken!
Enrich some other with your ruinous dower!

(*She pauses; and then, as her mantle slips to the ground by no act of her
own, turns about*)

    Oh, see! it is Apollo! his own hands
Strip off my mantle. He who brooked to see me
E'en in his priestly vesture jeered and mocked
When steadfastly I preached my people's folly,—
And I, named by his name, lit with his light,
Endured their scorn, like some poor starveling trull
That cries her amulets abroad,—he now
Hath brought me to this mortal casualty,
Where, for my father's altar-stone, there stands
A block still reeking with another's blood.
    Yet not all unregarded of the Gods
Shall be our death; another yet shall come
To avenge our cause, begotten to this end,
To make atonement with his mother's blood
For his dead sire. Outcast be he and exile,
A wanderer in strange lands, he shall come home
And on the horrors of this guilty house
Shall set the coping-stone. For God most high
Hath sworn that lo! the hand of his dead sire,
Stricken and prostrate, still shall beckon him.
    Oh! why stand I lamenting, I whose doom
Was ever sorrowful? Have I not seen
How Ilium fared? And they that vanquished her,
Do they go scatheless at God's judgement-seat?
I too will venture; I'll not shrink from dying.

        (*She turns to the palace gates*)

Open, ye gates of Death, and let me pass!
I pray only that on one mortal stroke,
With ne'er a tremor, when my blood hath ebbed
Gently away, my eyes may close in peace.

ΧΟ. ὦ πολλὰ μὲν τάλαινα, πολλὰ δ' αὖ σοφὴ   1295
    γύναι, μακρὰν ἔτεινας. εἰ δ' ἐτητύμως
    μόρον τὸν αὑτῆς οἶσθα, πῶς θεηλάτου
    βοὸς δίκην πρὸς βωμὸν εὐτόλμως πατεῖς;
ΚΑ. οὐκ ἔστ' ἄλυξις οὔ, ξένοι, χρόνοι πλέῳ.
ΧΟ. ὁ δ' ὕστατός γε τοῦ χρόνου πρεσβεύεται.   1300
ΚΑ. ἥκει τόδ' ἦμαρ· σμικρὰ κερδανῶ φυγῇ.
ΧΟ. ἀλλ' ἴσθι τλήμων οὖσ' ἀπ' εὐτόλμου φρενός.
ΚΑ. οὐδεὶς ἀκούει ταῦτα τῶν εὐδαιμόνων.
ΧΟ. ἀλλ' εὐκλεῶς τοι κατθανεῖν χάρις βροτῷ.
ΚΑ. ἰώ, πάτερ, σοῦ σῶν τε γενναίων τέκνων.   1305

    φεῦ φεῦ.
ΧΟ. τί τοῦτ' ἔφευξας; εἴ τι μὴ φρενῶν στύγος.
ΚΑ. φόβον δόμοι πνέουσιν αἱματοσταγῆ.
ΧΟ. καὶ πῶς; τόδ' ὄζει θυμάτων ἐφεστίων.   1310
ΚΑ. ὅμοιος ἀτμὸς ὥσπερ ἐκ τάφου πρέπει.
ΧΟ. οὐ Σύριον ἀγλάισμα δώμασιν λέγεις.
ΚΑ. ἰὼ ξένοι,   1315
    οὔτοι δυσοίζω θάμνον ὡς ὄρνις φόβῳ
    ἄλλως· νοούσῃ μαρτυρεῖτέ μοι τότε,
    ὅταν γυνὴ γυναικὸς ἀντ' ἐμοῦ θάνῃ,
    ἀνήρ τε δυσδάμαρτος ἀντ' ἀνδρὸς πέσῃ.
    ἐπιξενοῦμαι ταῦτα δ' ὡς θανουμένη.   1320
ΧΟ. ὦ τλῆμον, οἰκτείρω σε θεσφάτου μόρου.

ΚΑ. ἅπαξ ἔτ' εἰπεῖν καὶ πορευθῆναι θέλω
    οἶμον τὸν αὑτῆς. ἡλίῳ δ' ἐπεύχομαι
    πρὸς ὕστατον φῶς τοῖς ἐμοῖς τιμαόροις
    ἐλευθέρους φόνευτρ' ἐμοῦ τίνειν πρόμους   1325
    δούλης θανούσης, εὐμαροῦς χειρώματος.
    ἀλλ' εἶμι τὰν δόμοισιν ὠκύνουσ',— ἐμὴν   1313
    Ἀγαμέμνονός τε μοῖραν. ἀρκείτω βίος.   1314

ELDER.   O hapless soul, so woeful and so wise,
         A long lament is thine; yet if in sooth
         Thou know'st thy destiny, how canst thou move,
         Like ox submissive to some mystic call,
         Patient and undismayed toward the altar?
CAS.   Sirs, there is no escape, when th' hour is ripe.
ELDER.   An hour of respite is an hour of life.
CAS.   My day hath come; small profit now were flight.
ELDER.   Oh! brave, brave is the spirit that sustains thee.
CAS.   They need no salve whom fortune hath not bruised.
ELDER.   Yet is there solace in a noble death.
CAS.   Oh father! oh to think of thee and thine!
              (*She recoils in horror from the palace gates*)
         Faugh! Faugh!
ELDER.   What qualms are these? Some sickness of thy spirit?
CAS.   Horror is here; blood taints the very air.
ELDER.   Nay then, 'tis but the smell of sacrifice.
CAS.   'Tis as the vapours of an open'd tomb.
ELDER.   That were indeed a bastard frankincense.
CAS.   Forbear, good Sirs!
         I am no timorous bird that idly dreads
         A snare in every brake; I see and know;
         Bear me that testimony in the day
         When dies another woman as I died
         And falls a man as man ill-mated fell.
         Grant me, I pray you, this last charity.
ELDER.   Hard is the prophet's part; thou hast my pity.
CAS.   Once more I fain would speak before I take
         My destined path. Unto yon Sun, whose light
         Shall never lighten me again, I pray
         That, though I die enslaved and set at naught,
         Yet at the hands of my justiciaries
         The free shall suffer for the bondswoman
         And princes' lives pay forfeit for the oppressed.
             Now will I go, and quicken to its close
         What waiteth here within these gates,—the doom
         Decreed for Agamemnon and for me.
         Enough of life!

ΧΟ. ἰὼ βρότεια πράγματ᾽· εὐτυχοῦντα μὲν
σκιά τις ἂν πρέψειεν· εἰ δὲ δυστυχῇ,
βολαῖς ὑγρώσσων σπόγγος ὤλεσεν γραφήν.
οὐ ταῦτ᾽ ἐκείνων μᾶλλον οἰκτείρω πολύ.   1330

τὸ μὲν εὖ πράσσειν ἀκόρεστον ἔφυ
πᾶσι βροτοῖσιν· δακτυλοδείκτων δ᾽
οὔτις ἀπειπὼν εἴργει μελάθρων,
μηκέτ᾽ ἐσέλθῃς, τάδε φωνῶν.
καὶ τῷδε πόλιν μὲν ἑλεῖν ἔδοσαν   1335
μάκαρες Πριάμου,
θεοτίμητος δ᾽ οἴκαδ᾽ ἱκάνει·
νῦν δ᾽ εἰ προτέρων αἷμ᾽ ἀποτίσῃ
καὶ τοῖς θείνουσι θανὼν ἄλλων
ποινὰς θανάτων ἐπικράνῃ,   1340
τίς ποτ᾽ ἂν εὔξαιτο βροτῶν ἀσινεῖ
δαίμονι φῦναι τάδ᾽ ἀκούων;

ΑΓ. ὤμοι, πέπληγμαι καιρίαν πληγὴν ἔσω.

ΧΟ. α΄. σῖγα· τίς πληγὴν ἀυτεῖ καιρίως οὐτασμένος;

ΑΓ. ὤμοι μάλ᾽ αὖθις, δευτέραν πεπληγμένος.   1345

ΧΟ. α΄. τοὔργον εἰργάσθαι δοκεῖ μοι βασιλέως οἰμώγματι.
ἀλλὰ κοινωσώμεθ᾽ αὐτοῖς ἀσφαλῆ βουλεύματα.

β΄. ἐγὼ μὲν ὑμῖν τὴν ἐμὴν γνώμην λέγω,
πρὸς δῶμα δεῦρ᾽ ἀστοῖσι κηρύσσειν βοήν.

γ΄. ἐμοὶ δ᾽ ὅπως τάχιστά γ᾽ ἐμπεσεῖν δοκεῖ   1350
καὶ πρᾶγμ᾽ ἐλέγχειν σὺν νεορρύτῳ ξίφει.

δ΄. κἀγὼ τοιούτου γνώματος κοινωνὸς ὢν
ψηφίζομαί τι δρᾶν· τὸ μὴ μέλλειν δ᾽ ἀκμή.

ELDER. Ah me! the vanity of human hap!
Prosperity? 'tis but a semblance limned
In colour unsubstantial. Misery?
Moisten thy sponge, sweep it this way and that,
And lo! her sombre lines are blotted out.
Scarce deem I one more pitiful than other.

CHORUS. Oh! ne'er hath Fortune's bounty brought
Contentment; still men covet more;
The homage that they have is naught.
None ever yet hath barred his door
Against her coming, or hath cried
  'Hold! I am satisfied'.
Lo! now by grace of God hath come
In pride of conquest to his home
  A prince who hath no peer;
But if his life must mend the score
Of murder done in days of yore,
And by his death he shall impose
On them that deal the mortal blows
  Fresh penalty of death,—
Oh! who, oh! who that hearkeneth
    Will venture still
To vaunt a birthright void of ill,
  And take no warning here?

AGAM. Help! help! I am sore stricken, I am sore stricken.

1st ELDER. Hark! it is the cry of murder; who is he that
    calleth here?

AGAM. Help! help! they smite me again. Oh God! Oh God!

1st ELDER. 'Tis the King; the blow is fallen; heard ye not that
    dying moan?
    Haste we and concert together counsels of security!

2nd ELDER. I advise to rouse the townsfolk, bid them arm, and
    muster here.

3rd ELDER. I to arrest the traitors boldly while their blades be
    wet with blood.

4th ELDER. I agree, I vote for action; 'tis no hour to hesitate.

LAA

6

ε΄. ὁρᾶν πάρεστι· φροιμιάζονται γὰρ ὡς
    τυραννίδος σημεῖα πράσσοντες πόλει.   1355

ς΄. χρονίζομεν γάρ· οἱ δὲ τῆς Μελλοῦς κλέος
    πέδοι πατοῦντες οὐ καθεύδουσιν χερί.

ζ΄. οὐκ οἶδα βουλῆς ἧστινος τυχὼν λέγω·
    τοῦ δρῶντός ἐστι, καὶ τὸ βουλεῦσαι πέρι.

η΄. κἀγὼ τοιοῦτός εἰμ᾽, ἐπεὶ δυσμηχανῶ   1360
    λόγοισι τὸν θανόντ᾽ ἀνιστάναι πάλιν.

θ΄. ἦ καὶ βίον τείνοντες ὧδ᾽ ὑπείξομεν
    δόμων καταισχυντῆρσι τοῖσδ᾽ ἡγουμένοις;

ι΄. ἀλλ᾽ οὐκ ἀνεκτόν, ἀλλὰ κατθανεῖν κρατεῖ·
    πεπαιτέρα γὰρ μοῖρα τῆς τυραννίδος.   1365

ια΄. ἦ γὰρ τεκμηρίοισιν ἐξ οἰμωγμάτων
     μαντευσόμεσθα τἀνδρὸς ὡς ὀλωλότος;

ιβ΄. σάφ᾽ εἰδότας χρὴ τῶνδε θυμοῦσθαι πέρι·
     τὸ γὰρ τοπάζειν τοῦ σάφ᾽ εἰδέναι δίχα.

α΄. ταύτην ἐπαινεῖν πάντοθεν πληθύνομαι,   1370
    τρανῶς Ἀτρείδην εἰδέναι κυροῦνθ᾽ ὅπως.

ΚΛ. πολλῶν πάροιθεν καιρίως εἰρημένων
    τἀναντί᾽ εἰπεῖν οὐκ ἐπαισχυνθήσομαι.
    πῶς γάρ τις ἐχθροῖς ἐχθρὰ πορσύνων, φίλοις
    δοκοῦσιν εἶναι, πημονῆς ἀρκύστατ᾽ ἂν   1375
    φράξειεν, ὕψος κρεῖσσον ἐκπηδήματος;
    ἐμοὶ δ᾽ ἀγὼν ὅδ᾽ οὐκ ἀφρόντιστος πάλαι
    νείκης παλαιᾶς ἦλθε, σὺν χρόνῳ γε μήν·
    ἕστηκα δ᾽ ἔνθ᾽ ἔπαισ᾽ ἐπ᾽ ἐξειργασμένοις.
    οὕτω δ᾽ ἔπραξα, καὶ τάδ᾽ οὐκ ἀρνήσομαι,   1380
    ὡς μήτε φεύγειν μήτ᾽ ἀμύνεσθαι μόρον·
    ἄπειρον ἀμφίβληστρον, ὥσπερ ἰχθύων,
    περιστιχίζω, πλοῦτον εἵματος κακόν.
    παίω δέ νιν δίς· κἀν δυοῖν οἰμωγμάτοιν

5th ELDER. Yes, 'tis plain; here is the preface and the proof of
power usurped.

6th ELDER. True; Discretion whom we honour, they do spurn,
and name her Sloth.

7th ELDER. Counsel have I none to proffer; words avail not here,
but deeds.

8th ELDER. I am with thee; I discern not how debate may raise
the dead.

9th ELDER. Shall we live in their dominion who have brought
this house to shame?

10th ELDER. God forbid that we endure it! Better death than
servitude!

11th ELDER. Shall surmise alone content us? He whose groans ye
heard may live.

12th ELDER. Aye, let anger wait on knowledge; be not guided
by a guess.

1st ELDER. All your counsels point one issue, and I deem your
censure right:

Ye are minded to discover clear and plain our
monarch's plight.

*(The interior of the palace is disclosed; CLYTEMNESTRA is seen standing
with AGAMEMNON and CASSANDRA lying dead at her feet)*

CLYT.   Much erstwhile have I said to serve the hour
Nor will not be ashamèd to gainsay it.
Else how might one matching himself in feud
With foes that pass for friends stake firm and high
Th' encircling net, that, though the quarry leap,
He break not free? For me this hour of stress,
Long knit with thought of olden enmity,
Hath come, hath come at last. There where I struck
I stand in triumph o'er my work achieved.
So wrought I,—yes, this too will I avow,—
That nor could flight avail him nor defence.
In folds entangling as a fisher's net
I drew about him death's imperial robe,
And twice I struck, and with two groans forthwith

6·2

μεθῆκεν αὐτοῦ κῶλα· καὶ πεπτωκότι   1385
τρίτην ἐπενδίδωμι, τοῦ κατὰ χθονὸς
Ἅιδου νεκρῶν σωτῆρος εὐκταίαν χάριν.
οὕτω τὸν αὐτοῦ θυμὸν ὁρμαίνει πεσών·
κἀκφυσιῶν ὀξεῖαν αἵματος σφαγὴν
βάλλει μ' ἐρεμνῇ ψακάδι φοινίας δρόσου,   1390
χαίρουσαν οὐδὲν ἧσσον ἢ Διὸς νότῳ
γαίει σπορητὸς κάλυκος ἐν λοχεύμασιν.
ὡς ὧδ' ἐχόντων, πρέσβος Ἀργείων τόδε,
χαίροιτ' ἄν, εἰ χαίροιτ', ἐγὼ δ' ἐπεύχομαι.
εἰ δ' ἦν πρεπόντων ὥστ' ἐπισπένδειν νεκρῷ,   1395
τάδ' ἂν δικαίως ἦν, ὑπερδίκως μὲν οὖν·
τοσῶνδε κρατῆρ' ἐν δόμοις κακῶν ὅδε
πλήσας ἀραίων αὐτὸς ἐκπίνοι μολών.

ΧΟ. θαυμάζομέν σου γλῶσσαν, ὡς θρασύστομος,
ἥτις τοιόνδ' ἐπ' ἀνδρὶ κομπάζεις λόγον.   1400

ΚΛ. πειρᾶσθέ μου γυναικὸς ὡς ἀφράσμονος·
ἐγὼ δ' ἀτρέστῳ καρδίᾳ πρὸς εἰδότας
λέγω· σὺ δ' αἰνεῖν εἴτε με ψέγειν θέλεις
ὅμοιον· οὗτός ἐστιν Ἀγαμέμνων, ἐμὸς
πόσις, νεκρὸς δέ, τῆσδε δεξιᾶς χερὸς   1405
ἔργον, δικαίας τέκτονος. τάδ' ὧδ' ἔχει.

ΧΟ.   τί κακόν, ὦ γύναι,   [στρ
        χθονοτρεφὲς ἐδανὸν
     ἢ ποτὸν πασαμένα ῥυτᾶς
        ἐξ ἁλὸς ὄρμενον
        τόδ' ἐπέθου θύος
        δημοθρόους τ' ἀράς;
        ἀπέδικες, ἀπέταμες·   1410
        ἀπόπολις δ' ἔσει,
        μῖσος ὄβριμον ἀστοῖς.

His limbs lay limp; and to the fallen corse
Yet a third blow I paid, in gratitude
To him who keepeth safe the dead in Hell.
Himself is victim now, his own soul sped.
Where he lay gasping out the blood that welled
From wounds deep-cleft,—'twas as a rain from heaven
Dropping in crimson drops, that gladdened me
E'en as the corn is glad when God hath bid
Soft southern shower bedew the swelling sheath.

    This is the truth, ye reverend Argive elders;
Joy, an ye will, or sorrow! I exult.
If for his funerals there might be poured
Such wine as doth beseem,—thus, thus, would I
Empty o'er him my vials of hate; 'twere just,
Aye, more than justice. May he take it hence,
Empoisoned with my curse, that cup which erst
He filled for me with miseries manifold,
And with his own lips drain it to the dregs!

ELDER.   Amazed are we to hear thy reckless tongue,
That o'er thy husband dares boast such a tale.

CLYT.   Ye do entreat me as a witless woman
And make essay of daunting me; but I,
Confessing undismayed the thing ye know,
Caring no whit whether ye praise or blame,
Make answer: this is Agamemnon here,
My lord, but dead; and 'tis this hand which wrought
That deed of righteousness. I do avow it.

CHORUS.   Woman, what hath so bewitched thee,—
    Yieldeth earth a food so baneful,
    Yieldeth flowing sea a potion
        So malign,—
    Thus to proffer thee as victim,
    Thus to challenge from thy townsfolk
        Curse condign?
    From his kingdom thou hast cast him,
    Of his breath thou hast bereft him,
        And thy fate
    Shall be outlawry and exile
     Laden with thy people's hate.

ΚΛ. νῦν μὲν δικάζεις ἐκ πόλεως φυγὴν ἐμοὶ
καὶ μῖσος ἀστῶν δημόθρους τ' ἔχειν ἀράς,
οὐδὲν τότ' ἀνδρὶ τῷδ' ἐναντίον φέρων·
ὃς οὐ προτιμῶν, ὡσπερεὶ βοτοῦ μόρον,   1415
μήλων φλεόντων εὐπόκοις νομεύμασιν,
ἔθυσεν αὑτοῦ παῖδα, φιλτάτην ἐμοὶ
ὠδῖν', ἐπῳδὸν Θρῃκίων ἀημάτων.
οὐ τοῦτον ἐκ γῆς τῆσδε χρῆν σ' ἀνδρηλατεῖν,
μιασμάτων ἄποιν'; ἐπήκοος δ' ἐμῶν   1420
ἔργων δικαστὴς τραχὺς εἶ. λέγω δέ σοι
τοιαῦτ' ἀπειλεῖν, ὡς παρεσκευασμένης
ἐκ τῶν ὁμοίων χειρὶ νικήσαντ' ἐμοῦ
ἄρχειν· ἐὰν δὲ τοὔμπαλιν κραίνῃ θεός,
γνώσει διδαχθεὶς ὀψὲ γοῦν τὸ σωφρονεῖν.   1425

ΧΟ.   μεγαλόμητις εἶ,   [ἀντ.
         περίφρονα δ' ἔλακες,
         ὥσπερ οὖν φονολιβεῖ τύχᾳ
         φρὴν ἐπιμαίνεται,
         λίπος ἐπ' ὀμμάτων
         αἵματος ἐμπρέπειν
         ἀτίετον· ἔτι σὲ χρὴ
         στερομέναν φίλων
         τύμμα τύμματι τῖσαι.   1430

ΚΛ. καὶ τήνδ' ἀκούεθ' ὁρκίων ἐμῶν θέμιν·
μὰ τὴν τέλειον τῆς ἐμῆς παιδὸς Δίκην,
Ἄτην τ' Ἐρινύν θ', αἷσι τόνδ' ἔσφαξ' ἐγώ,
οὔ μοι φόβου μέλαθρον ἐμπελάσσεται,
ἕως ἂν αἴθῃ πῦρ ἐφ' ἑστίας ἐμῆς   1435
Αἴγισθος, ὡς τὸ πρόσθεν εὖ φρονῶν ἐμοί.
οὗτος γὰρ ἡμῖν ἀσπὶς οὐ σμικρὰ θράσους.
κεῖται γυναικὸς τῆσδ' ὁ λυμαντήριος,
Χρυσηίδων μείλιγμα τῶν ὑπ' Ἰλίῳ,
ἥ τ' αἰχμάλωτος ἥδε καὶ τερασκόπος   1440

CLYT.   So now thou doomest me to banishment,
        To townsfolk's hate and people's curse, though once
        Thou madest ne'er a move against this man.
        Heeding no more than 'twere a beast that perished,
        While his rich pastures teemed with fleecy flocks,
        He slew his child, the child whose love made sweet
        My travail,—all to allay the Thracian winds.
        Why spared ye him? Did his foul sin deserve
        No wage of banishment? Yet my confession
        Finds thee a stern judge. Hearken then; I warn thee,—
        An thou wouldst threaten, know that I am ready
        To face thee till thy might hath won thee right
        To rule; but if God order th' issue else,
        For all thine age, thou shalt be schooled to wisdom.
CHORUS.   High and haughty is thy temper,
            Rash and arrogant thy boasting;
            Only madness bred of murder
                    So could dream;
            Thou, whose guiltiness is blazoned
            On thy blood-bespattered forehead,
                    Durst thou deem
            Thou shalt haply 'scape unpunished?
            Retribution shall o'ertake thee;
                    Thou shalt go
            In thy turn forlorn and friendless,
                Blow be paid to thee for blow.
CLYT.   Hark then; let oath attest mine arrogance!
        By Justice for my child now satisfied,
        By the twin powers of Sin and Retribution
        To whom I gave this victim's blood, I vow
        This house shall have no neighbourhood with Fear,
        While at my hearth the gleaming firelight shows
        Aegisthus, as of old befriending me.
        He is my shield wherein I greatly trust.
        Low lies the wronger of my womanhood,
        The fondling of strange damsels by Troy's walls;
        And with him lies his captive prophetess,

καὶ κοινόλεκτρος τοῦδε, θεσφατηλόγος
πιστὴ ξύνευνος, ναυτίλων δὲ σελμάτων
ἰσοτριβής. ἄτιμα δ᾽ οὐκ ἐπραξάτην.
ὁ μὲν γὰρ οὕτως, ἡ δέ τοι κύκνου δίκην
τὸν ὕστατον μέλψασα θανάσιμον γόον   1445
κεῖται φιλήτωρ τῷδ᾽, ἐμοὶ δ᾽ ἐπήγαγεν
εὐνῆς παροψώνημα τῆς ἐμῆς χλιδῆς.

ΧΟ. φεῦ, τίς ἂν ἐν τάχει, μὴ περιώδυνος,   [στρ. α.
      μηδὲ δεμνιοτήρης,
      μόλοι τὸν αἰεὶ φέρουσ᾽ ἄμηνιν   1450
      Μοῖρ᾽ ἀτέλευτον ὕπνον, δαμέντος
      φύλακος εὐμενεστάτου
      πολέα τλάντος γυναικὸς διαί·
      πρὸς γυναικὸς δ᾽ ἀπέφθισεν βίον.

      ἰὼ ἰὼ παράνους Ἑλένα   1455
      μία τὰς πολλάς, τὰς πάνυ πολλὰς
        ψυχὰς ὀλέσασ᾽ ὑπὸ Τροίᾳ,
        νῦν δὲ τελείαν
      πολύμναστον ἐπήκρισεν δι᾽ αἷμ᾽ ἄνιπτον,
        ἥτις ἦν τότ᾽ ἐν δόμοις   1460
      ἔρις ἐρίδματος, ἀνδρὸς οἰζύς.

ΚΛ. μηδὲν θανάτου μοῖραν ἐπεύχου
      τοῖσδε βαρυνθείς·
      μηδ᾽ εἰς Ἑλένην κότον ἐκτρέψῃς,
      ὡς ἀνδρολέτειρ᾽, ὡς μία πολλῶν   1465
      ἀνδρῶν ψυχὰς Δαναῶν ὀλέσασ᾽
      ἀξύστατον ἄλγος ἔπραξε.

ΧΟ. δαῖμον, ὃς ἐμπίτνεις δώμασι καὶ διφυί-   [ἀντ. α.
      οισι Τανταλίδαισιν,
      κράτος δ᾽ ἰσόψυχον ἐκ γυναικῶν   1470
      καρδιόδηκτον ἐμοὶ κρατύνεις.
      ἐπὶ δὲ σώματος δίκαν
      κόρακος ἐχθροῦ σταθεῖσ᾽ ἐκνόμως
      ὕμνον ὑμνεῖν ἐπεύχεται δίκας.

The partner of his bed, the seer inspired,
The faithful spouse who at his side could brook
The ship's hard boards. Oh! they had earned their lot:
He—'tis his due; and she, her wailing o'er,
The dying swan's last lamentation sung,
Lies in his loving arms, and with the spice
Of these her nuptials seasons my delight.

CHORUS.   Oh! quickly now may death draw near
            Bringing no durance nor distress
        But endless sleep untouched of angry strife!
            Our kind protector, who did bear
            For woman's sake long weariness,
        By woman's hand is strick'n and reft of life.

            Oh frenzied Helen, by whose guilt
            That multitude of souls was sent
            To death at Troy, thy monument
            Doth stand complete; naught shall atone
        For this last deed of blood; that olden feud firm-built
        Hath now our sovran's doom for coping-stone.

CLYT.   Nay, pray not thus for the portion of death
                In thy burden of grief;
            And turn not aside 'gainst Helen thy wrath;
        Deem not that her carnage of men and her waste
        Of manifold souls in the Danaan host
                Was a cruelty all-transcending.

CHORUS.   Spirit malign, by whom opprest
            Sinks Tantalus' twin dynasty,
        Thy power, though wielded here by women's hands,
            Availeth still to pierce my breast.
            Like crow o'er carrion perched, she stands,
        And boasts of Justice in discordant glee.

ΚΛ. νῦν ὤρθωσας στόματος γνώμην,   1475
    τὸν τριπάχυντον
    δαίμονα γέννης τῆσδε κικλήσκων.
    ἐκ τοῦ γὰρ ἔρως αἱματολοιχὸς
    νείκει τρέφεται· πρὶν καταλῆξαι
    τὸ παλαιὸν ἄχος, νεόχμ' ὦρτο.   1480

ΧΟ. ἦ μέγαν οἰκοσινῆ   [στρ. β.
    δαίμονα καὶ βαρύμηνιν αἰνεῖς,
    φεῦ φεῦ, κακὸν αἶνον, ἀτη-
    ρᾶς τύχας ἀκόρεστον·
    ἰὴ ἰὴ διαὶ Διὸς   1485
    παναιτίου πανεργέτα·
    τί γὰρ βροτοῖς ἄνευ Διὸς τελεῖται;
    τί τῶνδ' οὐ θεόκραντόν ἐστιν;

    ἰὼ ἰὼ βασιλεῦ βασιλεῦ,
    πῶς σε δακρύσω;   1490
    φρενὸς ἐκ φιλίας τί ποτ' εἴπω;
    κεῖσαι δ' ἀράχνης ἐν ὑφάσματι τῷδ'
    ἀσεβεῖ θανάτῳ βίον ἐκπνέων,
    ὤμοι μοι, κοίταν τάνδ' ἀνελεύθερον,
    δολίῳ μόρῳ δαμεὶς   1495
    ἐκ χερὸς ἀμφιτόμῳ βελέμνῳ.

ΚΛ. μὴ δῆτ' αὔχει τόδε τοὔργον ἐμόν,
    μηδ' ἐνιδεχθῇς
    Ἀγαμεμνονίαν εἶναί μ' ἄλοχον·
    φανταζόμενος δὲ γυναικὶ νεκροῦ   1500
    τοῦδ' ὁ παλαιὸς δριμὺς ἀλάστωρ
    Ἀτρέως χαλεποῦ θοινατῆρος
    τόνδ' ἀπέτισεν,
    τέλεον νεαροῖς ἐπιθύσας.

ΧΟ. ὡς μὲν ἀναίτιος εἶ   [ἀντ. β.
    τοῦδε φόνου τίς ὁ μαρτυρήσων;   1506
    πῶ πῶ; πατρόθεν δὲ συλλή-
    πτωρ γένοιτ' ἂν ἀλάστωρ·
    βιάζεται δ' ὁμοσπόροις
    ἐπιρροαῖσιν αἱμάτων   1510

CLYT.   This time do thy lips give judgement aright
In naming the fiend who has waxèd fat
On the flesh of this race.
'Tis he who finds fresh quarrel to feed
Their craving for blood; ere the mischief of old
Hath an end, fresh mischief is risen.

CHORUS.   Aye, strong and merciless is he,
That fiend whose tale of anger thou dost tell,
Plaguing this house malignantly
With cruel woes that naught may ever quell.
Alas, alas, that Zeus so willed,
Who causeth and contriveth all!
Against his will what mortal thing can ever be fulfilled?
Hath not God sanctioned what doth now befall?

My king, my king! No falling tear,
No word of love, availeth here.
Entoiled like spider's prey thou liest,
Dishonoured in the death thou diest,
Laid on no princely couch, but where
With poignard bared for mortal blow
The hand of treachery drew near
And laid thee low.

CLYT.   Proclaim thou not that the deed was mine;
Say not in thy heart
That 'tis Agamemnon's mate stands here:
The Avenger of yore, still stern to requite
The merciless banquet of Atreus,
Hath taken the guise of the dead man's wife,
And in him hath a full-grown victim found
To atone for the slaying of children.

CHORUS.   That thou herein art innocent
What witness shall attest? It may not be,
Save of his forefathers were sent
Some fiend of vengeance bearing part with thee;
There strideth onward, while his wake
Is red with kinsmen's blood outpoured,

μέλας Ἄρης, ὅποι δίκαν προβαίνων
πάχνᾳ κουροβόρῳ παρέξει.

ἰὼ ἰὼ βασιλεῦ βασιλεῦ,
    πῶς σε δακρύσω;
φρενὸς ἐκ φιλίας τί ποτ᾽ εἴπω;   1515
κεῖσαι δ᾽ ἀράχνης ἐν ὑφάσματι τῷδ᾽
ἀσεβεῖ θανάτῳ βίον ἐκπνέων,
ὤμοι μοι, κοίταν τάνδ᾽ ἀνελεύθερον,
    δολίῳ μόρῳ δαμεὶς
ἐκ χερὸς ἀμφιτόμῳ βελέμνῳ.   1520

ΚΛ. ὧδε γὰρ αὔτως δολίαν ἄτην
    οἴκοισιν ἔθηκ᾽
ἐμὸν ἐκ τοῦδ᾽ ἔρνος ἀερθέν·   1525
τὴν πολύκλαυτόν τ᾽ Ἰφιγένειαν
ξένα δὴ δράσας ἄξια πάσχων
μηδὲν ἐν Ἅιδου μεγαλαυχείτω,
    ξιφοδηλήτῳ
θανάτῳ τίσας ἅπερ ἦρξεν.

ΧΟ. ἀμηχανῶ φροντίδος στερηθεὶς   [στρ. γ.
    εὐπάλαμον μέριμναν   1531
ὅπα τράπωμαι, πίτνοντος οἴκου.
δέδοικα δ᾽ ὄμβρου κτύπον δομοσφαλῆ
τὸν αἱματηρόν· ψεκὰς δὲ λήγει.
Δίκα δ᾽ ἐπ᾽ ἄλλο πρᾶγμα θηγάνει βλάβας   1535
πρὸς ἄλλαις θηγάναισι Μοίρας.

ἰὼ γᾶ γᾶ, εἴθε μ᾽ ἐδέξω
πρὶν τόνδ᾽ ἐπιδεῖν ἀγκυλοτοίχου
    δροίτας κατέχοντα χαμεύνην.   1540
τίς ὁ θάψων νιν; τίς ὁ θρηνήσων;
ἢ σὺ τόδ᾽ ἔρξαι τλήσει, κτείνασ᾽
ἄνδρα τὸν αὑτῆς ἀποκωκῦσαι,

A warrior from the courts of Hell, advancing till he take
    The vengeance due for infant-flesh devoured.

        My king, my king! No falling tear,
        No word of love, availeth here.
        Entoiled like spider's prey thou liest,
        Dishonoured in the death thou diest,
        Laid on no princely couch, but where
        With poignard bared for mortal blow
        The hand of treachery drew near
           And laid thee low.

CLYT.   And wherefore not? 'Twas treachery too
          His hand once wrought
    Who snatched from me the flower I loved.
    He shall not boast in the courts of Death
          O'er pitiful Iphigeneia;
    For his deed so drear he hath taken his due;
    'Twas he who first set hand to the sword,
        And now by the sword he is perished.

CHORUS.   My mind doth falter; no resource
    Of ready counsel guides her course.
    Oh! where shall be a refuge found?
    This house doth totter to the ground.
    And lo! I dread lest torrents now of blood
      Beat down and shatter it, out-poured
    No more in scattered drops, but very flood.
      Justice, on each new purpose set,
    Doth find new hones of fate whereon to whet
          Her vengeful sword.

O earth, o earth, would thine embrace
Had held me, or ever I lived to behold
My lord laid low, all huddled and pent,
   With a trough for his humble pallet!
Whose hand shall bury? Whose voice shall bewail?
Wilt thou adventure to do this thing,
To lament o'er the mate thine own hand slew,

ψυχῇ τ' ἄχαριν χάριν ἀντ' ἔργων   1545
μεγάλων ἀδίκως ἐπικρᾶναι;
τίς δ' ἐπιτύμβιον αἶνον ἐπ' ἀνδρὶ θείῳ
σὺν δακρύοις ἰάπτων
ἀλαθείᾳ φρενῶν πονήσει;   1550

ΚΛ. οὐ σὲ προσήκει τὸ μέλημ' ἀλέγειν
τοῦτο· πρὸς ἡμῶν
κάππεσεν, ἡμεῖς καὶ καταθάψομεν,
οὐχ ὑπὸ κλαυθμῶν τῶν ἐξ οἴκων,
ἀλλ' Ἰφιγένειά νιν ἀσπασίως   1555
θυγάτηρ, ὡς χρή,
πατέρ' ἀντιάσασα πρὸς ὠκύπορον
πόρθμευμ' ἀχέων
περὶ χεῖρε βαλοῦσα φιλήσει.

ΧΟ. ὄνειδος ἥκει τόδ' ἀντ' ὀνείδους·   [ἀντ. γ.
δύσμαχα δ' ἔστι κρῖναι.   1561
φέρει φέροντ', ἐκτίνει δ' ὁ καίνων.
μίμνει δὲ μίμνοντος ἐν θρόνῳ Διὸς
παθεῖν τὸν ἔρξαντα· θέσμιον γάρ.
τίς ἂν γονὰν ἀραῖον ἐκβάλοι δόμων;   1565
κεκόλληται γένος πρὸς ἄτᾳ.

ΚΛ. ἐς τόνδ' ἐνέβης ξὺν ἀληθείᾳ
χρησμόν. ἐγὼ δ' οὖν
ἐθέλω δαίμονι τῷ Πλεισθενιδῶν
ὅρκους θεμένη τάδε μὲν στέργειν,   1570
δύστλητά περ ὄνθ'· ὃ δὲ λοιπόν, ἰόντ'
ἐκ τῶνδε δόμων ἄλλην γενεὰν
τρίβειν θανάτοις αὐθένταισιν·
κτεάνων τε μέρος
βαιὸν ἐχούσῃ πᾶν ἀπόχρη μοι |
μανίας μελάθρων   1575
ἀλληλοφόνους ἀφελούσῃ.

And unto his soul unrighteously pay
A thankless oblation, in hope to atone
  For the wrong thou hast recklessly compassed?
    Oh! who shall lift his voice to sound
    Above the grave, with flowing tear,
    The praises of our lord renowned,
    With travail of a soul sincere?

CLYT.   Not thine is the task to fulfil; 'twas I
Who laid him low, and 'tis I will bury;
No kin shall escort him and wail his dirge;
But Iphigeneia will wait, as is meet,
At the marge of the swift-flowing sorrowful stream
With greeting of daughter to father dear
  And throw her arms round him and kiss him.

CHORUS.   Insult for insult, blow for blow!
  What Justice wills, 'tis hard to know.
  The spoiler is despoiled again,
  The slayer by the sword is slain.
For lo! 'tis firmly founded as God's throne,
  An ordinance that ever stands,
That man shall garner e'en as he hath sown.
  Sin haunts this house, and none may chase
Her cursèd brood away; she holds the race
    In iron bands.

CLYT.   'Tis the spirit of Truth that guides thee now
To take thy stand on Heaven's decree.
But I for my part would covenant make
With the fiend who hath troubled the line so long,
To endure my lot, be it ne'er so hard,
And that he be gone from this house henceforth
    And find other folk
  To plague with the murder of kinsmen.
Of goods I ask but an humble share,
And am full content to have saved this house
    And brought her feuds
  Of frenzied revenge to an ending.

ΑΙΓΙΣΘΟΣ

ὦ φέγγος εὖφρον ἡμέρας δικηφόρου.
φαίην ἂν ἤδη νῦν βροτῶν τιμαόρους
θεοὺς ἄνωθεν γῆς ἐποπτεύειν ἄγη,
ἰδὼν ὑφαντοῖς ἐν πέπλοις Ἐρινύων   1580
τὸν ἄνδρα τόνδε κείμενον φίλως ἐμοί,
χερὸς πατρῴας ἐκτίνοντα μηχανάς.

Ἀτρεὺς γὰρ ἄρχων τῆσδε γῆς, τούτου πατήρ,
πατέρα Θυέστην τὸν ἐμόν, ὡς τορῶς φράσαι,
αὑτοῦ δ᾽ ἀδελφόν, ἀμφίλεκτος ὢν κράτει,   1585
ἠνδρηλάτησεν ἐκ πόλεώς τε καὶ δόμων.
καὶ προστρόπαιος ἑστίας μολὼν πάλιν
τλήμων Θυέστης μοῖραν ηὗρετ᾽ ἀσφαλῆ,
τὸ μὴ θανὼν πατρῷον αἱμάξαι πέδον
αὐτοῦ· ξένια δὲ τοῦδε δύσθεος πατὴρ   1590
Ἀτρεύς, προθύμως μᾶλλον ἢ φίλως, πατρὶ
τὠμῷ, κρεουργὸν ἦμαρ εὐθύμως ἄγειν
δοκῶν, παρέσχε δαῖτα παιδείων κρεῶν.
τὰ μὲν ποδήρη καὶ χερῶν ἄκρους κτένας
ἔκρυπτ᾽ ἄνευθεν ἀνδρακὰς καθημένους·   1595
ἄσημα δ᾽ αὐτῶν αὐτίκ᾽ ἀγνοίᾳ λαβὼν
ἔσθει,—βορὰν ἄσωτον, ὡς ὁρᾷς, γένει.
κἄπειτ᾽ ἐπιγνοὺς ἔργον οὐ καταίσιον
ᾤμωξεν, ἀμπίπτει δ᾽ ἀπὸ σφαγὴν ἐρῶν,
μόρον δ᾽ ἄφερτον Πελοπίδαις ἐπεύχεται,   1600
λάκτισμα δείπνου ξυνδίκως τιθεὶς ἀρᾷ,
οὕτως ὀλέσθαι πᾶν τὸ Πλεισθένους γένος.

ἐκ τῶνδέ σοι πεσόντα τόνδ᾽ ἰδεῖν πάρα,
κἀγὼ δίκαιος τοῦδε τοῦ φόνου ῥαφεύς.
τρίτον γὰρ ὄντ᾽ ἐπίδικον ἀθλίῳ πατρὶ   1605
συνεξελαύνει τυτθὸν ὄντ᾽ ἐν σπαργάνοις·

(*Enter* AEGISTHUS)

AEG.   O dawn of Justice radiant and benign!
Now will I e'en confess that Gods on high
Take vengeful cognisance of earthly guilt,
Now that mine eyes have seen the blessèd sight
Of this my foe, clad in Hell's livery,
Taking the wages of his father's work.
   Atreus, his sire, who then held sway in Argos,
Fearing a challenge to his sovereignty,
Drave out my sire, Thyestes, his own brother,
From home and city; who, when he came again
An humble suppliant claiming sanctuary
At Atreus' hearth, thus far had sufferance
That Atreus spared him, and spilled not his blood
To stain forthwith the stones his fathers trod,
But welcomed him as guest, blasphemer he!
And with an eagerness that spake no love,
Feigning a day of feasting and good cheer,
Served him for meat the flesh of his own children.
The feet, the spreading fingers, he did keep
Hid from their sight whose seats were set aloof;
Naught could Thyestes know; no clue was there;
He took and ate. Look hither now and answer,—
Did prodigal e'er sup at such expense
Of his own kith and kin? Then presently,
Apprisèd of the abomination done,
One shriek he gave, then retching reeled away
And cried perdition on his house and name,
And with his foot drave crashing to the ground
Th' accursèd board, in sign and sacrament
Of ruin that should o'erwhelm th' whole royal race.
   That curse hath laid your monarch low; that curse
Did warrant my contrivance of his death.
Third in inheritance was I,—a babe
Still wrapped in swaddling-bands, and taken to share
The miseries and the exile of his sire;

LAA

7

τραφέντα δ' αὖθις ἡ Δίκη κατήγαγεν.
καὶ τοῦδε τἀνδρὸς ἡψάμην θυραῖος ὤν,
πᾶσαν συνάψας μηχανὴν δυσβουλίας.
οὕτω καλὸν δὴ καὶ τὸ κατθανεῖν ἐμοί,   1610
ἰδόντα τοῦτον τῆς Δίκης ἐν ἕρκεσιν.

ΧΟ. Αἴγισθ᾽, ὑβρίζειν ἐν κακοῖσιν οὐ σέβω·
σὺ δ᾽ ἄνδρα τόνδ᾽ εἰ φὴς ἑκὼν κατακτανεῖν,
μόνος δ᾽ ἔποικτον τόνδε βουλεῦσαι φόνον,
οὔ φημ᾽ ἀλύξειν ἐν δίκῃ τὸ σὸν κάρα   1615
δημορριφεῖς, σάφ᾽ ἴσθι, λευσίμους ἀράς.

ΑΙ. σὺ ταῦτα φωνεῖς νερτέρᾳ προσήμενος
κώπῃ, κρατούντων τῶν ἐπὶ ζυγῷ δορός;
γνώσει γέρων ὢν ὡς διδάσκεσθαι βαρὺ
τῷ τηλικούτῳ, σωφρονεῖν εἰρημένον.   1620
δεσμὸς δὲ καὶ τὸ γῆρας αἵ τε νήστιδες
δύαι διδάσκειν ἐξοχώταται φρενῶν
ἰατρομάντεις. οὐχ ὁρᾷς ὁρῶν τάδε;
πρὸς κέντρα μὴ λάκτιζε, μὴ παίσας μογῇς.

ΧΟ. τί δὴ τὸν ἄνδρα τόνδ᾽ ἀπὸ ψυχῆς κακῆς   1643
οὐκ αὐτὸς ἠνάριζες, ἀλλὰ σὺν γυνή,
χώρας μίασμα καὶ θεῶν ἐγχωρίων,
ἔκτειν᾽; Ὀρέστης ἀρά που βλέπει φάος,
ὅπως κατελθὼν δεῦρο πρευμενεῖ τύχῃ
ἀμφοῖν γένηται τοῖνδε παγκρατὴς φονεύς;   1648

ΑΙ. καὶ ταῦτα τἄπη κλαυμάτων ἀρχηγενῆ.
Ὀρφεῖ δὲ γλῶσσαν τὴν ἐναντίαν ἔχεις·
ὁ μὲν γὰρ ἦγε πάντ᾽ ἀπὸ φθογγῆς χαρᾷ,   1630
σὺ δ᾽ ἐξορίνας νηπίοις ὑλάγμασιν
ἄξει· κρατηθεὶς δ᾽ ἡμερώτερος φανεῖ.

ΧΟ. ὡς δὴ σύ μοι τύραννος Ἀργείων ἔσει,
ὃς οὐκ, ἐπειδὴ τῷδ᾽ ἐβούλευσας μόρον,
δρᾶσαι τόδ᾽ ἔργον οὐκ ἔτλης αὐτοκτόνως.   1635

And 'twas as heir, grown now to man's estate,
That Justice brought me home. I, the disowned
And banished, yet reached out and touched my foe;
Mine was the malice that did weave the plot.
Now death itself might come, and I not care,
Who now see him caught in the toils of Justice.

ELDER.   Aegisthus, contumely I disdain
Where sorrow is; but an thou dost avow
That thou of plan prepense didst slay this man
And didst alone devise his piteous doom,
This say I: Justice shall not pass thee by;
Upon thine own head be it! The people's curse
Shall sentence thee, the people's hands shall stone thee.

AEG.   Think'st thou the helmsman seated at the poop
Will brook such insolence from one who plies
A menial oar? Thy latter end shall prove
How hard a thing is wisdom taught so late.
Yet age may learn: bonds and the pangs of hunger
Have wondrous wizardry for cure of folly.
Canst thou have eyes and see no warning here?
Kick not against the pricks, lest thou be maimed.

ELDER.   Oh! why, thus hating him, didst thou not make
Essay of mortal combat, man to man?
Why tookest thou to share thy crime a wife
Whose guilt defiles our country and affronts
Our country's Gods? Oh! if Orestes lives!
If gracious Fortune bring him home again
To slay them both and triumph in their fall!

AEG.   Words again,—words whose sure posterity
Is woe! Ill dost thou mimic Orpheus' tongue
That charmed all things to follow where he led;
Thy puny whining doth but vex, and thou
Shalt go where others lead; captivity
Shall chasten thee, and teach a gentler tone.

ELDER.   What! thou to play the tyrant here in Argos!
Who, when thy malice had conceived this plot,
Durst not adventure thine own arm to strike!

ΑΙ. τὸ γὰρ δολῶσαι πρὸς γυναικὸς ἦν σαφῶς·
ἐγὼ δ' ὕποπτος ἐχθρὸς ἦ παλαιγενής.
ἐκ τῶν δὲ τοῦδε χρημάτων πειράσομαι
ἄρχειν πολιτῶν· τὸν δὲ μὴ πειθάνορα
ζεύξω βαρείαις—οὔτι μὴ σειραφόρον   1640
κριθῶντα πῶλον· ἀλλ' ὁ δυσφιλὴς σκότῳ
λιμὸς ξύνοικος μαλθακόν σφ' ἐπόψεται.

ΧΟ. γύναι, σὺ τοὺς ἥκοντας ἐκ μάχης νέον;   1625
οἰκουρὸς εὐνὴν ἀνδρὸς αἰσχύνων ἅμα
ἀνδρὶ στρατηγῷ τόνδ' ἐβούλευσας μόρον.   1627

ΑΙ. εἶα δή, φίλοι λοχῖται, τοὔργον οὐχ ἑκὰς τόδε.   1650

ΧΟ. ἀλλ' ἐπεὶ δοκεῖς τάδ' ἔρδειν κοὐ λέγειν, γνώσει τάχα·
εἶα δή, ξίφος πρόκωπον πᾶς τις εὐτρεπιζέτω.

ΑΙ. ἀλλὰ μὴν κἀγὼ πρόκωπος οὐκ ἀναίνομαι θανεῖν.

ΧΟ. δεχομένοις λέγεις θανεῖν σε· τὴν τύχην δ' αἱρούμεθα.

ΚΛ. μηδαμῶς, ὦ φίλτατ' ἀνδρῶν, ἄλλα δράσωμεν κακά.
ἀλλὰ καὶ τάδ' ἐξαμῆσαι πολλὰ δύστηνον θέρος·   1655
πημονῆς δ' ἄλλης ὕπαρχε μηδέν· ἡματώμεθα.
στείχετ', αἰδοῖοι γέροντες, πρὸς δόμους, Πεπρωμένης,
πρὶν παθεῖν, στέρξαντες οὖρον· χρῆν τάδ' ὡς ἐπράξαμεν.
εἰ δέ τοι μόχθων γένοιτο τῶνδ' ἅλις, δεχοίμεθ' ἄν,
δαίμονος χηλῇ βαρείᾳ δυστυχῶς πεπληγμένοι.   1660
ὧδ' ἔχει λόγος γυναικός, εἴ τις ἀξιοῖ μαθεῖν.

ΑΙ. ἀλλὰ τούσδ' ἐμοὶ ματαίαν γλῶσσαν ὧδ' ἀπανθίσαι
κἀκβαλεῖν ἔπη τοιαῦτα δαίμονος πειρωμένους,
σώφρονος γνώμης δ' ἁμαρτεῖν τὸν κρατοῦντά θ' ὑβρίσαι.

AEG. The guile, 'tis manifest, was woman's work;
And I had long been suspect for his foe.
But now, seized of his substance and his realm,
I will essay to rule: the mutinous
I will coerce and curb; they shall not prance
Unruly as a corn-fed colt; their stall
Shall be a dungeon, where grim hunger schools
The disobedient to humility.

ELDER. Thou craven weakling, thou coerce and curb
Their spirit who but now have fought and won!
'Twas by thy dalliance and thy lecheries
That thou didst compass this their captain's doom.

AEG. Ho! my trusty men, make ready! action now is forward
here.

ELDER. Nay, if action be thine answer, thou shalt learn a lesson
soon.
Ho! my comrades, draw and face them! hold ye ready
for the fray!

AEG. Nay, I too will draw and face thee; I am ready too to
die.

CHORUS. Die thou shalt; we hail the omen; be it so! we are
content.

CLYT. Forbear, dear lord; do we no mischief more!
The harvest we have reaped is rich in hurt.
Sow no new sorrow; we have done with blood.
    Ye reverend signors, get you to your homes;
Tempt not your fate, but go your way resigned
To Destiny, howe'er she blow; we wrought
As she ordained. Yet oh! how glad were we
Would she but deem these sufferings enough!
Sore bruised are we beneath her heavy heel.
Will ye not let a woman counsel you?

    (The CHORUS *begin to file out*)

AEG. What! I to bear with these, whose idle tongues
Run riot, who defy their fate and hurl
Insult upon me, who know not the path
Of soberness, but vilify their master!

ΧΟ. οὐκ ἂν Ἀργείων τόδ᾽ εἴη, φῶτα προσσαίνειν κακόν. 1665
ΑΙ. ἀλλ᾽ ἐγώ σ᾽ ἐν ὑστέραισιν ἡμέραις μέτειμ᾽ ἔτι.
ΧΟ. οὔκ, ἐὰν δαίμων Ὀρέστην δεῦρ᾽ ἀπευθύνῃ μολεῖν.
ΑΙ. οἶδ᾽ ἐγὼ φεύγοντας ἄνδρας ἐλπίδας σιτουμένους.
ΧΟ. πρᾶσσε, πιαίνου, μιαίνων τὴν δίκην, ἐπεὶ πάρα.
ΑΙ. ἴσθι μοι δώσων ἄποινα τῆσδε μωρίας χάριν. 1670
ΧΟ. κόμπασον θαρσῶν, ἀλέκτωρ ὥστε θηλείας πέλας.

ΚΛ. μὴ προτιμήσῃς ματαίων τῶνδ᾽ ὑλαγμάτων· ἐγὼ
καὶ σὺ θήσομεν κρατοῦντε τῶνδε δωμάτων σέβας.

ELDER. We Argives do not fawn upon a coward.
AEG.   Think not to escape mine arm; thine hour will come.
ELDER. Not, if some God escort Orestes hither.
AEG.   I have known exile; I have fed on hopes.
ELDER. Aye,—to wax fat on heritage foul-gotten.
AEG.   Know, sirrah, thou shalt pay thy folly's price.
ELDER. Crow on! Thy mate doth listen thee. Crow on!

(*Exit* the last ELDER)

CLYT.   Heed not their feeble snarling; thou and I
        Conjoined in sovereign power will so dispense
        That this our house be held in reverence.

NOTES

1–19. The balance of this passage as given in the MSS. is defective. Nothing is more reasonably certain in Greek idiom than that a μέν in the opening sentence of any piece of literature will be duly answered by δέ in the next main sentence. The required δέ occurs in *v.* 12, and, as it happens, owing to the length of the sentence, is resumed and repeated in *v.* 16. The antithesis thereby indicated is between complete release (ἀπαλλαγὴν πόνων) and temporary alleviation (ὕπνου τόδ᾽ ἀντίμολπον ἄκος). This balance of sentences is disturbed in the traditional text by the intrusion of another main sentence, καὶ νῦν φυλάσσω..., but may very simply be restored by placing a comma in lieu of a full stop at the end of the clause governed by κάτοιδα, and by reading καὶ νῦν φυλάσσων,—the καὶ being coupled with νῦν to give the sense of 'still'.

The view which Headlam among others adopts,—that 'καὶ νῦν answers to μέν in *v.* 1, which is itself intended to qualify φρουρᾶς ἐτείας μῆκος: *as throughout the year...so now...*',—cannot, I feel, be sustained; indeed his very rendering by means of 'as...so...' implies similarity and not contrast, and merely glosses over the difficulty.

If we were to translate the first sentence, as Headlam wishes, 'for a whole year I have been asking the gods for release', we should logically render καὶ νῦν either as 'but now' or as 'but still'. But the latter is indefensible as Greek; for, if the words καὶ νῦν must be coupled to produce the sense of 'still', the indispensable 'but' is missing, and the initial μέν remains unanswered; while the former (though just defensible on grounds of idiom, in that τε or καί is occasionally found in lieu of δέ) would produce a strangely inverted antithesis: 'for a whole year I have been praying for release, but now I am keeping watch', whereas the true and natural antithesis might have been, 'for a whole year I have kept watch, but now I ask for release'. Headlam's view, that is, imputes to Aeschylus at the opening of this masterpiece either faulty Greek or false antithesis; and when I put to myself the question, 'Is it more likely that Aeschylus committed one of these offences or that some scribe accidentally wrote φυλάσσω instead of φυλάσσων and thereby impaired the balance of the whole passage?' my answer is that the latter is vastly more likely.

For my own part, moreover, I am convinced that the rendering of φρουρᾶς ἐτείας μῆκος, which Headlam's view involves, as an accusative of duration, is in itself wrong. I take φρουρᾶς to be in apposition to πόνων, and may point out that the addition of μῆκος to ἐτείας is no unnecessary pleonasm; ἔτειος alone means 'yearly' just as often, I think, as 'year-long', and the insistence upon long duration is in any case appropriate here.

7. ἀστέρας, ὅταν φθίνωσιν, ἀντολάς τε τῶν : I have omitted this line, which has long been suspect. Metrically the opening dactyl (see Paley ad loc.) is contrary to the normal use of Aeschylus, but, what is more important still, the construction of the phrase ὅταν φθίνωσιν is hardly defensible. Its position and its correspondence with ἀντολάς τε τῶν preclude us from regarding it as a purely relative temporal clause dependent on φέροντας; but, if it be treated as an indirect interrogative clause dependent on κάτοιδα, a parallel for such usage is far to seek. There is a wide gulf between this usage of ὅταν and that of ὅτε or ὅποτε following certain verbs denoting remembrance or expectancy. I reject the line therefore as a clumsy interpolation designed merely to explain the preceding line.

12. I conceive that εὖτ' ἂν δέ introduces the topic of the alleviations of toil which the watchman can himself effect as opposed to the complete release from his labours which lies on the knees of the gods. If so, ἔχων is vastly preferable to ἔχω, the main thought thereafter being interrupted by φόβος γὰρ...ὕπνῳ, but resumed, in the form originally intended, by the line ὅταν δ' ἀείδειν κ.τ.λ.

14-15. The lines as given in the MSS.

φόβος γὰρ ἀνθ' ὕπνου παραστατεῖ
τὸ μὴ βεβαίως βλέφαρα συμβαλεῖν ὕπνῳ

involve an awkward and unpleasing repetition of the word ὕπνος. In one or other line some correction has been felt to be needed. Wecklein suggested ἀντίπνους in place of ἀνθ' ὕπνου, but I feel that that word does not consort well with παραστατεῖ, but should rather be associated with some verb suggesting movement. I regard my own suggestion ἀντίος as more probable. If the last syllable -ος were once lost, a scribe who found φόβος γὰρ ἀντὶ... παραστατεῖ in his text might readily have argued that 'fear' was present instead of 'sleep', and have inserted ὕπνου. An alternative correction would be to read τάδε (cf. v. 1294) in place of ὕπνῳ, assuming in this case too that the one word had fallen out of the text and the other was inserted conjecturally in its place. Of these two possibilities I prefer the former, because, with the reading ἀντίος, the following line is definitely required in order to complete the sense, whereas, with τάδε in place of ὕπνῳ, the line, though quite relevant, would be almost superfluous.

26. σημαίνω is to be read as subjunctive, but the emphasis of the line lies not on the verb but on Ἀγαμέμνονος γυναικὶ and τορῶς, so that the resulting meaning is 'Let this cry of mine pierce the ears of Clytemnestra'. The present subjunctive is rarer than the aorist in such usage, but is here correct. The watchman conceives of his ἰοὺ ἰού as a cry still ringing through the palace; had his exhortation to himself preceded, instead of following, that cry, he would have used the aorist σημήνω.

From the literary point of view there is a wide difference between σημαίνω read as subjunctive and σημαίνω read as indicative. The former is addressed by the watchman to himself as an exhortation which forms part of a genuine soliloquy; the latter would be an explanation addressed to the audience after the manner of an Euripidean prologue.

32. The scholiast's explanation of θήσομαι by οἰκειώσομαι is interesting. He understood the watchman to mean 'I will score my master's good fortune as my own'. The term θέσθαι was used of the moves made in such games as backgammon, and, the moves available being determined by the fall of the dice, the same term might well cover both the score made by each throw of the dice and the actual move which, as it were, marked that score.

33. τρὶς ἕξ: this on the evidence of Plautus, *Curculio* II. 3. 80, was known as the *iactus basilicus*, and there is every likelihood that βασιλικός was applied in the same manner in the age of Aeschylus. If so, an Athenian audience would have quickly seized this allusion to a 'royal' throw.

43–4. διθρόνου...τιμῆς: I believe this genitive to be directly dependent on the adjective ὀχυρόν. There is no difficulty in supposing that an adjective derived directly from ἔχω included in its range of meanings the active sense of 'possessing'. So too Calder (*Class. Review* XXXVII. 23).

50. ὕπατοι λεχέων: It has been contended that this phrase cannot mean 'high above their nests', on the ground that ὕπατος is always a superlative, so that a genitive following it should be a partitive genitive. That this is the primary and general usage of the word is abundantly proved; but the *Agamemnon* itself provides evidence of a laxer usage. At *v.* 55 ὕπατος δ᾽ ἀίων ἤ τις Ἀπόλλων ἢ Πὰν ἢ Ζεύς... the word does not suggest a true superlative, for, as such, it should be applied (as often in Homer) to Zeus alone. At *v.* 89 again (πάντων δὲ θεῶν...ὑπάτων, χθονίων...) it merely indicates the gods above as opposed to those whose habitation is this earth. And finally at *v.* 509 (ὕπατός τε χώρας Ζεύς), where a genitive is associated with it, if χώρας is in effect the equivalent of τῶν ἐγχωρίων, the genitive will be partitive, but I am more inclined to see in it a parallel to the present passage, differing only in this, that whereas here ὕπατοι λεχέων has reference to locality only, ὕπατος χώρας in *v.* 509 suggests sovereignty as well. I therefore retain the reading of the MSS.

70. ἀπύρων ἱερῶν is interpreted by the scholiast in its technical meaning,— offerings, such as those made to the Μοῖραι and Ἐρινύες, which were not burnt. I am at a loss to reconcile this interpretation with the tenor of the passage. I believe the phrase to mean simply sacrifices, such as Cain's sacrifice, which refuse to take fire and thereby indicate the stubborn anger (ὀργὰς ἀτενεῖς) of gods who refuse to be propitiated.

I retain the reading of the MSS. in the preceding line, οὔθ᾽ ὑποκλαίων οὔθ᾽ ὑπολείβων, and concur therefore in the deletion of οὔτε δακρύων as a mere gloss on the former. The suggested readings ὑποκαίων (Casaubon) and ἐπιλείβων (Schütz) indicate more practical expedients than tears for igniting difficult material, but here after all we are dealing with poetry.

97. The ordinary reading λέξασ'...παιών τε γενοῦ has no claim to elegance and would, I feel, be merely slipshod writing; I give therefore λέξαι θ'. The infinitive in the imperative sense followed by an actual imperative is by no means rare. In *v.* 1431 a not dissimilar error of copying has produced ἀκούεις where I believe ἀκούεθ' should be read.

101. ἀγανὰ which the MSS. give has been changed by most editors to ἀγανή. I have suggested ἀγάν' αὖ as giving an equally satisfactory construction and sense, and accounting more easily for the error of the MSS.

102–3. The reading of M is ἐλπὶς ἀμύνει φροντίδ' ἄπλειστον | τὴν θυμοφθόρον λύπης φρένα, while *f* has θυμοβόρον for θυμοφθόρον. I believe the correct reading to be τὴν θυμοβόρον φρενὶ λύπην, and that φροντίδα and ἄπληστον represent glosses respectively on λύπην and θυμοβόρον. The vagueness of the word λύπην in itself may well have led some annotator to explain that it here means 'painful anxiety', though indeed the emphatic τὴν should make it clear enough that λύπην refers back to μερίμνης in *v.* 99. The words φροντίδ' ἄπληστον being once incorporated in the text, τὴν θυμοβόρον would have appeared to agree with φροντίδα, and the sentence have ended in confusion.

By omitting φροντίδ' ἄπληστον we obtain the half line which Aeschylus favours before the final paroemiac.

104–7. κύριός εἰμι...αἰών: The restoration of the text of these four lines may most conveniently be discussed in a single note, for the reason that the scholia on the second sentence (ἔτι γὰρ...αἰών) bear also upon the interpretation of the first sentence. The scholia are at this point of real value; they run as follows: (1) δύνατός εἰμι εἰπεῖν τὸ συμβὰν αὐτοῖς σημεῖον ἐξιοῦσιν, (2) τὸ ἐν τῇ ὁδῷ ὀφθέν, (3) πείθει γάρ με ἡ παρὰ θεῶν πίστις μέλπειν καὶ λέγειν ὅτι εὖ πράξουσιν οἱ Ἀτρεῖδαι ὅσον ἀπὸ τοῦ σημείου, (4) ὁ γὰρ σύμφυτός μοι αἰών, ὅ ἐστι τὸ γῆρας, διὰ τὴν εἰς θεοὺς πειθὼ μολπήν μοι καὶ ἀλκὴν καταπνεῖ, ὅ ἐστιν, εἰ καὶ γέρων εἰμί, ὅμως μέλψω τὰ γεγονότα· πέποιθα γὰρ ὅτι εἰς πέρας αὐτὰ ἄξουσιν οἱ θεοί.

The first point that emerges is that the commentators who wrote these notes believed that some word in the text could be fairly interpreted by σημεῖον. Francken, observing this, suggested τέρας in place of κράτος, and Headlam adopted the suggestion; but the fact that this line is quoted in the *Frogs* of Aristophanes in the form in which the MSS. of Aeschylus give it seems to me an insuperable objection to such emendation; for we should have to assume either that τέρας was corrupted into κράτος independently in the MSS. both of Aristophanes and of Aeschylus, which would be too astounding a coincidence, or that, such corruption having occurred in the MSS. of one author, it was deliberately copied as a correction into the MSS. of the other, which is almost equally incredible; for no one would wish to change the easy τέρας into the difficult κράτος.

The authenticity of κράτος being thus guaranteed, which was the word that the scholia explain by means of σημεῖον? My answer is ὅδιον,—not an adjectival ὅδιον agreeing with κράτος, but the accusative of a substantival ὅδιος. Hesychius vouches for its existence: ὅδιος—οἰωνὸς αἴσιος, καὶ ἐπίθετον Ἑρμοῦ. The word ὅδιος, he means, could be used substantivally to denote a roadside omen, just as in fact σύμβολος is several times found used substantivally to denote an auspicious or inauspicious 'meeting' (e.g. Aesch. P.V. 487, Aristoph. Aves 721). Indeed we may well infer that Hesychius when he wrote οἰωνὸς αἴσιος had this very passage in mind; for αἴσιον is the adjective here used. It may however be questioned whether every ὅδιος or roadside omen was favourable; more probably Hesychius was generalising on the basis of this single passage.

I suspect moreover that the substantival ὅδιος should be read in another passage of Aeschylus. In Eumenides 770 Orestes in his farewell speech swears that there shall be an everlasting alliance between Argos and Athens, and, if after his death the Argives fail to respect the oath he has sworn, 'we', he says, picturing himself as a δαίμων, 'will bring them to repentance, ὁδοὺς ἀθύμους καὶ παρόρνιθας πόρους τιθέντες'. It is fair criticism of the passage, I think, to say that, if ὁδούς and πόρους mean in effect the same, we could dispense with one of them, and that ὁδίους in place of ὁδούς would still maintain the balance of the line while imparting to its two members a little more variety of expression,—'disheartening omens and inauspicious paths'.

This substantival usage of adjectives is not rare. At v. 1392 σπορητός is used without the addition of ἀγρός, and similarly ζύγιος and σειραφόρος may be used without ἵππος, ὁλκὰς and πεντηκόντορος without ναῦς, μελιττοῦττα and οἰνοῦττα without μᾶζα. Indeed the usage is carried so far, particularly in language in any way technical, that ὀρθή actually possesses four substantival senses according to context,—a direct road, a straight line, a right angle, and a nominative case, according as ὁδός, γραμμή, γωνία, or πτῶσις is implied. The use of ὅδιος as implying οἰωνός presents therefore no difficulty, particularly as it may have been a technical term in augury, the adjective in current use otherwise being ἐνόδιος.

But if ὅδιον αἴσιον constitutes one accusative, which is masculine, what is its relation to the other accusative κράτος ἀνδρῶν, which is neuter? Clearly some verb must connect them in order to complete the construction.

This brings us to the word ἐκτελέων, which may quite possibly be corrupt; for (1) it is not guaranteed as genuine by the Aristophanic quotation,—that quotation is made merely to illustrate Aeschylus' penchant for a particular metre and therefore breaks off at ἀνδρῶν,—(2) the word in itself presents such difficulty that some scholars have wished to read it as participle of ἐκτελέω, others as genitive of ἐκτελής, and others again to read ἐντελέων in its place, and yet (3) in spite of this uncertainty of interpretation the scholia I have cited ignore the word totally as if it had not been present in the text which they were explaining. I therefore suggest in its place ἐκτελεοῦν, present participle of ἐκτελεόω, agreeing with κράτος and governing ὅδιον αἴσιον. The whole phrase will then form the composite object of the verb θροεῖν,—'it is mine to tell of the endeavour of mighty men to bring to its fulfilment a favourable omen seen by the roadside'.

This interpretation agrees in its general meaning with the third of the scholia quoted above, but the paraphrase εὖ πράξουσιν οἱ Ἀτρεῖδαι ὅσον ἀπὸ τοῦ σημείου is not close enough to the original to indicate what the writer of it then had in his text. He may have had ἐκτελεοῦν and, believing ὅδιον to be a neuter substantive, have inverted the construction so as to make it mean 'a favourable omen tending to bring the might of warriors to a successful issue', 'making their might τέλειον', a rendering which, so far as the usage of the verb is concerned, might be correct; or again he may have known ὅδιον to be masculine and have had in his text ἐκτελεοῦντ' in agreement with it; or finally he may have read the passage exactly as I read it, with ἐκτελεοῦν in agreement with κράτος, and given a fairly free paraphrase. Personally I consider that the verb ἐκτελεόω is more likely to have been used of men 'striving to bring to fulfilment' the omen shown to them, than of the omen 'tending to crown with success' those men's efforts, and I give therefore in my text ἐκτελεοῦν in preference to ἐκτελεοῦντ'.

The second sentence under consideration, ἔτι γάρ...αἰών, has no light thrown upon it by the scholia relating to it. They represent merely an attempt to make something out of the jumble of words in the traditional text.

The easiest method of obtaining a grammatical construction is that which Headlam adopts; he reads μολπᾶν ἀλκάν as an accusative in apposition to πειθώ. But this adjustment does not affect that which I regard as the crux of the passage,—the usage of καταπνεύει. If we had the simple verb πνέω, I should feel that the passage might bear the construction which Headlam puts upon it, — 'I, though old, by God's grace still breathe words of enchantment'. But καταπνέω appears to me to be regularly used not of the poet who breathes charm, but of the divine or other influence which inspires the poet or breathes down upon some person any kind of grace. An excellent example occurs in Aristophanes, *Lysistrata* 551:

ἀλλ' ἥνπερ ὅ τε γλυκύθυμος Ἔρως χἠ κυπρογένει' Ἀφροδίτη
ἵμερον ἡμῶν κατὰ τῶν κόλπων καὶ τῶν μηρῶν καταπνεύσῃ...

I claim therefore that the appropriate subject of καταπνεύει is not αἰών but θεός, and suggest accordingly that we should read not θεόθεν καταπνεύει but θεὸς ἐγκαταπνεύει. That the double compound ἐγκαταπνέω is not elsewhere found is hardly a serious objection in my judgement; for both ἐμπνέω and καταπνέω are used of divine inspiration, and an amalgamation of the two will bear the same meaning.

If this emendation be adopted, it will necessarily follow that the whole sentence, containing now two nominatives, θεός and αἰών, consists of two short clauses. The first of these will be ἔτι γὰρ θεὸς ἐγκαταπνεύει πειθώ, and the second will almost inevitably become μολπᾶν τ' ἀλκᾷ σύμφυτος αἰών (sc. ἐστι), a phrase which utilises σύμφυτος to the full, as a predicate associated with the dative ἀλκᾷ, whereas in the text otherwise treated it appears to me to be a somewhat ineffective epithet of αἰών.

I may add that similar textual difficulties, due, as I conceive it, to small verbal corruptions accompanied by the compression of two clauses or sentences into one, occur at vv. 423–4 and 1228–31.

The form -πνεύει is preferred to -πνείει by Wilamowitz-Moellendorff and has strong support in this passage from the MSS.; and, though there is no parallel for it elsewhere in Tragedy, I have retained it.

The literary interest of these lines, whether with the emendations which I propose or otherwise, should not be overlooked. It is easy to imagine the personal significance with which these opening lines of the veteran Aeschylus—veteran both in war and in minstrelsy—would have fallen on the ears of an Athenian audience who still gloried in the memories of Marathon. I am tempted indeed to wonder whether, as they listened to the closing line of the whole trilogy,

$$\mathrm{ὀλολύξατε\ νῦν\ ἐπὶ\ μολπαῖς,}$$

they were not inevitably reminded of this earlier phrase, and felt that Aeschylus had indeed vindicated his claim—μολπᾶν ἀλκᾷ σύμφυτος αἰών.

119–120. λαγίναν...βλαβέντα: The puzzle presented by βλαβέντα following upon λαγίναν γένναν perplexed the scholiast as it has perplexed modern editors. But tucked away and, as I think, probably overlooked among the many conjectural emendations collected in Wecklein's Appendix there is one attributed to Beckmann which I believe to be right and on which, as it happens, I had hit independently. It turns on the word λαγίναν. If λαγίναν is the accusative of a masculine substantive λαγίνης, and not the accusative feminine of an adjective λάγινος, it will be necessary only to read γέννας in lieu of γένναν and the whole construction will be rectified. What then is the evidence concerning λαγίναν? Of the adjective λάγινος there is, so far as I can discover, apart from this passage, no trace to be found; the ordinary adjective was λαγῷος, with λάγειος as a rarer by-form. On the other hand the substantive λαγίνης does occur as a by-form of λαγώς, albeit only in a Byzantine historian (Manasses, Chron. 171). So then by a narrow margin the evidence of usage favours the view that λαγίναν is a masculine substantive; and since this view at once explains βλαβέντα, I adopt it. The use of a masculine word to denote a female hare presents of course no difficulty; Aristotle (H.A. 6. 24. 1) uses ὁ θῆλυς ὀρεύς to denote the female mule.

126–155. Calchas in his interpretation of the omens makes three points. First, the capture and destruction of the hare by the two eagles represents the capture and destruction of Troy by Agamemnon and Menelaus; and possibly the fact that the hare's brood is involved in the destruction indicated to him that the destruction of Troy would involve all the flocks and herds belonging to the city. Secondly, the killing of the hare with her unborn brood, which could be described as an αὐτότοκος θυσία (see my note on *v.* 137), foreshadowed an αὐτότοκος θυσία of another kind, the sacrifice of Iphigeneia by her own father, as involved in the enterprise. Thirdly, the wrath of Artemis against the eagles betokened wrath of the same goddess against the chieftains.

Now Calchas' interpretation has often been criticised by editors as illogical, and obviously it is so. The hare represents in one aspect Troy, and in another aspect Iphigeneia; and again whereas, in the case of the hare, the killing of it is the cause of Artemis' anger, in the case of Iphigeneia Artemis' anger (why aroused, we are not told) is the cause of Iphigeneia's death,— cause and effect being inverted. Obviously, as I say, the logic, if logic were the prescribed instrument for interpreting omens, would be condemned as faulty; but of course it was just because ordinary reasoning was of no avail that recourse was had to the services of a prophet. It was not the omens only that were god-given; the interpreter too was inspired by the gods.

131–5. The consecutive phrases στόμιον μέγα Τροίας στρατωθέν and οἴκῳ γὰρ ἐπίφθονος are open to the following criticisms: (1) the first sentence would end happily and easily at Τροίας; (2) στρατωθέν (or στρατευθέν, for the ω is possibly only a scribe's error) is a harsh usage in connexion with στόμιον; (3) στρατωθέν (or στρατευθέν) may have been a gloss on προτυπέν, due to an annotator who argued that προτύπτω in its normal military sense 'to push forward' was roughly equivalent to στρατεύω and that therefore προτυπέν might be an equivalent of στρατευθέν; (4) οἴκῳ is obviously wrong, and οἴκτῳ (Scaliger) is not a convincing substitute; the emphasis it would receive as the leading word is misplaced; (5) ἐπίφθονος has to be taken in the sense of φθονερός, an usage for which I can find no parallel or authority L. and S. indeed cite as parallel Appianus, *Punica* 59, μάχαις ἐν αἷς καὶ τὸ δαιμόνιον ἀνώμαλον καὶ ἐπίφθονόν ἐστι, but, as indeed ἀνώμαλον tends to show (cf. Eurip. *Fr.* 685, ἀνώμαλοι τύχαι), τὸ δαιμόνιον is no longer personal as it was in earlier Greek, but means merely 'the element of luck', which is described as *inconstans et malignum*. I submit therefore that ἐπίφθονος never meant 'feeling ill-will', but that, as applied to persons, it meant regularly 'incurring ill-will', while it was occasionally applied more loosely to things (as in *Eumen.* 376) in the sense of the Latin 'malignus'. The analogy of ἐπίζηλος and ἔποικτος in Aeschylus, and of ἐπίχαρις and ἐπίμωμος elsewhere, supports this view: as applied to persons, they all denote not those who feel the particular emotion but those who excite it in others and incur it.

In view of these accumulated criticisms I argue the text corrupt at this point. In attempting to emend it I would start with ἐπίφθονος. The general notion of φθόνος is obviously appropriate to the passage, and if, as I have pointed out, ἐπίφθονος is not admissible, as an epithet of Artemis, in the nominative, the only other form of the word which will fit the metre is the accusative ἐπίφθονον. To complete the sentence we should then have to find a substantive in the accusative with which the epithet would agree, and a verb to govern that accusative. The substantive might well be νεῖκος, which is not too far removed from οἴκῳ, especially if the initial ν might have been misread as the ending of the word preceding it. The verb required will then have to take the place of στρατωθέν, which—if I have rightly explained it as a gloss on προτυπέν, and if that gloss has ousted the verb from its place—will afford no clue in *ductus litterarum* to the form of the verb. As a matter of fact the choice of a probable verb is restricted; if the tense is to be present as in the following phrase, στυγεῖ δὲ δεῖπνον, metre demands a verb in -μι, and of those available τίθησι, which Aeschylus uses so freely in such phrases, appears to me the most likely. I conjecture therefore τίθησι νεῖκος γὰρ ἐπίφθονον. I may add that the position of γάρ as third word may have had some influence in inducing the corruption, as Headlam has observed in a later passage (see his note on v. 222).

137. αὐτότοκον πρὸ λόχου μογερὰν πτάκα θυομένοισι: The climax of Calchas' prophecy is reached in this phrase, and Aeschylus never wrote a more wonderful line. The function of Calchas was to interpret the omen of the eagles and the hare; but the words which God puts in his mouth as he interprets bear in themselves the double import of an oracle. That the word θυομένοισι foreshadows θυσίαν ἑτέραν ἄνομόν τιν', ἄδαιτον in v. 151 is obvious and has been generally recognised by editors; but they appear to have missed the double import of all the other words. The descriptive πτάκα rather than the specific λαγῶς is deliberately used because Iphigeneia too may be termed a 'poor shrinking' victim, just indeed as in *Eumen.* 326 the other form πτῶκα is applied specifically to Orestes. The epithet αὐτότοκον is no less applicable to Agamemnon's 'own child' slain by his hand than to the hare which perishes 'unborn brood and all'. And finally in πρὸ λόχου we have a play upon words such as Greek only, I think, could not merely tolerate but admire (cf. *vv.* 687 and 699). As applied to the hare, the words mean 'before the birth' of her young; as applied to the sacrifice of Iphigeneia, they mean 'on behalf of the host'. In my rendering I have devised a form of words which, I hope, is equally equivocal; but, if the Greek needs a note, my own rendering may require elucidation too. 'For deliverance' in relation to the hare is intended to mean 'instead of the deliverance of her brood', while in relation to the sacrifice of Iphigeneia it will mean 'with a view to the deliverance' of the host from their plight.

140–5. τόσον περ εὔφρων...φάσματα [στρούθων]: The MSS. vary between καλά as vocative and ἁ καλά as nominative. I prefer the latter, for I judge it fitting that Calchas should amplify his statement of Artemis' attitude, rather than pray to her and then immediately assume her deaf and divert his prayer to Apollo. And the scholiast concurs; for he treats αἰτεῖ as 3rd person active: αἰτεῖ με φάναι, 'requests me to announce' is his comment. Mazon, taking this seriously, conjectures μ' αἰτεῖ and adopts Hermann's κρῖναι—'m'invite à expliquer'. I regard this interpretation as incongruous, and attach to the scholium no value save that it confirms ἁ καλά. For αἰτεῖ, which most editors question or condemn, I conjecture ἴεται (cf. σπευδομένα, v. 151)—or possibly μῶται (see Hesychius), if the scholiast really had μ' αἰτεῖ in his text—the gist of the passage being, as I think, 'Artemis, though so gentle to young animals, seeks now a girl's death', or (to render the words more literally) 'she is eager for the accomplishment of the things portended by these omens in their favourable aspect but also...'. And it is there precisely, I believe, that the sentence breaks off; for my emendation in the last phrase of the sentence gives a new turn of expression to the remaining words. The word στρουθῶν is by common consent impossible both in metre and in meaning. What clues are there to the correct reading? Two only. First, στρουθῶν itself must either be a corrupted form of the last word of the line, or a gloss which has superseded it. But the only word on which it might be a gloss is τούτων, and any annotator who had wished to explain that pronoun would surely have written αἰετῶν or οἰωνῶν. The word therefore is not a gloss, but is a corrupt form, and the word to seek is one which resembles it. Secondly, φάσματα helps us, for φάσματα does not simply repeat ξύμβολα. This latter word means properly a 'tally', and in connexion with omens may be used either of the sign itself which tallies with the event foreshewn by it, or of that event as tallying with the omen. Here τούτων ξύμβολα means clearly 'the events which will tally with these omens'; it is the events which Artemis is eager to bring to pass. But φάσματα means 'portents' only, and not the events portended. In other words, the subject of thought, and, as it happens too, the subject of the sentence, changes after δεξιὰ μέν—. Calchas pauses, and then avoids the untoward ending of the sentence for which we look; he substitutes κατάμομφα δὲ φάσματα σούσθω, 'but as for the omens of ill, let them begone!' and by that final turn of expression leads up naturally to his direct prayer to Apollo.

The form σούσθω (which occurs in Soph. *Aj.* 1414) is quite rare enough to have puzzled a copyist who was not even expecting a verb at this point.

141. The MSS. vary between δέλπτοις and δέπτοις. For once I think the inferior MSS. with a meaningless form are nearer the true reading than the best. I have no hesitation in reading ἀόπτοις, 'sightless', even though in so doing I am imputing to Aeschylus a zoological inexactitude. The young of several species of *felidae*, including the domestic cat, are born with their eyes closed; this is not the case with lion-cubs, so I learn from Larousse, but the belief that they were was a pardonable error. Most editors adopt Wellauer's λεπτοῖς (—should it not be λεπταῖς?—), but the little support which the reading of M, δέλπτοις, might be thought to give to this is discounted by the scholium thereon (τοῖς ἔπεσθαι τοῖς γονεῦσι ⟨μὴ⟩ δυναμένοις) which implies the existence of δέπτοις as the earlier reading.

The word ἄοπτος in the sense required here is not otherwise known; but Harpocration and Suidas quote it from Antiphon in the sense of 'unseen'.

168. The MSS. give οὐδ' ὅστις πάροιθεν ἦν μέγας. The words οὐδ' ὅστις cannot, I submit, be accepted as genuine. I suspect that they have arisen from a marginal comment Οὐρανός τις—'a god named Ouranos'. The sequence of the following passage ὃς δ' ἔπειτ' ἔφυ... and Ζῆνα δέ τις... practically demands ὃς μὲν in the first clause. The choice of reading seems therefore to lie between ὃς μὲν γὰρ and ὃς μὲν τοῖς. I prefer the latter as giving more point to the participial phrase παμμάχῳ θράσει βρύων,—'he that was great in the eyes of men of old time as defying all challenge etc.'

180. I believe σωφρονεῖν to furnish both the object of στάζει (used transitively) and the subject of ἦλθε. The position of the τε in coupling the two members of the sentence is in that case slightly irregular but not unpleasingly so, since ἐν ὕπνῳ and παρ' ἄκοντας are naturally balanced against each other. I have therefore given only a comma after πόνος.

184 ff. For the method which I have adopted of breaking up this long sentence in my translation I am indebted not a little to Headlam's rendering.

192. Some critics, in their desire that each epithet or descriptive phrase should be strictly relevant to the situation, have made heavy weather of these northern gales. But is there any need to suppose that each phrase has specific reference to the plight of the Achaean armies? The epithets κακόσχολοι and νήστιδες are indeed directly relevant, but in the following phrases δύσορμοι βροτῶν ἄλαι and νεῶν τε καὶ πεισμάτων ἀφειδεῖς Aeschylus passes, I think, to a general description of the gales. The word βροτῶν in itself seems to indicate the transition from the particular case of the Achaeans to the storm's more general characteristics. In my translation I have grouped the relevant epithets in one phrase and the general epithets in another.

197. The MSS. give, as the ending of this line, ἄνθος 'Αργείων, which cannot be metrically equated with -ας βωμοῦ πέλας in v. 210. One or other phrase must be at fault, but there can be no justification for altering both as Sidgwick for example does. Blomfield suggested (and Wilamowitz-Moellendorff accepts) πέλας βωμοῦ, but πέλας normally follows its substantive and I distrust an emendation which involves the inversion of the familiar order. Moreover v. 210, as it stands with βωμοῦ πέλας, is of a metrical form common in Aeschylus (cf. vv. 242 and 252, 410-1 and 427-8). Of the two phrases involved therefore I suspect ἄνθος 'Αργείων, and I suggest that 'Αργείων should be replaced by the rarer form 'Αργολᾶν. The form occurs in lyrics in the *Rhesus*, v. 41, στρατὸς 'Αργόλας, and also in dialogue in a fragment of Aristophanes (ed. Holden, no. 174):

> A. οὐκ ἠγόρευον; οὑτοσί γ' οὐκ 'Αργόλας.
> B. μὰ Δί' οὐδέ γ' Ἕλλην, ὅσον ἔμοιγε φαίνεται.

From this latter passage it would appear that the Doric form in -ας was retained in ordinary Attic, as was the practice with personal names like Βρασίδας.

8-2

212. It is obvious that λιπόναυς is required by the context to mean not 'deserting my ships' but 'deserted by my ships', 'ship-less'. Later Greek, as the lexicon will show, has a considerable number of compound adjectives of like form, to which λιπο- contributes the sense of 'lacking'; e.g. λιπόθριξ = 'bald'.

220. τόθεν: I take τόθεν as relative, and have therefore placed a comma only after μετέγνω. The sentence βροτοὺς…πρωτοπήμων is then a parenthesis, and ἔτλα δ᾽ οὖν resumes the main sentence.

229. I follow Wilamowitz in reading αἰῶ τε in place of αἰῶνα. The emendation is that of O. Müller and is based on Bekk. An. 363 (αἰῶ τὸν αἰῶνα κατὰ ἀποκοπὴν Αἰσ.). It allows the insertion of the required τε at the natural place for it.

233. παντὶ θυμῷ, the MS. reading, appears to me intolerable. Some have supposed the phrase to go with λαβεῖν ἀέρδην and would render it 'to take heart and lift her...', in defiance of the order of the words; others, having regard to the position of the phrase, have tried to associate it with προνωπῆ, as it were 'fainting in all her soul', a suggestion which does violence to the natural meaning of προνωπῆ, which the scholiast rightly interprets by προνενευκυῖαν. I conjecture πάντ᾽ ἄθυμον, and suggest that this was misread by some scribe as πάντα θυμόν and altered to a dative.

With this alteration the three phrases πέπλοισι περιπετῆ, πάντ᾽ ἄθυμον, προνωπῆ form a perfect description of Iphigeneia crouching low in utter despair and huddled in her robes, not daring to look on that which awaits her. To detach προνωπῆ, as some editors have done, and to combine it with λαβεῖν ἀέρδην in the sense 'to seize her and lift her so that her head should hang over the altar', is to spoil a beautiful passage. The scholiast was right when he rendered περιπετῆ and προνωπῆ by two perfect participles, περιεσκεπασμένην and προνενευκυῖαν; the words picture the posture of Iphigeneia before the serving-men advance to seize her. The companion and contrasted picture is found in the next stanza, when Iphigeneia rises to her feet (for this is implied), letting fall to the ground the veil or mantle which had covered her face, and takes courage in the supreme moment to confront death with open eyes.

239. The MS. reading ἐς πέδον χέουσα is faulty both in metre and in tense. I conjecture ἐκ πέδονδε χέυασ᾽, surmising that ἐκ was read as ἐς and the termination of πέδονδε then omitted as a redundant δέ. The form χέυασα in place of χέασα is old, and has the support of -πνεύω for -πνέω in v. 105.

251-2. τὸ μέλλον δ᾽…: I understand the passage thus: 'it is only from the sufferings of the past that wisdom comes; foreknowledge of the future, seeing that the future is predestined, would be no benefit; rather it would be a foretaste of sorrow'. Accordingly I would read ἐπεὶ γένοιτ᾽ ἂν κλύουσι as a subordinate clause, 'seeing that the future would still befall men though they should foreknow it', and let the simple χαιρέτω close the sentence. Whence then the προ which the MSS. attach to χαιρέτω? I imagine that it was originally written in over κλύουσι to show that προκλύουσι was really meant; several MSS. include in the text after μέλλον the phrase τὸ δὲ προκλύειν, which might quite logically have formed the subject of this clause in place of τὸ μέλλον, if Aeschylus had chosen so to express his thought, and does in effect form the subject of ἴσον δὲ τῷ προστένειν. But the simple κλύουσι is fully intelligible; to know the future by hearing it from a prophet's mouth, which is what the whole context implies, is the same as foreknowing it; and κλύειν itself, it should be remembered, means often in tragic usage 'to have heard' and so 'to know', rather than merely 'to hear' (cf. L. and S. s.v.). So then I would dismiss προχαιρέτω with a final χαιρέτω.

275. The reading of the MSS. οὐ δόξαν ἂν λάβοιμι has rightly fallen under suspicion. The phrase δόξαν λαβεῖν means normally 'to get an impression of' something, and λάβοιμι cannot be forced here to have the full meaning of δεξαίμην. I am not however satisfied with Karsten's λάκοιμι either. The word λάσκειν is used—in no derogatory sense—of any loud announcement; Clytemnestra now might be said λάσκειν the fall of Troy; and, that being so, Greek idiom would require οὐ δόξαν ἂν ἔλασκον..., 'if it were only a sleeper's fancy I should not now be crying it abroad'. Headlam, who accepts λάκοιμι, shows clearly by his translation that he overlooked this objection. Two other possible corrections suggest themselves, σέβοιμι and λαλοῖμι. The former might indeed fall under the same condemnation as λάκοιμι—if, that is, the sense required us to translate: 'if it were only a sleeper's fancy I should not now be respecting it'; but as an answer to πότερα...σέβεις; it might bear the true optative sense 'you would not find me at any time respecting a mere dream'. But obviously σέβοιμι following so closely on σέβεις would be less liable to be mistaken for λάβοιμι than would the other possible reading λαλοῖμι. Here the optative too would be correct. Clytemnestra at the moment may be said λάσκειν, 'to cry her news aloud', but not λαλεῖν, 'to chatter'; λαλοῖμι then becomes just as fully emphasised as the remainder of the sentence: 'I am not one to *chatter* over a mere *dream*'. An accusative after λαλεῖν, though not frequent, does occur.

276. ἄπτερος φάτις: The usage of ἄπτερος is so curious that if we had to judge of its meaning by its derivation we should probably assign to it almost the reverse of its actual significance, or be tempted to emend our text and substitute εὔπτερος. But Hesychius accepted the word as correct here, and explains it thus: ἄπτερος· αἰφνίδιος παρὰ Ὁμήρῳ ὁ προσηνὴς ἢ ταχύς. Αἰσχύλος Ἀγαμέμνονι: and he has also ἄπτερα: ἰσόπτερα, ταχέα, ἡδέα. To his evidence may be added that of the scholiast on the present passage, who explains the word by ἰσόπτερος, κούφη, and of the scholiast on the word ἀπτερέως in Apoll. Rhod. IV. 1765, who renders it by τάχιστα. We may not fully agree with Hesychius' interpretation of the Homeric use, which recurs in a set phrase of the *Odyssey*: τῇ δ' ἄπτερος ἔπλετο μῦθος, and appears there to indicate a speech which does not fully enlighten the hearer but rather puzzles her. But the evidence that ἄπτερος φάτις meant here a 'light' or 'fleeting rumour' seems to me adequate, though I can hazard no guess as to the process by which it attained this sense.

278. ποίου χρόνου δὲ καὶ πεπόρθηται πόλις; The use of a genitive denoting time along with a perfect tense is rare, and the idiom deserves investigation. The genitive in relation to time denotes normally the period within which some event did or did not, will or will not, occur, and the appropriate tense is then aorist or future. Thucydides begins many chapters with τοῦ δ' ἐπιγιγνομένου χειμῶνος and the like followed by an aorist, and examples with the future or a periphrasis implying future time are also common (*e.g.* Soph. *El.* 478, 817, *O.C.* 397; Arist. *Wasps* 260).

The same usage was, I think, logical too in conjunction with a tense expressing duration (whether perfect or present) when the verb was negatived; for then, it may be argued, the sense of duration is itself negatived; there can be no duration of that which has not occurred or is not occurring. From this point of view Aristophanes' line (*Plut.* 97)

πολλοῦ γὰρ αὐτοὺς οὐχ ἑόρακά που χρόνου

is perfectly defensible, and Porson's emendation οὐχ ἑώρακ' ἀπὸ χρόνου is not necessary. There is a parallel in the *Thesmophoriazusae* (806–7), πρὸς Ἀριστομάχην δὲ χρόνου πολλοῦ...οὐδεὶς οὐδ' ἐγχειρεῖ πολεμίζειν, where either present or perfect tense would have been admissible without sensible difference of meaning.

But the case is different when we have the perfect tense unaccompanied by a negative. The logical temporal questions relating to a past occurrence are 'at what date' or 'within what period' did it occur; those relating to an established state of things are 'since what date' or 'during what period' has it continued. If then πεπόρθηται indicates, as the perfect must, the state in which Troy has been and is, the question of the Chorus must be put in one of two ways,—either 'since what date' or 'during what period' has Troy been captive and despoiled. But if 'during what period' be the question, the accusative should naturally be used, and not the genitive, as in a line of Euripides (*Hel.* 111) closely resembling this:

πόσον χρόνον γὰρ διαπεπόρθηται πόλις

And alternatively, if the question be 'since what date', the normal usage is a genitive accompanied by ἐκ (*e.g.* Thuc. I. 68) or ἀπό (*e.g.* Thuc. I. 18). It would appear then that ποίου χρόνου has to be regarded logically as an equivalent either of πόσον χρόνον or of ἐκ πόσου χρόνου—for no third

form of the question can logically be formulated. Given that choice, no
one, I imagine, will hesitate; it would be foreign to all known use of the
genitive that it should express duration of time and do duty for an accusative. I conclude therefore that the question put by the Chorus means
properly 'Since when has the city been a conquered city?' or (to give a
French rendering in which the correspondence of idiom is still closer)
'*Depuis combien de temps est-ce que la ville est prise* (or more colloquially
a été prise)?', to which the answer may be, as here, '*depuis la veille*'. In
the only parallel case which I can find, this interpretation fits. A fragment
of Eupolis (Bothe, *Comic. Graec. Fragm.* p. 177) runs:

> a. πόσου χρόνου γὰρ συγγεγένησαι Νικίᾳ;
> β. οὐδ᾽ εἶδον, εἰ μὴ ᾿ναγχος ἑστῶτ᾽ ἐν ἀγορᾷ.

'Since when have you been in association with Nicias?' 'I never saw him
till just now—standing in the market-place.'

How then did this idiom arise? Two explanations are possible. One is
that the genitive, besides denoting the period within which an event
occurred, may have denoted also the date as from which some state of
things has continued; for the pure genitive, no less than a genitive
governed by ἐκ or ἀπό, is intrinsically capable of denoting the point of
departure; πόσου χρόνου, that is, may be only a poetical or old-fashioned
variant for ἐκ πόσου χρόνου. The other explanation is that the normal
usage of the genitive denoting the 'period within which' has been extended
from the cases in which the perfect tense was accompanied by the negative
to the cases in which there is no negative. Where there is a negative the
idiom, as I have said, is logical; the passage of the *Plutus* quoted above,

> πολλοῦ γὰρ αὐτοὺς οὐχ ἑόρακά που χρόνου,

may be logically rendered 'Within a long time past I have not seen them'.
But observe that 'within a long time' (or, in the ordinary idiom of English,
'for a long time') in such sentences means in effect the same as 'since a
long time ago', '*depuis longtemps*'; and if the genitive had once come to
be understood in this latter sense in a negative sentence, its extension to
positive sentences might readily follow.

A passage of Aristophanes (*Ach.* 83–4) which has been discussed in this
connection,

> Δικ. πόσου δὲ τὸν πρωκτὸν χρόνου ξυνήγαγε;
> Πρε. τῇ πανσελήνῳ,

has, I think, no bearing upon it, for the reason that the tense used is the
aorist, and the answer is given by means of a dative of time denoting the
'date at which'. Here 'within what time did he...?' is equivalent to 'how
long was it before he did so?' and the answer is 'he did so at the time of
the full moon'. The passage is peculiar only in this, that, though the tense
is past, the 'within what period' accompanying it has a prospective force
(as normally when a future is used) instead of a retrospective force, which

is naturally more common with a past tense. But 'within what period' means either 'within what past period' (looking back from the present or other assumed date) or 'within what future period' (looking forward from the present or other assumed date), and the precise meaning is determined by context only. In the *Acharnians* here it means 'within what future period' as from the date of the occurrence previously mentioned.

The use of ποίου χρόνου by Aeschylus rather than πόσου χρόνου, as well as the emphasis given to the perfect tense by καί, lends clearly some tone of incredulity to the question, 'Since when has this alleged plundering of Troy been an accomplished fact?'—and καὶ τίς at the opening of the next question is in the same vein.

I judge that Mazon would concur with me in my interpretation of the line in all respects; for his translation is 'Depuis quand Ilion serait-elle conquise?'

288. ἐπεῦκτο: This emendation of πεύκη τὸ is one which I published some years ago in the *Classical Review* (Vol. xxxv. p. 100). The conditions of the problem, as I see them, are:

(1) πεύκη in apposition to ἰσχὺς πορευτοῦ λαμπάδος is intolerable;

(2) the sentence needs a main verb at this point;

(3) τὸ is not required with χρυσοφεγγὲς σέλας, and is probably the detached termination of the missing verb;

(4) the verb must be such as will allow παραγγείλασα, an *aorist* participle, to be associated with it. This condition at once excludes such suggestions as πέμπει (Enger) and ἐπέσυτο (Koch), which would be accompanied by a present or future participle.

I am convinced that no word but ἐπεῦκτο can satisfy all these conditions. There is a parallel for the participial construction in Plato, *Soph.* 235 c. Of the form as compounded with ἐπί, there is, so far as I know, no other instance, but the simple form εὖκτο is found in *fragment* 3 of the *Thebais*, and possibly ηὔγμην too in Soph. *Trach.* 610, which L. and S. record as a pluperfect, should be regarded as aorist.

Calder (*Classical Review* xxxvi. 158), who argues the corruption of this passage to be due to the loss of a line, approves ἐπεῦκτο on palaeographic grounds and admits the possibility of the participial construction; 'but', he says, 'the result is to make nonsense of ὥς τις ἥλιος. No beacon, εἰ φωνὴν λάβοι, would say παρήγγειλα σέλας ὥς τις ἥλιος. The phrase ὥς τις ἥλιος is obviously the poet's comparison...'. For myself I should hesitate to assert what a beacon might or might not say, εἰ φωνὴν λάβοι, but I am at a loss to understand why it is nonsense for a beacon to vaunt itself as 'a second sun' and yet good sense for Aeschylus to make the same comparison.

NOTES 121

301. πλέον καίουσα τῶν εἰρημένων: I have retained the reading of the MSS. as preferable to the phrase recorded by Hesychius, προσαιθρίζουσα πόμπιμον φλόγα, which Dindorf wished to introduce in its place. The sequence of πομποῦ πυρός, φάος τηλέπομπον, and πόμπιμον φλόγα in three consecutive lines would be tedious.

314. The line, as I read it, means literally 'The victor is the one who first reaches the goal though he was the last to take up the running'. It is quite likely that in practice the fastest runner of a team should be reserved for the last stage of the relay race; and, if his team won, he himself (more particularly if he were captain, as the fastest runner might well be) would naturally be acclaimed as victor. But there is, I suspect, a concealed irony in this phrase. Clytemnestra is thinking of herself. In the contest with Agamemnon she has not yet 'taken up the running', but the last stage will give her the victory. It is the same thought which reappears in vv. 1377–8,

ἐμοὶ δ' ἀγὼν ὅδ' οὐκ ἀφρόντιστος πάλαι
νείκης παλαιᾶς ἦλθε, σὺν χρόνῳ γε μήν.

In my translation I have deliberately given a somewhat free rendering of the passage, such as may, I hope, suggest some of this hidden meaning.

341. ἐμπίπτοι: The MSS. give some indication of a variant reading ἐμπίπτῃ. Either is possible Greek, but inasmuch as there is a strong tendency to use aorist rather than present in the subjunctive construction, whereas the present optative is frequent in the expression of wishes, the fact that the tense is present inclines me to prefer the optative mood.

345. I concur with the majority of critics in holding that ἀναμπλάκητος can give no true sense here, and that the positive ἀμπλάκητος is required. Of the corrections suggested I prefer Bamberger's θεοῖς δ' ἄρ' ἀμπλάκητος.

346. τὸ πῆμα τῶν ὀλωλότων: Such is the traditional and, so far as I know, universally accepted reading. But what does it mean? The word πῆμα does not denote a feeling; it denotes the concrete calamity or bane which causes the emotions of grief or pain. The phrase might mean the wrong or hurt done to the dead; but it is not the objective wrong or hurt which may wake and become active to the undoing of the Argive host, but rather some resentment or anger harboured by the dead. In fact the sense of the passage seems to call for μήνιμα in place of τὸ πῆμα. It will then be used in precisely the same sense in which Antiphon (p. 127. 1) has it: μὴ ὀρθῶς δὲ καταληφθεὶς ὑφ' ὑμῶν, ὑμῖν καὶ οὐ τούτῳ τὸ μήνιμα τῶν ἀλιτηρίων προστρίψομαι (or, as I think we should write, προστρέψομαι). Μήνιμα in this usage hardly differs from μῆνις, and denotes the slow and lurking anger of the dead or of those ἀλιτήριοι θεοί who seek vengeance on their behalf. And the following line supports the conjecture: πρόσπαια, 'sudden', is not antithetic to anything in the phrase τὸ πῆμα τῶν ὀλωλότων, but does introduce a natural contrast to μήνιμα which implies a sullen anger slow to wake to activity.

350. I accept Hermann's τήνδ' for τήν, and understand the line to mean : 'for in expressing this hope (τήνδε)—(namely the vague and general hope that right may prevail)—I chose the fruition of *many* blessings'. The pronoun τήνδε agrees idiomatically with ὄνησιν, but is actually the direct object of εἱλόμην, whereas πολλῶν ἐσθλῶν ὄνησιν, with the emphasis on πολλῶν, forms a predicate.

353. I have adopted Paley's suggestion of αὖ in place of εὖ. The line then naturally recalls what the Chorus said in *v.* 317.

367. Headlam, following Blomfield, rightly takes πλαγὰν ἔχουσιν as equivalent to πεπληγμένοι εἰσί and places it in inverted commas. But his εἰπεῖν πάρεστιν, τοῦτό τ' ἐξιχνεῦσαι seems to me awkward in respect of the emphasis thrown on τοῦτο. The fact that one MS. had originally ἔχουσαν which was corrected to ἔχουσ', not to ἔχουσιν, suggests another reading, 'Διὸς πλαγὰν ἔχουσ',' ἀνειπεῖν· πάρεστίν τοι τόδ' ἐξιχνεῦσαι, where ἀνειπεῖν, with imperative force, 'proclaim!' is eminently suitable to the context, and τοι τόδ' in place of the τοῦτ' or τοῦτό γ' of the MSS. removes the undesirable emphasis on the pronoun. The correction τοι τόδ' is Karsten's.

374–5. πέφανται δ' ἐγγόνους ἀτολμήτων : I agree with the general verdict on ἐγγόνους. Even if it could be fitted into the construction, the sense of the passage excludes it. We are not considering here the visiting of the sins of the fathers upon the children, but the chastisement which befalls such as Paris in their own person. But Headlam's objection to τῶν Ἄρη πνεόντων μεῖζον ἢ δικαίως—namely that it would 'condemn Paris for a spirit *over-bellicose!*'—fails to do justice to δικαίως. I have translated the phrase as meaning those 'who breathe defiance and transgress the boundaries of righteousness'—οἷος καὶ Πάρις.

Hartung's emendation of the passage, ἐκτίνουσα τόλμα τῶν Ἄρη..., is, in my judgement, on the right lines as (1) supplying a subject for πέφανται and (2) detecting in the corrupt ἐγγόνους a participle agreeing with that subject; but ἐκτίνουσα used absolutely, with no accusative following it, is not entirely satisfactory.

Following the same lines, I would suggest ἐγγὺς οὖσα λύμα τῶν.... A scribe who had once written ἐγγόνους might well have combined the remnants -α λ(ύ)μα των into ἀτολμάτων. Let me add that Headlam's objection to Hartung's suggestion on metrical grounds—namely that πέφανται δ' ἐκτίνουσ- | -α τόλμα τῶν Ἀρη would involve 'an unparalleled caesura'— would apply to my suggestion too; but the arrangement of the lines in the form

πέφανται δ' ἐγγὺς οὖσα λύμα
τῶν Ἄρη πνεόντων
μεῖζον ἢ δικαίως

cuts away that ground, and has some support in the ract that one MS. does write πνεόντων in the same verse with Ἄρη. So arranged, the two lines πέφανται δ᾽ ἐγγὺς οὖσα λύμα and φλεόντων δωμάτων ὑπέρφεν repeat pleasantly the rhythm of the first two lines of the strophe.

378–80. ἔστω...λαχόντα: The construction of this sentence deserves a word of explanation. The ὥστε-clause (which includes ἀπήμαντον, placed as first word in it for emphasis) depends simply on ἔστω, as in Soph. *Philoct.* 656, ἆρ᾽ ἔστιν ὥστε κἀγγύθεν θέαν λαβεῖν;. Written more in the manner of prose, the sentence would run: ἔστω δ᾽ ὥστε ἀπαρκεῖν ἀπήμαντον ὄντα τὸν εὖ πραπίδων λαχόντα. The idiom is used again, with an exactly similar position for the emphatic word, in *v.* 1395, on which see my note.

381–4. οὐ γὰρ...ἀφάνειαν: A correct translation of these lines involves two questions: (1) does πλούτου depend on ἔπαλξις or on κόρον, and (2) is πρὸς κόρον used adverbially, qualifying λακτίσαντι, or may it be construed closely with ἔπαλξις? I prefer to take πλούτου as dependent on κόρον and the whole phrase πλούτου πρὸς κόρον as closely associated with ἔπαλξις—'there is no defence against the κόρος that arises from wealth for a man who has once abandoned all reverence for Justice'. If πλούτου be read as dependent on ἔπαλξις, one of two meanings must result—either 'Wealth provides no defence against κόρος...' or 'Wealth provides no protection (presumably against the punishment due) when once a man has insolently spurned Justice'. The former is barely possible, for no one would conceive of wealth as a protection against κόρος which it is apt to engender. The latter, though good sense, is a little defective in clarity of expression. The translation which I have preferred is supported by passages of Theognis and Solon which Aeschylus would seem to have had in mind: Τίκτει τοι κόρος ὕβριν, ὅταν κακῷ ὄλβος ἔπηται ἀνθρώπῳ, καὶ ὅτῳ μὴ νόος ἄρτιος ᾖ (Theogn. 153, cf. Solon VIII ed. Bergk); οὐ γὰρ ἐπίστανται κατέχειν κόρον...οὐδὲ φυλάσσονται. σεμνὰ θέμεθλα Δίκης (Solon IV. 9 and 14); and in a similar context ὁππότ᾽ ἀνὴρ ἄδικος...ὑβρίζῃ πλούτῳ κεκορημένος (Theogn. 749–751), in which last I find definite confirmation of my view that πλούτου πρὸς κόρον forms a single phrase.

386. προβουλόπαις: The objections to this, the MS. reading, are two-fold: (1) metrically it should in all probability repeat the preceding line; (2) the compound itself is hardly possible if παῖς denotes, as one would expect, the relationship of Πειθώ to Ἄτη. Verrall indeed retains the compound and claims that παῖς here denotes the function of slave, so that προβουλόπαις would mean 'counsellor-servant'; but that colloquial usage of παῖς lacks the dignity suited to this passage. Hartung's emendation προβούλου παῖς is an easy correction, but does not satisfy me; Πειθώ, 'Temptation', is the subject of thought, and it is surely she who 'prepares the decrees' of Ate. Her parentage is of minor importance, though in point of fact her mother was generally said to be not Ate but Aphrodite. I would read therefore προβουλευτάς, a word not found elsewhere until

Byzantine times; a scribe familiar with the common word πρόβουλος, who took the longer form for a compound of it, might easily have read τας as παις.

412–13. The MSS. have σιγᾶς ἄτιμος ἀλοίδορος | ἄδιστος ἀφεμένων. I accept Hermann's σιγὰς ἀτίμους ἀλοιδόρους as a certain correction; but neither Enger's ἄλγιστ' for ἄδιστος nor Dindorf's ἀφημένων for ἀφεμένων satisfies me, though the latter in itself, if the gap preceding it could be satisfactorily filled, would give a reasonable sense. The objection to ἄλγιστ' is that it would mean, not 'in deep pain', but 'most distressingly (to others)'. In favour of my own conjecture ἄστοις ἐφημμένων, 'clinging to what is vanished', I would urge the following points: the sense is precisely what the context (πόθῳ ὑπερποντίας κ.τ.λ.) requires; the form ᾶστος for ἄιστος is Aeschylean (*Eumen.* 565); and the dative after ἐφάπτεσθαι is justified by Pindaric usage in a passage where the verb denotes 'clinging to' rather than 'aiming at'. Κελεύθοις ἁπλόαις ζωᾶς ἐφαπτοίμαν, says Pindar (*Nem.* VIII. 61), 'May I cleave unto simple paths of life!' Cf. also *Pyth.* VIII. 60, *Ol.* I. 86.

423. μάταν γὰρ, εὖτ' ἂν ἐσθλά τις δοκῶν ὁρᾶν, παραλλάξασα...: Headlam (*Class. Rev.* XII. 246), followed by Verrall, would retain the MS. reading. ' "For vainly, when, dreaming that he beholds his joy, (*he would embrace her*), the vision slips through his hands and is gone". The construction, which has given much trouble, is an ellipse, the verb being suppressed εὐφημίας ἕνεκα.' Thus quotes Verrall with approval, citing Theocr. I. 105, οὗ λέγεται τὰν Κύπριν ὁ βουκόλος—and other similar aposiopeses collected by Headlam from 'the lighter literature'. 'But', he continues, 'it is then imperative to suppose that this whole passage, *vv.* 419–434, is satirical or semi-satirical in tone.... All Dr Headlam's examples (except Soph. *O.T.* 1288, a peculiar case) are from comedy or the like, and indeed such an aposiopesis is plainly incompatible with pure pathos or perfect dignity.'

I agree with this criticism, but whereas Verrall, who made it, accepted the text thus interpreted as suiting his own conception of the δόμων προφῆται in whose mouths the words are put, I reject the interpretation. Of emendations offered in the latter half of the line, Housman's εὖτ' ἂν ἐς θιγὰς δοκᾶν ὁρᾷ, 'when he looks to touch the phantom,' is highly ingenious, but I believe the simple and natural phrase ἐσθλά τις δοκῶν ὁρᾶν to be sound, and the corruption to lie in the preceding words. I conjecture ματᾷ γὰρ εὐχᾶν, and place a stop at ὁρᾶν. The clause παραλλάξασα κ.τ.λ. then follows by way of fuller explanation and needs no connecting particle; indeed its very abruptness is appropriate to the sense. The use of a genitive after ματᾶν follows the analogy of ἁμαρτάνειν, etc., and occurs once in Oppian, *Halieut.* III. 102—βουλῆς δὲ σαόφρονος οὐκ ἐμάτησε. This is not the only passage in which the text of the *Agamemnon* has suffered from the telescoping of two clauses (cf. above on *v.* 105, and below on *vv.* 1228 ff. and 1625 ff.).

430. The τλησικάρδιος of the MSS. is hardly possible. The gloss τὴν καρδίαν τήκουσα found in one MS. represents probably the true reading, and I accept τηξικάρδιος (Auratus).

444. I retain the εὐθέτου of the MSS. There is more bitterness or tone if the epithet belong to σποδοῦ than if it be transferred to λέβητας.

450. φθονερὸν is to be read as part of the predicate.

454. εὔμορφοι: used of those whose bodies were interred without cremation.

478. The MSS. have ἤ (or εἰ) τοι θεῖόν ἐστι (or ἐστιν) μὴ ψύθος. The negative μή ruins the balance of the clauses and must go. I have suggested ἤ τι θεῖον οὖν ἐστὶ ψύθος, and assume that οὖν was absorbed in the final -ον of θεῖον and the line wrongly restored.

485. I accept Blomfield's ἔρος for the MS. ὄρος. There is, I feel, no likelihood of ἐπινέμεται being used as a passive to mean 'is encroached upon', the sense which ὄρος would postulate; whereas the verb in its normal middle sense was used commonly of fire spreading (e.g. Herod. v. 101) and is therefore appropriate and picturesque with ἔρος as its subject. The imagery of fire which suggested πυρωθέντα in v. 481 recurs again here.

489–500. It is a matter of doubt to whom this speech should be assigned. The two lines which follow it sound like the conventional comment of the leader of the Chorus upon the speech of some other person. The list of the *dramatis personae* as given in the MSS. includes an ἄγγελος, but we cannot have a messenger outrunning by a minute or two the herald himself. Moreover the speaker speaks as one on or near the stage who is in a better position than others to observe the herald's approach. I have therefore assigned the lines to the Watchman, who might well remain at his post to catch the first sight of the returning army.

539. The metrical difficulty involved in finding a substitute for the τεθνάναι of the MSS. is best met by Schneidewin's τὸ τεθνάναι, which as a substantival phrase (instead of a pure infinitive) fits better with the normal usage of ἀντιλέγω—'as regards death, I will not gainsay the gods'.

547. The MSS. have στύγος στρατῷ; The best emendation offered is in my judgement Jacob's στύγος; φράσον, where φράσον is quite happily answered by πάλαι τὸ σιγᾶν.... The suggestion στυγοστράτῳ (M. Schmidt), which Headlam adopts, and translates by 'mislikers of our war', seems to me peculiarly inapposite after the line ποθεῖν ποθοῦντα τήνδε γῆν στρατὸν λέγεις.

557. The MSS. give τί δ' οὐ | στένοντες οὐ λάχοντες ἥματος μέρος; I suspect that οὐ στένοντες and οὐ λαχόντες are portions of alternative lines at this point, and that those lines were each provided with a main verb which completed the construction; *e.g.* τί δ' οὐ στένοντες ἐξηντλοῦμεν ἥματος μέρος, and τί δ'οὐ λαχόντες ἠλγύνθημεν ἥματος μέρος. If so, the restoration of the exact text is a matter of guesswork only, but I regard the reading which I have given as a nearer approximation than is the text of the MSS. to what Aeschylus wrote.

558. The order of the words in the MSS. is καὶ προσῆν πλέον στύγος. Wilamowitz rightly, I think, condemns the position of καί, but the order he proposes, καὶ πλέον στύγος προσῆν, appears less likely to me than καὶ πλέον προσῆν στύγος which Headlam suggests in his notes.

560-2. ἐξ οὐρανοῦ γὰρ κἀπὸ γῆς λειμώνιαι δρόσοι...τιθέντες...:
If we do not suspect Aeschylus of making an elementary grammatical mistake, and if metre forbids us to substitute τιθεῖσαι for τιθέντες, it must follow that the sentence had a masculine subject, or a composite subject of which one member was masculine. Now a composite subject is indicated: from heaven there fell ὄμβροι; the dews, δρόσοι, were of the earth. But ὄμβροι cannot be inserted without displacing ἐξ οὐρανοῦ γάρ. Is this phrase then above suspicion? On the contrary, the γάρ is in the text a false connection, which modern editors, following Pearson's suggestion, have tried to rectify by changing γάρ to δέ. But the same γάρ would be a genuine part of the phrase if the whole phrase were a gloss on some epithet attached to ὄμβροι. What epithet then would earn such a gloss? One, and perhaps one only—δῖοι. I read therefore ὄμβροι δὲ δῖοι κἀπὸ γῆς....

561-2. The MSS. have κατεψέκαζον ἔμπεδον σίνος | ἐσθημάτων τιθέντες ἔνθηρον τρίχα. Two methods of punctuation have been advocated, but neither is satisfactory in the phrasing which results. According to one method, the phrase ἔμπεδον σίνος ἐσθημάτων is treated as being in apposition to the subject (or to the sentence) preceding; but (1) τιθέντες as opening word of the next phrase would acquire an undue emphasis and offend the ear, and (2) it may be questioned whether Aeschylus regarded rain and dew as the cause of a verminous condition of the hair, or would have expressed such meaning in any case by the word ἔνθηρον.

According to the other method, ἔμπεδον σίνος alone stands in apposition to what precedes, and ἐσθημάτων is part of the following phrase. This arrangement rectifies the position of τιθέντες, but I cannot believe that ἐσθημάτων τρίχα means (as Headlam would have it) 'our woolly garments'—Aeschylus surely would have written λάχνην, not τρίχα.

Moreover both interpretations ignore the fact that κατεψέκαζον is probably transitive; for if the effect of the κατα compounded with ψεκάζω were not to make the verb transitive but merely to emphasise the sense of

'downward', it would follow that Aeschylus went out of his way to select
an inappropriate compound; for the dews cannot be said to drip 'downward'
ἀπὸ γῆς.

I assume then that κατεψέκαζον was transitive in meaning, and that in
this passage it governed τρίχα. The herald's complaint will then be the
same as that made by the seamen who form the Chorus in the *Ajax* of
Sophocles (v. 1206),

> κεῖμαι δ' ἀμέριμνος οὕτως,
> ἀεὶ πυκιναῖς δρόσοις τεγγόμενος κόμας,
> λυγρᾶς μνήματα Τροίας.

It is the poet's way of stating that the troops lay in the open, with no roof
over their heads.

This construction of the passage involves the interchange of the two
words τρίχα and σίνος, and, this being effected, the second line in the form
ἐσθημάτων τιθέντες ἔνθηρον σίνος becomes entirely satisfactory. The place
of the participle is correct; and ἔνθηρον will bear what I believe to be its
normal meaning—not 'infested with lice', as editors have supposed, but
'infested with maggots' or, more generally, 'corrupt' and 'rotten'. It is
thus that Sophocles (*Phil.* 698) applies the word to the festering wound of
Philoctetes; and the medical usage of θηριοῦσθαι and θηρίωμα in connection
with malignant ulcers bears this out.

It will, I think, necessarily follow that we should read ἐμπέδως in place
of ἔμπεδον; for though the latter form is used adverbially in Homer and
once at any rate in the lyrics of Sophocles, Aeschylus regularly uses ἐμπέδως.
One may assume that the copyist, when he had written κατεψέκαζον ἐμπεδ,
allowed his eye to wander to the next line and finished with ον σίνος instead
of ως τρίχα, and that the subsequent correction, when the words which he
had omitted were written in, was ill made.

612. χαλκοῦ βαφάς: Clytemnestra is protesting her own sincerity, and
I believe therefore that this expression has reference to some process of
making base metal pass for genuine—bronze for gold. But there is irony
too; the usage of βάπτειν with ἔγχος or ξίφος was familiar, and χαλκός often
does duty in poetry for one of those words.

613-14. I follow Hermann in assigning these two lines to Clytemnestra:
the comment τῆς ἀληθείας γέμων cannot be put into the mouth of the herald.

615-16. The phrase αὕτη μὲν οὕτως εἶπε is the customary phrase for
dismissing what has been said by one speaker and leading up to a question
put to another, σὺ δ' εἰπέ, κῆρυξ.... But Clytemnestra's speech is not dis-
missed without comment. This comment is not easy Greek. If the text be
assumed sound (and the scholiast, to judge by his rendering, knew some
other text), εὐπρεπῶς explains οὕτως, μανθάνοντί σοι depends on εὐπρεπῶς,
τοροῖσιν ἑρμηνεῦσιν is an instrumental dative going closely with μανθάνοντι

('learning at the mouth of clear interpreters the real meaning of the speech'), and λόγον is governed by μανθάνοντι (for, if it were governed by εἶπε, εὐπρεπῆ would be almost inevitable to agree with λόγον in place of εὐπρεπῶς). The resulting meaning of the comment then is: 'speciously, if you take the meaning of her speech as shrewd interpreters would interpret it'.

634. A mark of interrogation at λέγεις gives the main question a more natural form. The direct answer to it is given in *v.* 649.

639. στυγνῷ προσώπῳ: Hesychius records the rare word σμοιός in the phrase σμοιῷ προσώπῳ and explains it by φοβερῷ ἢ στυγνῷ, σκυθρωπῷ. It is possible that either here or in Eurip. *Alc.* 777, where also στυγνῷ προσώπῳ occurs, σμοιῷ may have been the original reading and have been ousted by a gloss στυγνῷ, but it is of course more probable that Hesychius was quoting from some work no longer extant.

677. καὶ ζῶντα καὶ βλέποντα: The phrase quoted by Hesychius, χλωρόν τε καὶ βλέποντα, which he explains by ἀντὶ τοῦ ζῶντα, may be a variant reading of this passage. But the tautology of καὶ ζῶντα καὶ βλέποντα is not such as to condemn it; for in the *Persae* (*v.* 299) we find similarly ζῇ τε καὶ βλέπει φάος.

696. κελσάντων has always been regarded as the genitive of the participle, depending on κατ' ἴχνος πλατᾶν ἄφαντον, and referring to Paris and Helen and their company. A main verb has then to be supplied out of ἔπλευσε in the previous clause, and whereas Σιμόεντος ἀκτὰς εἰς ἐριφύλλους obviously goes with κελσάντων, δι' ἔριν αἱματόεσσαν has to be associated with a verb which is implied only and not expressed. This is awkward Greek, and I believe the passage to have been generally misread. My view is that κελσάντων is a bold imperative, ringing out suddenly in the description like a word of command. I can adduce no parallel; but—and it is a large 'but'—is it too daring an usage for Aeschylus? The historic present was part and parcel of Greek idiom: might not an imperative, no less than an indicative, though bearing normally a present sense, be applied on occasion to the past? Read the passage both ways, I would say, and if this reading is finer and more arresting than the other, then be sure that Aeschylus intended it to be so read.

697. The MSS. vary between ἀκτὰς εἰς ἀεξιφύλλους and ἀκτὰς ἐπ' ἀξιφύλλους. The corresponding line of the antistrophe is αἰῶν' ἀμφὶ πολιτᾶν. I therefore take ἀκτὰς εἰς and, in place of ἀεξιφύλλους, conjecture ἐριφύλλους, a word recorded by Hesychius. If this conjecture is right, ἀεξίφυλλος, which is found here only, I believe, will have no further claim to existence. Apart from Hesychius' evidence, ἀρίφυλλος would be as likely a form as ἐρίφυλλος, and possibly the superscription of an *a* over the ε led to the corruption.

717-19. Conington's correction of λέοντα σίνιν into λέοντος ἶνιν is universally accepted; but ἀγάλακτον οὕτως, which the MSS. give, still requires attention. Few, I imagine, will follow Verrall in retaining it; if the lion-cub was φιλόμαστος and its owner intended to rear it, he would not have denied it some milk. The emendation which has hitherto found most favour is Wecklein's ἀγάλακτα βούτας,—based on Hesychius, ἀγάλαξ· ὁμότιτθος. The word βούτας with ἀνήρ is obviously a quite happy suggestion; but what of ἀγάλακτα? In the first place it may be questioned whether Aeschylus would have used the form when the Attic equivalent ὁμογάλακτες was in use; but the more important point is the meaning. It means definitely 'suckled at the same breast' as, presumably, the herdsman's own children, and φιλόμαστον could only reinforce that literal meaning. Did Aeschylus mean to present us with a picture of the herdsman's wife—with a baby held in one arm and a lion-cub in the other—discharging that maternal function? Wecklein's ingenuity was, I think, superior to his sense of humour.

My own correction (published in the *Classical Review*, Vol. xxxv. p. 100) is slightly nearer than Wecklein's to the text of the MSS. I read ἀγελακτόνου τέως, giving to λέοντος an appropriate epithet before we pass on to the description of the whelp. The word is not elsewhere found, but its formation is unexceptionable; ἀγεληνόμος, 'tending herds', is found in Nonnus, and Attic has ἀγορανόμος and the like. And the relevance of the epithet goes far towards justifying the conjecture. The whelp, we are told, ἀπέδειξεν ἦθος τὸ πρὸς τοκέων, 'displayed the temper of his parents'; but how? μηλοφόνοισι σὺν ἄταις. The lion had attacked the kine; the whelp, as soon as he was big enough, began with sheep. And what of τέως? Clearly it is equally appropriate; it is first amplified by ἐν βιότου προτελείοις, and then answered by χρονισθεὶς δέ.

738. Whether πάραντα means here 'for the nonce' or 'in like manner' is not certain. Either sense fits, and in rendering by 'so at the first' I have combined both meanings and confessed my doubt as to which is intended.

755. γένει should be read with βλαστάνειν, emphasising it, 'in direct descent'.

758. The emphasis is on τὸ δυσσεβὲς ἔργον: it is not good fortune but impiety, says Aeschylus, which produces a brood of misery.

767-9. I accept H. L. Ahrens' φάος τόκου in place of the corrupt νεαρὰ φάους κότον, and Hermann's τὰν ἄμαχον for τὸν ἄμαχον. The sense then is: the old ὕβρις has twin offspring, a new ὕβρις and θράσος, who may both be called ἄται, 'powers of perdition', and resemble the stock from which they spring. Aeschylus was here, I think, regarding ὕβρις as insolence and violence towards men, while θράσος, as its epithet ἀνίερον indicates, was rather defiance of the gods. The phrase δαίμονά τε τὰν ἄμαχον ἀπόλεμον, 'that other irresistible fiend', suggests that θράσος is even worse than ὕβρις.

778. The MSS. have ὅσια προσέβα τοῦ. I take the τοῦ to be a corruption of the last syllable of an aorist middle ending in -το, and προσέβα to be a gloss on the verb in question. Ahrens' προσέσυτο appears to me the best correction.

788 ff. Many editors, including Verrall, Headlam, and Mazon, have misread this passage, though Paley had interpreted it rightly; they have treated παρα-βάντες as if it were a loosely used aorist where a present would be correct. 'Many rate semblance above reality, and do injustice so' is Verrall's rendering, whereas the real meaning is 'Many men, when they have transgressed justice, prefer dissimulation to candour on the part of their neighbours'. 'And', continues the Chorus in effect, 'they get what they want—pretence of sympathy in their troubles, pretence of congratulation in their joys. But such pretence will not deceive one who can judge of his flock; and we will be sincere. At Aulis we did not approve your actions: now in all honesty we welcome you and wish you joy.'

794 ff. The hiatus between βιαζόμενοι and ὅστις was rightly taken by Hermann for evidence that a line had fallen out. That line included the main verb; for ξυγχαίρουσιν is not present indicative, but dative of the present participle depending on ὁμοιοπρεπεῖς. What was the substance of the missing line? A clue is provided by Agamemnon's reply (830 ff.): 'I agree with your sentiments,' he says; 'to few men does it belong φίλον τὸν εὐτυχοῦντ᾽ ἄνευ φθόνου σέβειν'. Now the Chorus have not mentioned or suggested φθόνος in the existing lines; but the incomplete sentence, 'and as for congratulation, while they assume the fitting expression and force their faces to smile...' might well end, 'they are merely hiding the φθόνος of their hearts'. I conclude therefore that φθονερὰς κλέπτουσι μερίμνας or the like should fill the gap.

803. Headlam's and Verrall's notes fail to convince me that the MS. reading (with merely θάρσος for θράσος) may be retained, and that θάρσος ἑκούσιον ἀνδράσι θνήσκουσι κομίζων can mean 'trying to recover *a consenting wanton* at the cost of men's lives'. The combined emendations, ἐκ θυσιῶν for ἑκούσιον and θρήσκοισι for θνήσκουσι, give an admirable sense; and a reference to the sacrifice of Iphigenia is at least as appropriate as a sugges-tion that the recovery of Helen was not worth a war; for the whole of the first chorus has been devoted to the doom of Iphigeneia, and it is that memory above all which has rendered the Chorus uneasy and anxious. The word θρῆσκος, in Aeschylus' time, may have been associated with the wilder aspects of religion; Hesychius interprets θρησκός (thus accented) by ἑτε-ρόδοξος as well as by εὐσεβής (so corrected from εὐγενής), and its by-form θρεσκός by περιττός and δεισιδαίμων, while the attempt to connect the verb θρησκεύειν, in its derivation, with 'Thracian' orgiastic rites appears to indicate the same connotation (see Suidas, *s.v.*).

805–6. I accept Headlam's insertion of ἔστιν ἐπειπεῖν (or some equivalent) as essential to the completion of the sentence.

812. I read νόστου not in the sense of 'return' but in that of 'expedition', as it is used in Eurip. *I.A.* 966 (πρὸς Ἴλιον νόστος) and 1261. Cf. also Soph. *Phil.* 43.

819. The reading of the MSS., συνθνήσκουσα, cannot in my opinion be sustained. There is nothing to which the συν- can refer; the blasts of Ate are not dying down but ζῶσι, and συνθνήσκειν τοῖς ζῶσι would be a sheer contradiction of terms. Nor can it well be maintained that the city is viewed as θνήσκουσα, since the true subject of the preceding line is not πόλις but ἁλοῦσα πόλις, 'the capture of the city'. But if nothing else is said to be 'expiring', there is nothing 'along with' which the ashes can be said to expire. I therefore reject συνθνήσκουσα and read συνθρώσκουσα in its place. The compound συνθρώσκειν is assigned by L. and S. to Aelian only, but so natural a compound could, I believe, have been used by any poet in any age.

820. In my rendering of προπέμπει I have deviated from the ordinary translation. The verb προπέμπειν normally means to 'escort' and 'accompany', and rarely (if ever) to 'send forth'. The passages cited by L. and S. under this latter heading include, besides the present passage, two others only: Aesch. *Sept.* 915, which is too corrupt to be of much assistance, though Paley there believes the sense to be that of 'escorting' and not 'sending out'; and Soph. *Phil.* 105, ἰοὺς ἀφύκτους καὶ προπέμποντας φόνον, where obviously it may be claimed that, whereas a bow would be said to 'send forth' death, the arrows may be said to 'escort' or 'accompany' it. Without extending my research into usage further I am content to accept the word here in what is manifestly its normal sense.

822. Tyrwhitt's emendation χἀρπαγὰς in place of καὶ πάγας gives the required sense, save that ἁρπαγὰς without the καί attached seems to me preferable. The doubled καί in χἀρπαγὰς ἐπραξάμεσθα καὶ γυναικός... would imply a contrast and difference between the two phrases, whereas the second merely explains the first. I have given therefore ἁρπαγὰς; the absorption of the initial ἁρ in the termination of ἐπείπερ is just as likely as the absorption of χἀρ. I accept also Heath's ὑπερκόπους for ὑπερκότους.

829. This seemingly simple line is easily misread. The emphasis, I believe, is entirely on φροίμιον and τόδε (which are in apposition rather than agreement),—'thus much by way of prelude'; the extended thanksgiving to the gods implied in πολύμνηστον χάριν τίνειν is still to come, and at *v.* 851 Agamemnon announces his intention of proceeding to that duty. The pronoun τόδε in effect limits the meaning of ἐξέτεινα and means 'only thus much', just as τοσοῦτοι may mean 'only so many' or, in other

words, 'so few'. Headlam's rendering 'To Heaven this lengthened preface',
and Verrall's 'having given to religion this ample precedence', both miss,
as I think, the true intonation of the line, as do also Swanwick, Davis, Mazon,
and other translators.

839. Headlam's criticism of the words ὁμιλίας κάτοπτρον is sound: 'It
is certain that ὁμιλία does not mean friendship (φιλία), nor is κάτοπτρον ever
used of a mere reflexion (σκιά or εἴδωλον)'. He accordingly punctuates in
such manner as to make κάτοπτρον the object of ἐξεπίσταμαι, and to leave
εἴδωλον σκιᾶς δοκοῦντας... to be governed by λέγοιμ᾽ ἄν: 'By knowledge
proven in companionship's true mirror, *ghost of a shadow* I can term
some seeming-absolute devotion to me'. But I find the accumulation of
accusatives governed by different verbs unpleasing to the ear, and believe
that the text has suffered slightly. At v. 307 the MSS. give κάτοπτρον
where κάτοπτον (or κατόπτην) is necessarily restored; and here too I would
read κάτοπτον in agreement with εἴδωλον, and ὁμιλίαις therefore for ὁμιλίας,
the whole phrase then meaning: 'I would describe their seeming devotion as a mere shadow-shape, for well I know that shape as reflected in
the mirror of daily intercourse'. By the term εἴδωλον σκιᾶς he means the
mere shape or outline without substance or depth.

868. There is no need to change πλέω to πλέον, for the accusative
τρήματα is suggested sufficiently by the verb τέτρηται: cf. v. 1068, οὐ μὴν
πλέω ῥίψασ᾽ ἀτιμασθήσομαι, where ῥίψασα implies a less kindred word,
namely ἔπη. Τέτρηται for τέτρωται is due to H. L. Ahrens.

870-1. After Γηρυὼν ὁ δεύτερος the MSS. have the line πολλὴν ἄνωθεν,
τὴν κάτω γὰρ οὐ λέγω. It is entirely pointless, and πολλὴν ἄνωθεν seems to
be due to a premature copying of v. 875, πολλὰς ἄνωθεν, the gap after it
having been filled by a *cliché* of singular banality. It was bracketed by
Schütz, and I omit it.

876. The MS. reading λελημμένης cannot be right. As Verrall well
observes, 'Of two proposed renderings for πρὸς βίαν λελημμένης, (1), supplying ἐμοῦ, "of me violently seized (by them)", would require ληφθείσης
the *act*, not λελημμένης the state, and (2), supplying δέρης, "my neck caught
violently in the noose", gives λαβεῖν a forced meaning'.
    I am not however satisfied with H. L. Ahrens' conjecture λελιμμένης,
which both Verrall and Headlam adopt,—'in spite of my eagerness'. I have
no doubt that in taking πρὸς βίαν as = βίᾳ, 'in spite of' (cf. *Eumen.* 5),
they are right; but the logic of the sentence requires at the end a word
which definitely governs ἀρτάνας. It is incorrect to say that 'others un-
loosed the nooses because of these malign rumours': it was Clytemnestra
who knotted them about her neck because of the rumours; the final word
should therefore govern the accusative ἀρτάνας even though it be governed

also by ἔλυσαν. I had on my own conjecture read ἐνημμένης, which is freely used as a middle with an accusative following it, but find that I have been anticipated long since by Emperius. The phrase then means 'in despite of me who had fitted the nooses on (my neck)'.

884. I retain καταρρίψειεν, and read βουλὴν in its pure abstract sense as meaning 'good counsel', the function of rulers, as opposed to ἀναρχία, also abstract, the quality of an unruly mob. Scaliger's καταρράψειεν, which several editors have preferred, would denote the hatching of a plot, but a mob which has reached the stage of anarchy has long passed the stage of plotting. Verrall retains καταρρίψειεν but translates 'might risk a plot against us', assuming that καταρρίπτω might bear this sense of ῥίπτω or ἀναρρίπτω. There is no evidence to justify the assumption.

886. μέντοι is used here not in the most familiar sense, 'however', but to emphasise a protestation, 'verily'; see L. and S. s.v.

890. κλαίουσα, the MS. reading, has apparently escaped criticism hitherto. Following on a present tense, βλάβας ἔχω, which does not read as historic in meaning, the present participle suggests that Clytemnestra is still weeping. κλαίουσι with ὄμμασιν can easily have the force of an imperfect,—'my eyes that were continually weeping'.

895–902. Dindorf rejects the whole of these lines, Headlam the last three. Headlam has some reason in urging (1) that κάλλιστον... ἐκ χείματος is little more than a repetition of γῆν φανεῖσαν κ.τ.λ. and (2) that the line τερπνὸν δέ... is an interruption; he would wish τοιοῖσδε... προσφθέγμασιν to follow immediately on the προσφθέγματα. Dindorf's position in rejecting all the προσφθέγματα but retaining the line which refers to them is to me quite unintelligible.

Though granting the truth of Headlam's first criticism, I would retain the lines. None of the imagery is irrelevant; the first three προσφθέγματα—κύνα, πρότονον and στῦλον—have reference rather to the maintenance of existing safety, the remainder to unlooked-for deliverance from fear or peril; but the general theme, as summed up in v. 902, is the gladness of safety or deliverance, and the several expressions of the thought are all appropriate.

It will be observed that the reason for the two phrases μονογενὲς τέκνον πατρί and γῆν φανεῖσαν ναυτίλοις παρ' ἐλπίδα being coupled by καί (when all the other phrases are disconnected) is that φανὲν παρ' ἐλπίδα is understood with πατρί. Previously we have had genitives, σταθμῶν, ναός, στέγης, and the dative πατρί indicates to the ear that the phrase is still to be completed. The dative having once been introduced is carried on in ὁδοιπόρῳ.

926. Headlam refers with approval to an explanation offered by Blass, *Mélanges Henri Weil*, 1898, p. 13. 'To walk merely over ποδόψηστρα

would be ἀνεπίφθονον; but it would have a different sound if rumour said that he had walked upon τὰ ποικίλα, which belong to the service of the gods.' He accordingly translates: 'the sound on Rumour's tongue Rings different far of *mats* and *broideries*'. I admire the ingenuity, but to make Agamemnon say, however elegantly, 'give me a mat, if you like, just to wipe my boots, but do not ask me to incur the opprobrium of soiling choicer materials'—this I find unconvincing. And yet in the line as the MSS. give it,

$$\chi\omega\rho\grave{\iota}s\ \pi o\delta o\psi\acute{\eta}\sigma\tau\rho\omega\nu\ \tau\epsilon\ \kappa a\grave{\iota}\ \tau\hat{\omega}\nu\ \pi o\iota\kappa\acute{\iota}\lambda\omega\nu,$$

the presence of the article with the one word, adjective though it be, and not with the other is not pleasing to the ear, I feel, but does tend to suggest such a contrast between the two members of the phrase as Headlam's rendering gives. I think it probable therefore that Aeschylus wrote ποικιλμάτων, and that, ποικίλων having once been erroneously written in its place, the τῶν was inserted to fill a metrical gap in the most obvious manner.

930. εἰ πάντα δ' ὡς πράσσοιμ' ἄν: Is the optative with ἄν in the protasis a solecism or a permissible usage which is rare merely because the precise shade of meaning which it carries is not frequently required? I take the latter view. It is obvious that λέγοιμ' ἄν (e.g. in v. 896) is merely a mild future in meaning, expressing inclination, where the actual future λέξω would express intention. If then Greek permits εἰ λέξω, there is no *logical* reason why it should reject εἰ λέγοιμ' ἄν. What then as regards idiom, which in judging of language is more important than logic? The pure future is ruled out here by idiom, for εἰ with the future in Attic almost invariably has a warning or threatening tone; e.g. Thuc. VI. 86, οὐκ ἄλλον τινὰ προσείοντες φόβον ἤ, εἰ περιοψόμεθα ὑμᾶς ὑπὸ Συρακοσίοις γενέσθαι, ὅτι καὶ αὐτοὶ κινδυνεύσομεν, and a second example at the end of the same chapter. But suppose that Agamemnon wishes to say here: 'If I incline to act thus in all things, my heart is serene'. May he not then use πράσσοιμ' ἄν, subordinated, in the same sense in which it was frequently used as a main verb? Plato does it: ὅτι δ' ἐστί τι ἀλλοῖον ὀρθὴ δόξα καὶ ἐπιστήμη, οὐ πάνυ μοι δοκῶ τοῦτο εἰκάζειν, ἀλλ' εἴπερ τι ἄλλο φαίην ἂν εἰδέναι (ὀλίγα δ' ἂν φαίην), ἓν δ' οὖν καὶ τοῦτο ἐκείνων θείην ἂν ὧν οἶδα (*Meno*, 98 B). And again: τὴν ἀρετὴν φῂς διδακτὸν εἶναι, καὶ ἐγὼ εἴπερ ἄλλῳ τῳ ἀνθρώπων πειθοίμην ἄν, καὶ σοὶ πείθομαι (*Protag.* 329 B). No one, I imagine, will doubt that in the first of these passages φαίην ἄν in the subordinate clause means precisely the same as φαίην ἄν in the parenthetic main clause which follows. (These two examples are quite different from those sentences in which a conditional clause itself contains a complete conditional sentence: e.g. εἰ μηδὲ δοῦλον ἀκρατῆ δεξαίμεθ' ἄν, πῶς οὐκ ἄξιον αὐτόν γε φυλάξασθαι τοιοῦτον γενέσθαι; (Xen. *Mem.* 1. 5. 3), where ἀκρατῆ in effect = εἰ ἀκρατὴς εἴη.) Since then εἰ πάντα δ' ὡς πράσσοιμ' ἄν is justified both by logic and idiom, *stet*. The

nuance which distinguishes εἰ πράσσοιμι from εἰ πράσσοιμ' ἄν may be fairly represented by the difference in English between 'if I should...' and the less common 'if I would...',—the difference between mere contingency and contingency tempered by volition.

931-3. The reading of the MSS. καὶ μὴν τόδ' εἰπέ... can only mean 'answer me this', and would lead directly to a question. This much may be taken as generally conceded. But does Clytemnestra's next line, ηὔξω θεοῖς δείσας ἂν ὧδ' ἔρδειν τάδε, constitute a question? 'Yes,' says Headlam, 'and it means "In hour of peril Would you have made performance of this act A promised vow to Heaven?"' and in his notes he makes it clear that by 'this act' he understands the trampling of embroideries under foot. 'The editors', he says, 'strangely imagine that ὧδ' ἔρδειν τάδε means "to refrain from treading on dyed robes"; having forgotten that when you made a vow to the gods you did not say οὐ θύσω, "save me, and I will—*not* sacrifice!"' But Headlam surely was neglecting his context. The question is not one of sacrificing or dedicating dyed robes to the gods: to that Agamemnon would have assented; θεούς τοι τοῖσδε τιμαλφεῖν χρεών are his own words. What Clytemnestra is urging is that he should accept for himself honours appropriate to gods only. And when he abruptly refuses, she assumes that his refusal must be due to some vow. What sort of vow then? A vow, I suppose, that if the gods should save him or grant him victory, he would claim no honour nor triumph for himself but ascribe to them only all might, majesty, dominion, and power. Such surmise on Clytemnestra's part is natural; Agamemnon has previously said τούτων θεοῖσι χρὴ πολύμνηστον χάριν τίνειν (v. 821) and θεοῖσι πρῶτα δεξιώσομαι (v. 852); and if he now refuses all pageantry in his own honour, a vow, she may argue, furnishes the explanation of his attitude.

So then I reject Headlam's interpretation of this line, and therewith necessarily the emendation which he adopts (viz. ἐξεῖπεν for ἐξεῖπον) and the meaning he requires in the following line.

The view which I take is that ηὔξω...τάδε is not a question; it is an inferential statement, an innuendo almost, which invites, and receives, denial, but it is no question. It means 'you must have vowed in some moment of fear that you would act thus'. Verrall understood it thus, and called the idiom 'the conjectural use of the past indicative with ἄν'. It is a natural development of the usage in conditional sentences, but the inference in such a case as this is not from a *past* contingency to a *past* conclusion (as in εἰ τούτῳ ἐπιστεύσατε, ἀπωλόμην ἄν, 'if you had believed this man, I should have been ruined'), but from a *present* contingency to a *past* conclusion. The present contingency here is 'if this is your present attitude', and then follows 'you must have vowed...'. An exactly similar case occurs in v. 1252. The Chorus, having at last been explicitly warned by Cassandra that Agamemnon is in danger of death, say to her: τίνος πρὸς ἀνδρὸς τοῦτ' ἄγος πορσύνεται; and she replies ἦ κάρτ' ἄρ' ἂν σὺ παρεκόπης χρησμῶν ἐμῶν, *i.e.* 'if you can put that question with the word ἀνδρὸς in it, you must have utterly missed the meaning of my prophecies'.

If then the line ηὔξω...τάδε is an inferential statement, and if the inference is drawn from Agamemnon's refusal, in the previous line, to change his mind, there is no question asked such as the words καὶ μὴν τόδ' εἰπέ would introduce.

What follows? My inference is that for εἰπέ we should read εἶκε, and let Clytemnestra strike the dominant note of the whole passage at the outset,— 'Yield!'

In that case μὴ παρὰ γνώμην ἐμοί will mean 'not contrary to my expectation', *i.e.* 'yield and do not disappoint me'. For (*pace* Headlam) phrases like παρὰ γνώμην *need* not mean 'contrary to the expectation or opinion' of the person who forms the subject of the sentence. They have that meaning in default of any indication to the contrary; but a dative may be added (as ἐμοί here) to show whose expectation or opinion is concerned: *e.g.* Plato, *Phaedo* 95 A, τὸν λόγον...θαυμαστῶς μοι εἶπες ὡς παρὰ δόξαν.

But then Agamemnon picks up the word γνώμην and uses it not in the sense of 'expectation' but in that of 'decision'. 'As regards γνώμην', he says (the μέν serving to mark his changed use of the word), 'be assured that *I* shall not change my decision', *i.e.* 'I shall not give way in this'.

And then comes Clytemnestra's inference and innuendo: 'if you are as determined as you say, you must have made some vow to the Gods that you would act thus,—some panic-vow'.

And Agamemnon replies to the taunt conveyed by δείσας. 'It was in no panic', he implies, 'but with full knowledge of what I was doing that I proclaimed this final decision.' And (once more *pace* Headlam) the γε in εἰδώς γ' εὖ is entirely appropriate, for Agamemnon in εἴπερ τις, εἰδώς γ' εὖ is giving every possible emphasis to εἰδώς in rebutting the suggestion made by δείσας. Headlam, treating the previous line as a question, and reading in this line ἐξεῖπεν for ἐξεῖπον, requires γε to mean 'Yes'; but I am at a loss to understand his denial of its appropriateness in emphasising one particular word. See Neil's edition of Aristoph. *Knights*, Appendix I. p. 188 (2).

For τέλος in the sense of a 'final decision' cf. Antiphon, v. 89, ἡ μὲν γὰρ τούτων αἰτίασις οὐκ ἔχει τέλος, ἀλλ' ἐν ὑμῖν ἐστι καὶ τῇ δίκῃ. Cf. also τέλος δίκης (*Eumen.* 243) and αἰτίας τέλος (*Eumen.* 434). These passages seem to indicate that ἐξεῖπον τέλος should be rendered by some phrase suggestive of a judicial decision.

942. ἦ καὶ σὺ νίκην τήνδε δήριος τίεις; Once more a line simple in appearance has produced a large crop of diverse renderings. Verrall removes the mark of interrogation and translates: 'Thou plainly, no less than I, thinkest the point worth fight'. He claims that τίειν is used in its rarer Homeric sense (*Il.* xxiii. 703 and 705) = 'to value at', and that δήριος is a

genitive of price. This is ingenious at any rate, if hardly probable; for even
in Homer the genitive is not found with τίειν. But by ignoring the fact
that ἦ καὶ time after time introduces a question, he puts his interpretation,
I think, out of court. His reading of the line would contain too many
curiosities of idiom.

Headlam is more brusque in his note on the line. 'ἦ καὶ σύ', he says,
'is *tu quoque*, and could not mean anything else.' This *dictum* will not
bear investigation; the three words may be combined in speech either as
ἦ καὶ σύ or ἦ καὶ σύ; the καί need not belong to the word following it, and
ἦ καί may form a single interrogative expression like ἦ γάρ, etc. Aeschylus
has it in vv. 424 and 434 of the *Eumenides*, and Sophocles is fond of it. ἦ καί,
φίλη δέσποινα, says Odysseus to Athene, πρὸς καιρὸν πονῶ; (*Ajax* 38.)
where the vocative interposed marks the isolation of καί from any specific
word in the sentence, and shows that ἦ καί is merely a more emphatic ἦ,
used, as Jebb notes *ad loc.*, 'in eager question'. He might indeed have
said 'in either eager or indignant question'; for in *O.T.* 368 indignation
is paramount. The passage occurs in the altercation between Oedipus and
Teiresias: ἦ καὶ γεγηθὼς ταῦτ᾽ ἀεὶ λέξειν δοκεῖς; says Oedipus, 'do you really
expect to go on talking in that strain and escape unpunished?' I need not
accumulate further evidence; other clear examples may be found in *Ajax* 44
and *O.T.* 757, while *Ajax* 48 and *Electra* 314 and 663 either may or should
be read otherwise. Among the ambiguous examples must be classed also
v. 1362 of the *Agamemnon*, though personally I consider that ἦ καί is better
read there as the indignant interrogative. In which manner then is ἦ καὶ
σύ... to be read here? Headlam, connecting καί with σύ, as I have said,
translates: 'And *thine* eyes, Do *they* account such conquest as a prize?'
i.e. 'Do you, no less than I (*tu quoque*), attach so much importance to having
your way in this controversy?' But this will not do when Agamemnon is
on the point of yielding; he should not reassert here his own strong
wishes in the matter. The key to the correct rendering lies, to my thinking,
in νίκην. Clytemnestra has used the word νικᾶσθαι. Agamemnon, thinking
of his own victories, retorts scornfully 'Do you really esteem this a victory?'
or something to that effect, thereby implicitly minimising the importance of
the point in dispute, and so making easier his final surrender.

Now, if it were not for δήριος, the line as it stands would naturally bear
the required sense: τήνδε would be the object of τίεις (attracted to the
gender of the predicate), and νίκην the predicate. But δήριος, if merely attached
to νίκην, is then so otiose as to be objectionable. I believe therefore that
Auratus' conjecture τῆσδε is right, and that the meaning is: 'Do you really
esteem so highly a victory resulting from such strife as this?' Whereupon
Clytemnestra, humbling herself and disclaiming the name of victor,—wins.

943. I accept Weil's correction κρατεῖς μέντοι παρείς (as improved by
Wecklein) in place of κράτος μέντοι πάρες γ'. The μέντοι here, as above in

v. 886, means 'verily'. Whether it should be written *divisim* as μέν τοι is an open question.

945. λύοι in place of the normal λυέτω is an usage which Aristotle, I imagine, would have approved as ξενικόν and so adding distinction to the style. In *Choeph.* 889 there is a similar case: δοίη τις ἀνδροκμῆτα πέλεκυν ὡς τάχος.

956. σοῦ receives a slight stress: 'as Cassandra is my bondswoman', it suggests, 'so am I at your command'.

961–2. οἶκος δ᾽ ὑπάρχει...ἔχειν is not Greek. Porson's οἴκοις is a simple remedy, but the two lines which result, if lucid enough, are somewhat dull. I believe that it is only the traditional punctuation that is at fault. I have placed a stop at ὑπάρχει,—'and (apart from the sea's bounty) we have our household store'. Then, with a gesture, '*These* things,' says Clytemnestra,— 'our house knows not how to stand possessed by God's grace of such riches as these, and yet to play the pauper'. The genitive τῶνδε would serve as a partitive genitive so far as ἔχειν is concerned, and fits again with πένεσθαι, which I take to indicate here not κτῆσις but χρῆσις, not actual poverty of possession, but an appearance of poverty in the use of wealth. This allows to οὐκ ἐπίσταται its full and right meaning. The ordinary rendering is 'and our house is not acquainted with poverty'; but I would have it mean ' our house does not *know how* to behave as if poor'. And the following line tends to corroborate this meaning; Clytemnestra is found to have passed from the question of possession to that of use: 'this house does not know how to behave as poor; thousands of robes would I have devoted to trampling in the dust'.... I conclude then that the contrast of ἔχειν πένεσθαι δ᾽ was adequate to give to πένεσθαι this sense. The lines so read fit well with the μεγαλοπρέπεια of Clytemnestra's character. Cf. *vv.* 1042 ff.

966–9. The lines as given in the MSS. run as follows:

ῥίζης γὰρ οὔσης, φυλλὰς ἵκετ᾽ ἐς δόμους,
σκιὰν ὑπερτείνασα σειρίου κυνός.
καὶ σοῦ μολόντος δωματῖτιν ἑστίαν,
θάλπος μὲν ἐν χειμῶνι σημαίνεις μολών.

This is deplorable Greek and not to be attributed to Aeschylus: as the lines stand in the MSS., ὑπερτείνασα is wrong in tense, and the construction of σοῦ μολόντος...σημαίνεις μολών is singularly awkward and unlikely. I will not discuss the various renderings by which an attempt has been made to introduce some relevance into these ungrammatical and disjointed remarks. I suggest simply that the lines are out of order. After saying what she would have sacrificed previously to secure Agamemnon's safe return, Clytemnestra almost necessarily, I feel, continues καὶ σοῦ μολόντος... 'and now that you have actually come...'; whereupon logically she should proceed

'I will sacrifice even more by way of thanksgiving'; but instead of this she breaks as it were into a psalm of thanksgiving, and in six exquisite lines (exquisite when restored) gives us the parable of the vine which brings both shelter and abundance to the house over which it rambles. With the small alterations ῥίζης παρούσης for ῥίζης γὰρ οὔσης, σκιάν θ' for σκιὰν, and σημαίνει μολόν for σημαίνεις μολών, the passage becomes a beautiful whole. The past tense ὑπερτείνασα is then right: it is when the vine has already spread her leaves to form a shelter against the coming heat, that men read her message—'winter is past and spring is here'.

972. ἐπιστρωφωμένου: I believe this unusual word to have been selected as being suitable to the vine as well as to the master of the house.

983–6. The reading of the MSS. χρόνος δ' ἐπεὶ (or ἐπὶ) πρυμνησίων ξυνεμβόλοις ψαμμίας ἀκάτας παρήβησεν is corrupt and meaningless. By common consent (*pace* Verrall) ξυνεμβόλοις must go; but can ξυνεμβολαῖς take its place? This abstract word occurs in *Persae* 396, κώπης ῥοθιάδος ξυνεμβολῇ,—'the simultaneous dipping of the oars',—but I know of no marine manœuvre which requires the simultaneous dropping of a number of cables whether into the sea or elsewhere; and no other legitimate sense can be got out of this compound. But Casaubon's ξὺν ἐμβολαῖς is another matter. What are the meanings of ἐμβάλλειν in connexion with ships? (1) 'To ram another ship abeam' (intransitive with dative); (2) in the phrase ἐμβάλλειν κώπαις, 'to strike in' with the oars (again intransitive, I think, and not, as Stephanus followed by L. and S. suggested, a condensed form of ἐμβάλλειν χεῖρας κώπαις, 'to set hands to the oars'); (3) 'to put on board', both active (*e.g.* Hom. *Od.* IX. 470) and middle (*e.g.* Lucian, *Ver. Hist.* I. 5, and II. 1) being used as equivalents of the more frequent ἐντιθέναι or ἐντίθεσθαι, just as the opposite ἐκβάλλειν is regularly used of putting things (whether εὖναι, 'anchor-stones', or cargo) overboard. If then πρυμνησίων ξὺν ἐμβολαῖς would mean 'along with the stowing of the cables on board', a phrase is found which fits the moment when the naval host ὦρτο—'made a start' for Troy; for the πρυμνήσια were cables fastened to some rock or tree ashore, and loosened and hove aboard before setting sail.

What then of the rest of the sentence? I would accept H. L. Ahrens' ψαμμὶς ἀκτὰ as the nominative, and read περιήχησεν for παρήβησεν. Wecklein suggested παρήχησεν, a word not actually known to exist in the active form or in the sense here required; but to obtain metrical correspondence with *v.* 998 in the form in which I have reconstructed it, περι- is required here instead of παρ-, and the form περιήχησεν has Homeric guarantee.

997. Aeschylus' conception of anatomy is not so clear to me that I would venture on any change of the text, but I acknowledge that Headlam's κυκώμενον for κυκλούμενον may be right.

998-9. The MSS. vary; *f* gives ἐξ ἐμᾶς ἐλπίδος, *h* gives ἀπ' ἐμᾶς τοι ἐλπίδος.

This difference is of more importance than might appear at the first glance. Judged on the analogy of other phrases, ἐξ ἐμᾶς ἐλπίδος should mean 'in accordance with my expectation', while the opposite sense, 'beyond' or 'contrary to my expectation', may be expressed by either ἀπ' ἐλπίδος or ἐκτὸς ἐλπίδος. It is this latter sense which the passage appears to require. How are the two readings to be reconciled in such a way as will produce that meaning?

I suggest that the true reading was ἐκτὸς ἐμᾶς, and that, in the archetype whence *f* and *h* derive, ἐκ ἐμᾶς had been accidentally written and that τος appeared as a superscript correction. Then, I suggest, the scribe of *f* corrected ἐκ ἐμᾶς into ἐξ ἐμᾶς and overlooked the τος, while the scribe of *h*, either to produce the right sense or to preserve the metre, substituted ἀπ' for ἐκ, and copied τος as τοι at the end of the line. The phrase ἐκτὸς ἐλπίδος is familiar in tragedy in the sense appropriate to this passage, save only that ἐλπίδος here is 'expectation' and not 'hope'.

1001. μάλα γάρ τοι τᾶς πολλᾶς ὑγιείας ἀκόρεστον τέρμα: Thus *f*, presenting a text which needs correction at three points. The first of these, μάλα γάρ τοι, is with general consent corrected to μάλα γέ τοι. The second, τᾶς πολλᾶς, is more difficult. Paley's suggestion, τὸ μεγάλας, though accepted in several editions, has no merit save the restoration of the metre. If τᾶς πολλᾶς, as is probable, represents a gloss on some harder word, that word was certainly not the commonplace μεγάλας. In my judgement we require an adjective or participle unaccompanied by the article, so that μάλα may be associated with it and not with ἀκόρεστον—or with ἀόριστον if this be accepted instead of ἀκόρεστον—since these are both absolute terms in themselves and need no qualification by μάλα. I suggest therefore τεταμένας, which might be read as equivalent to τᾶς πολλᾶς but would suggest also more clearly the ancient view of health as a harmony of the body's humours without an excess of any one of them; 'requiritur enim', as Wilamowitz-Moellendorff observes, 'sententia Hippocratea αἱ ἐπ' ἄκρον εὐεξίαι σφαλεραί'.

This emendation, I think, fits in well with Karsten's ἀόριστον, which I adopt, in place of ἀκόρεστον. Whether ἀκόρεστον be interpreted in an active or a passive sense, I cannot extract any satisfactory meaning from it or see how the next clause could logically be connected with it by γάρ. But ἀόριστον τέρμα is a readily intelligible phrase; I understand it to mean a boundary which is no true frontier and gives no security, for the reason that (γάρ) sickness is lodged close against it in readiness to encroach.

The penultimate syllable of ὑγιείας is treated as short ; possibly some other spelling should be used.

1005. A line is missing here. H. L. Ahrens' suggestion,

ἀνδρὸς ἔπαισεν < ἄφνω
δυστυχίας πρὸς > ἄφαντον ἕρμα,

is attractive (1) as suggesting how the omission was caused—namely by the copyist's eye straying from ἄφνω to ἄφαντον—and (2) as giving the more familiar construction with παίω used in this sense. But as against this I feel that ἀνδρός requires qualification. As ὑγίεια alone is not perilous, but ὑγίεια μάλα τεταμένη, so πότμος εὐθυπορῶν in itself is good, and dangerous only when the man concerned presumes upon it; as Wilamowitz observes, *desideramus 'nimii' notionem in cursu directo*. I would prefer therefore to insert ἱεμένου θρασέως or words to that effect before ἀνδρός. The rest then stands; for the construction of παίω in this sense with a direct accusative has a parallel in Soph. *Electra*, 745. With this reading θρασέως provides a natural contrast to ὄκνος in the next sentence.

1012. πημονᾶς γέμων ἄγαν : Some of those who have believed the line to refer to the ship's proper freight have found πημονῆς difficult, and Verrall, adopting Housman's suggestion, gave παμονᾶς, a possible (though not known) equivalent of πᾶμα (*i.e.* κτῆμα). But does the line refer to the cargo, or to the water pouring in through the breach in the ship's hull? Surely the real πῆμα is the mounting water; by the jettisoning of some of the cargo, if the breach affects one hold only or is near the water-line, the ship though partially flooded may still be kept afloat; she is not *too full* (γέμων ἄγαν) ot the water that constitutes her πῆμα.

1015. I have placed a comma after ἀμφιλαφής τε to indicate that the construction is πολλά...ἀμφιλαφής τέ ἐστι, καὶ... .

1016. ἤλασεν (Schütz) for ὤλεσεν of the MSS. is justified by the scholiast's explanation διεσκέδασε.

1022-4. οὐδὲ...ἀπέπαυσεν ἐπ᾽ ἀβλαβείᾳ (or εὐλαβείᾳ); is the text usually accepted. But the awkwardness of the question introduced by οὐδὲ is obvious, and Hartung's ἀπέπαυσεν in place of the MS. αὔτ᾽ ἔπαυσ᾽ is not therefore a good correction. I read ἂν ἔπαυσεν instead, and remove the mark of interrogation.

The choice between ἀβλαβείᾳ and εὐλαβείᾳ is not easy; I slightly prefer the latter, taking it to mean 'by way of precaution' (as in Plato's *Republic*, 539 D), or 'with a view to encouraging caution among mankind'.

1041. The MSS. present two versions of this line: *f* has

while *h* gives

πραθέντα τλῆναι δουλείας μάζης βία,

πραθέντα τλῆναι καὶ ζυγῶν θιγεῖν βία.

Headlam accepts the reading of *f* in the amended form δουλίας μάζης βία, and translates 'spite of the slave's fare'. But I can find no confirmation of this use of βία, which normally has a genitive of the person, not of the thing, and means 'against the will of'. Greek said βία Σωκράτους or indeed βία φρενῶν as equivalent to *invito Socrate* or *invito animo*, but not, I think, μάζης βίᾳ. If this be so, the line is obviously faulty, for δουλίας μάζης would remained ungoverned.

Wilamowitz-Moellendorff adopts, *faute de mieux* as he acknowledges, a mixed reading, δουλίας μάζης θιγεῖν. He admits that βία as well as πραθέντα τλῆναι must have been in that archetype from which *f* and *h* derive, but holds too that the introduction of θιγεῖν is not of the type of emendation which he would impute to Triclinius; and what is true of θιγεῖν is true also, I assume, of καὶ ζυγῶν.

Can we then account for the two readings on the assumption that one represents the text and the other a gloss thereon—either or both having been incorrectly copied?

The only word in either reading likely to provoke a gloss is μάζης. I will assume therefore that δουλίας μάζης represents the text and that καὶ ζυγῶν θιγεῖν represents a gloss.

In what words would a commentator be likely to explain μάζης?

The μᾶζα in its simplest form was a mixture of ἄλφιτα (barley or other meal), as opposed to ἄλευρα (wheat-flour), with water and oil (Hesych. *s.v.*). It was not baked (Herod. i. 200, Plato, *Rep.* 372 B), but presumably hardened of its own accord as the meal absorbed the liquid. More palatable forms of μᾶζα contained wine, honey, or other ingredients, and were known as οἰνοῦττα, μελιτοῦττα, etc., but a δουλία μᾶζα may be assumed to have been made without such additions.

Now Tryphon of Alexandria in a monograph on Ἄρτοι (Athen. 109 *b, c*) classified breads, (*a*) according to their basic substance, as σεμιδαλίτην (made of fine flour), χονδρίτην (made of coarse meal), and συγκομιστόν (made o unbolted meal, *i.e.* that in which the offal has not been sifted and separated off from the finer material), and (*b*) according to the method of preparation, as leavened (ζυμίτην) and unleavened (ἄζυμον); and he mentions particularly that the coarse (χονδρίτης) is made ἐκ τῶν ζειῶν, *i.e.* from some grain resembling barley (κριθή) but inferior thereto, possibly spelt (cf. Hesych. *s.v.* ζειά). This is confirmed by one Mnesitheos (Athen. 115 *f*), who described τὸν ἐκ τῶν ζειῶν ἄρτον as heavy and indigestible.

Tryphon devoted a section of his work to μᾶζαι (Athen. 114 *e*). The details here are not preserved by Athenaeus, but it may be assumed that the μᾶζαι provided for slaves (1) were made from the coarsest material, viz. ἐκ ζειῶν, and (2) were included in the class of ἀζύμων. I suggest therefore that καὶ ζυγῶν in Triclinius' MS. was due to faulty reading of either ἐκ ζειῶν or ἀζύμων, either of which would be a reasonable gloss on μάζης. As between the two it is hard to judge of probability, nor does it matter; in the case of ἀζύμων, the plural is no objection, for biblical Greek would have made τὰ ἄζυμα familiar; it was used both of the bread itself (Exodus xii. 15 and Luke xxii. 1) and of the feast-day (Mark xiv. 1); while on the other hand the accent, and also the pronunciation (if similar to that of Modern Greek), are more in favour of ἐκ ζειῶν.

The word θιγεῖν remains. Is that also a gloss, and, if so, on what word?
Let it first be noted that the sense of the passage may permit but does
not require both τλῆναι and βίᾳ. It would suffice to say 'he endured to
eat' or 'he perforce ate' : it is unnecessary to say 'he endured to eat perforce'.
Hence τλῆναι is not indispensable and may be a corruption of some rarer
verb governing μάζης—a verb which was explained by θιγεῖν. The gloss
θιγεῖν, that is, may date back to some MS. earlier than the archetype of our
existing MSS. and may have survived the corruption of that word which
it was originally designed to explain. I suggest accordingly that τλῆναι is a
corruption of πλῆσθαι; the π once mistaken for a τ, any scribe might have
been tempted to correct, as he would have thought, a wrong termination of
the infinitive.

Now πλῆσθαι belongs to two different verbs, πελάζω and πίμπλημι; Homer
uses ἔπλητο and the like freely as aorist middle of either ; and further both
verbs may govern the genitive; πίμπλημι does so regularly, πελάζω occasionally. A commentator therefore who should have explained πλῆσθαι (as if
belonging to πελάζω) by θιγεῖν would have been justified by poetic usage,
even though he were in fact wrong. Actually, I believe, ἔπλητο as an aorist
of πελάζω was obsolete by the time of Aeschylus (being superseded by
πλαθῆναι or πελασθῆναι), whereas ἔπλητο as aorist of πίμπλημι was still used
even in ordinary Attic. Aristophanes uses it freely (in the compound ἐμπίμ-
πλημι); indicative, imperative, optative, and participle all occur. And later
on, even Apollonius Rhodius, with all his borrowing of Homeric language,
used ἔπλητο etc. only as aorist of πίμπλημι, and did not attempt to revive
the other usage. We need therefore have no hesitation in assuming that
Aeschylus might have used πλῆσθαι in the sense of 'to take one's fill'. The
genitive μάζης will then be governed by πλῆσθαι, and βίᾳ will mean simply
'perforce'.

I conclude therefore that we should read here

πραθέντα πλῆσθαι δουλίας μάζης βίᾳ,

treating τλῆναι of f and h as an old corruption of πλῆσθαι, θιγεῖν of h as an
intelligent, if mistaken, gloss on πλῆσθαι, dating from a time when τλῆναι
had not yet invaded the text, and καὶ ζυγῶν of h as a misreading of a gloss
on μάζης—either ἐκ ζειῶν or ἀζύμων.

1056-7. The reading of the MSS. is τὰ μὲν γὰρ ἑστίας μεσομφάλου
ἔστηκεν ἤδη μῆλα πρὸς σφαγὰς πυρός. It has rightly been felt that the
expression σφαγὰς πυρός is not sense, and that the genitive ἑστίας needs a
word to govern it. Hence Musgrave's suggestion of πάρος for πυρός.
Headlam accepts this; but the interval between ἑστίας and πάρος is in my
judgement too long. I suspect disorder in the arrangement of the words
as we now have them. Instead of μεσομφάλου after ἑστίας I suggest that we
should read μεσομφάλους after σφαγὰς, and the lines would then run :

τὰ μὲν γὰρ ἑστίας ἤδη πάρος
ἔστηκε μῆλα πρὸς σφαγὰς μεσομφάλους.

It may well have happened that a scribe's eye wandered from ἑστίας to σφαγὰς and that he wrote μεσομφάλους accordingly in place of ἤδη πάρος, and that the omitted words which he subsequently wrote in a margin or elsewhere were taken to be a complete line and their order adjusted for metrical purposes. The order of the words as I have edited them appears to me simpler and more rhythmical; and I would therefore ascribe that order to Aeschylus, and impute the traditional order to the blunder of some copyist.

1059. σὺ δ'—εἴ τι δράσεις...: The line should be spoken with the slight pause after σὺ δ' which I have indicated by a dash. In the preceding sentence Aeschylus has deliberately delayed the word μῆλα so that τὰ μὲν may suggest 'some of the victims—the sheep—are ready for sacrifice', and then follows 'but thou—'. This is a light touch of irony which should not be missed—the irony of what is almost an aposiopesis.

1091. Headlam's suggestion of ἄρταμα (or ἀρταμάς, which I prefer) in place of ἀρτάνας is clearly right. The house of Atreus was not addicted to the use of the noose, but preferred ἀρταμή, 'butchery'. The formation of the word is correct, and it matters little that it is not found elsewhere; ἄρταμος, 'a butcher', and the verb ἀρταμέω are sufficient warranty for it.

1092. I adopt Porson's πέδου for πέδον, but cannot accept ῥαντήριον as correct. There is no horror attaching to 'sprinkling the ground' unless blood, for example, is used for the purpose; and the word 'blood' cannot therefore be fitly omitted. I read χραντήριον instead; neither word is elsewhere found, and χραίνειν, 'to defile', instead of ῥαίνειν, 'to sprinkle', completes the sense.

I have adopted also Dobree's ἀνδροσφαγεῖον.

1098–9. The MSS. have ἠμὲν (sic) before προφήτας. It may be assumed to be a mere duplication of the opening of the previous line. I accept Weil's τούτων in its place. The sense then is: 'we had heard of your skill in prophecy (and expected to hear something difficult to understand); but in respect of what you have now said no expounder of prophecies is needed; they are quite clear'.

Headlam at this point is unfortunate both in text and in translation; he conjectures τὸ μὲν κλέος σοῦ μαντικὸν, meaning apparently τὸ μὲν μαντικόν σου κλέος, and in his rendering does not distinguish between the meanings of μάντις and προφήτης.

1100. The subject of μήδεται is intentionally left unexpressed. In English the easiest rendering is by means of the passive.

1110. προτείνει δὲ χεὶρ...: The vision which Cassandra sees is that of a fisherman hauling on a rope. In her next speech that which 'comes to view' (φαίνεται) at the end of the rope is a net.

1115. I have substituted a full stop for the mark of interrogation usually given after Ἄιδου. Cassandra, I think, answers her own question; she has already half anticipated what now appears; ' yea, verily ', she says, ' it is a net, a net of destruction '. If ἦ, as I suppose, is affirmative, the γε can stand; if it were interrogative, γε would hardly be needed.

1118. θύματος λευσίμου: Cf. v. 1616. Death by stoning was doubtless the traditional Greek punishment for the gravest crimes. Plato (*Laws* ix. 873 B), in prescribing the penalty for the wilful murder of a near kinsman, allows indeed a more humane method of execution, but requires the ceremony of stoning to be carried out on the dead body.

1123. ξυνανύτει: The intransitive usage of ξυνανύτει which the sense of the passage requires brings the form under suspicion. The simple verb in all its forms, ἀνύω, ἀνύτω, and ἄνω, is, I believe, always transitive. It is permissible indeed to use ἀνύτειν absolutely, in the sense of ὁδὸν or δρόμον ἀνύτειν, to indicate the completion of a course or the reaching of a goal; and there is also the colloquial usage of ἀνύσας in conjunction with an imperative with no expressed object. But these I regard as abbreviations of the transitive usage rather than as constituting an intransitive usage. Nor indeed can ξυνανύτει here be treated as akin even to the former of these; for ἀνύτειν (δρόμον) always implies some effort or striving, a notion foreign to the present passage. On the other hand, the passive of ἄνω is regularly used of a period of time (*e.g.* νύξ in *Iliad* x. 251, ἔτος in Herod. vii. 20, ἦμαρ in Apoll. Rhod. ii. 494) which draws to a close. Here therefore, in combination with βίου δύντος αὐγαῖς, ξυνάνεται appears to me far more probable than ξυνανύτει. Moreover Hesychius definitely quotes ξυνάνεσθαι = συνανύεσθαι, and his authority, added to what I consider the probabilities of usage, seems to me reasonably conclusive in weighing one ἅπαξ λεγόμενον against another. I read therefore ξυνάνεται.

1129. λέβητος τύχαν: The word τύχαν seems to me to have little point unless it have an epithet. I have therefore written δολοφόνον in place of δολοφόνου.

1137. Headlam's ἐπεγχύδαν for the unmetrical ἐπεγχέασα of the MSS. seems to me a highly probable correction, and I have adopted it.

1163. The reading of the MSS. is νεογνὸς ἀνθρώπων μάθοι. The correction which I have adopted is a slight modification of Karsten's suggestion. Instead of writing νεόγονος, as he proposed, I have written καὶ νεογνός.

1166. The MS. reading θραύματα presents a difficult problem. I have little doubt that there is a reference to this passage in Hesychius when he writes θραῦσμα=λύπη. πληγή. κατάπτωμα γῆς. καταστολή. παῦσμα, παῦσις. But λύπη and πληγή may represent no more than some old annotation of this passage made by some reader who connected πέπληγμαι with θραύματα and assumed θραύματα therefore equivalent to πληγάς, ignoring its connection with ἐμοὶ κλύειν. There are plenty of scholia preserved in our MSS. which are quite as bad as that would be. My objection to reading θραύματα and interpreting it in this sense is twofold : (1) it is unlikely that a word normally meaning 'fragments' should on occasion possess the meaning of ' heart-breaking things', and (2) a word meaning λύπας or πληγάς would be tautologous and ineffective at the finish of a sentence which began with πέπληγμαι δ' ὑπαὶ δάκει φοινίῳ. That vigorous expression leaves no room for a commonplace 'I am grieved to hear it' at the end.

As a stronger word I suggest θράγματα. The form θράσσω is freely used in place of ταράσσω, and there can be no improbability in postulating θράγμα as a by-form of τάραγμα. Now τάραγμα and ταραγμός were strong words denoting a state of consternation and bewilderment ; e.g. Eurip. H. F. 1091,

$$\text{ὡς δ' ἐν κλύδωνι καὶ φρενῶν ταράγματι}$$
$$\text{πέπτωκα δεινῷ....}$$

The word θράγματα here would therefore definitely add something to the sentence instead of merely repeating in feebler form the opening words. Cassandra's lamentations over her own lot not only pierce the Chorus to the heart but leave them utterly confounded,—as they confess again at the end of their next utterance, τέρμα δ' ἀμηχανῶ.

1171-2. The MSS. give: τὸ μὴ πόλιν μὲν ὥσπερ οὖν ἔχειν (or in one MS. ἔχει) παθεῖν, ἐγὼ δὲ θερμόνους τάχ' ἐμπέδῳ βαλῶ. Neither ἔχει nor (pace Verrall) ἔχειν can be sustained. Greek idiom required ἔχειν ὥσπερ ἔχει or παθεῖν ὥσπερ ἔπαθε, and did not admit a mixture of the two. For ἔχειν I read ἔχρων. This gives a good sense: 'nothing availed to save my city from suffering exactly as I kept foretelling'. It is noteworthy too that the same word, ἔχρων, has been, as I conceive, the source of trouble later at v. 1272, on which see my note.

What general sense then may be expected in the contrasted clause ἐγὼ δὲ...? Either (1), the meaning which editors by one means or another have endeavoured to extract from it, 'and I too shall soon perish as did my city', or (2), in view of my correction of ἔχειν into ἔχρων, 'and still my prophecies are as vain as they were then'. It is this latter line of thought which I follow in suggesting ἐγὼ δ' ἔθ' ὁρμαίνουσα τἀμποδὼν ματῶ,—'and still my musing on that which confronts me and Agamemnon is all in vain'.

In this emendation the assumed corruption of ματῶ into βαλῶ may seem to many a considerable assumption ; but a similar error (not so far as I know hitherto observed) has occurred in Soph. O.C. 1054, where a variant on ἐγρεμάχαν occurs in the form ὀρειβάταν. Now ὀρειβάταν would give no suitable sense, and is presumably a corruption of ὀρσιμάχαν,—which therefore, as an otherwise unknown form, has some claim to oust ἐγρεμάχαν. The nearest known form ὀρσίμαχος occurs in Bacchylides, xv. 3 (Kenyon, 1897), in the phrase < Π >αλλάδος ὀρσιμάχου. If μάχαν can produce βάταν, there is no reason why ματῶ should not produce βαλῶ.

I claim two points of literary likelihood in favour of this emendation. First there is a pathetic corroboration of Cassandra's complaint—that still her prophecy is in vain—in the reply of the Chorus, who while acknowledging her inspiration (καί τίς σε...δαίμων) confess that they have learnt nothing from it (τέρμα δ' ἀμηχανῶ). Secondly the theme of the vanity of Cassandra's prophecies pervades the whole of her following speeches and dialogues with the Chorus. Analysing the whole scene beginning at 1178 and ending at 1330, we find that it falls into three sections; (1) vv. 1178-1213, concerning the past history of the house of Atreus, and repeating in fuller and clearer form the lyrical passage 1072-1097; (2) vv. 1214-1255, dealing with the fate of Agamemnon, and repeating similarly 1100-1135; (3) vv. 1256-1326, dealing with Cassandra's own fate, and repeating in like manner 1136-1177, though adding now a prophecy of Orestes' destined part. But in these passages Cassandra does not merely expand and elucidate her previous utterances; throughout them she pleads for the Chorus' belief. In the first section we have μαρτυρεῖτε...ῥινηλατούσῃ (1184), and ἦ ψευδόμαντίς εἰμι...; ἐκμαρτύρησον...τό μ' εἰδέναι... (1195-6), leading up to the Chorus' reply ἡμῖν γε μὲν δὴ πιστὰ θεσπίζειν δοκεῖς (1213). And so again in the second section, Cassandra's main speech ends with the same plea: καὶ σύ μ' ἐν τάχει παρὼν | ἄγαν γ' ἀληθόμαντιν οἰκτείρας ἐρεῖς (1240). And similarly in the third section: μαρτυρεῖτέ μοι... (1317). I claim then that my restoration τὸ μὴ πόλιν μὲν ὥσπερ οὖν ἔχρων παθεῖν, ἐγὼ δ' ἔθ' ὁρμαίνουσα τἀμποδὼν ματῶ, prepares in a manner characteristic of Aeschylus for the whole scene that follows.

In the *Classical Review* (Vol. xxxv. p. 100) I formerly suggested this emendation with γ' ἐμπέδως after ὁρμαίνουσα. On later thought I have preferred τἀμποδών.

1190. συγγόνων 'Ερινύων: Various renderings are given. Verrall gives 'sister-fiends' and Headlam 'Kindred-Avengers', making συγγόνων, I presume, dependent on 'Ερινύων. I prefer a third rendering: 'the Furies who are akin to this house', its 'familiar' fiends.

1193. Some editors wish to take δυσμενεῖς as nominative: I prefer to read it with εὐνάς, and have translated the passage in that sense.

1198. καὶ πῶς ἂν...: I take this, though interrogative in form, to be the expression of a wish, like φεῦ, τίς ἂν ἐν τάχει... in v. 1448. An *indignant* question, such as καὶ πῶς, καὶ τίς etc. usually introduce, would be out of tone here. The καὶ after all only affects a question by emphasising the interrogative, and in this case it may equally well emphasise the wish.

1216. στροβεῖ ταράσσων: The MSS. give the participle; but Hesychius' explanation of στροβεῖ suggests to me that the original form may have been

NOTES

the indicative ταράσσει. It has been generally assumed (as by M. Schmidt in his edition of Hesychius and by Wilamowitz-Moellendorff in his edition of Aeschylus) that Hesychius had this passage in mind. His text actually gives στροβεῖται ταράσσει κινεῖ, and I think this should probably be edited in the form στροβεῖ ταράσσει=κινεῖ rather than, as Schmidt gives, στροβεῖ= ταράσσει κινεῖ. The verb στροβεῖν by itself is dealt with almost immediately afterwards; and here therefore it seems likely that Hesychius, *more suo*, is quoting an actually occurring phrase as his lemma, though he means to explain only one word in that phrase. Exactly similarly σμοιῷ προσώπῳ= φοβερῷ ἢ στυγνῷ, σκυθρωπῷ is given side by side with the word σμοιός by itself. The emphatic asyndeton στροβεῖ ταράσσει is moreover characteristic of Aeschylus; cf. *Choeph.* 287–9, μάταιος ἐκ νυκτῶν φόβος...κινεῖ ταράσσει. For these reasons I prefer ταράσσει to ταράσσων.

The end of this line also presents a problem; for the MSS. give ἐφημένους there as well as at the end of the next line, where it properly belongs. What was the word which has accidentally been ousted? The suggestions offered are mainly epithets for φροιμίοις, it being assumed that φροιμίοις is an instrumental dative with ταράσσων. But I suggest that φροιμίοις is definitely contrasted with ὀρθομαντείας, and refers back to the lyrical and less comprehensible prophecies contained in vv. 1100–1135, while ὀρθομαντεία is another way of expressing the χρησμὸς οὐκέτ' ἐκ καλυμμάτων δεδορκώς of vv. 1178–9. In that case we shall need a word which will couple ὀρθομαντείας with φροιμίοις, and I propose ξυνηγόρου. Cf. Soph. *Trach.* 1165, μαντεῖα καινὰ τοῖς πάλαι ξυνήγορα.

1227–31. The MSS. here give:

> νεῶν τ' ἄπαρχος Ἰλίου τ' ἀναστάτης
> οὐκ οἶδεν οἷα γλῶσσα μισητῆς κυνὸς
> λέξασα καὶ κτείνασα φαιδρόνους δίκην
> ἄτης λαθραίου τεύξεται κακῇ τύχῃ.
> τοιάδε τολμᾷ......

With the substitution of κἀκτείνασα (Canter) for καὶ κτείνασα, some sense may be extracted from the passage on one assumption—the assumption that τεύξομαι, normally the future of τυγχάνω, could be used alternatively, in place of τεύξω, as the future of τεύχω.

What grounds are there for this assumption? L. and S. cite two reputed examples of the use in Homer. These are (1) *Iliad* v. 652–3

> σοὶ δ' ἐγὼ ἐνθάδε φημὶ φόνον καὶ κῆρα μέλαιναν
> ἐξ ἐμέθεν τεύξεσθαι...

and (2) *Iliad* xix. 205–8

> ἦ τ' ἂν ἔγωγε
> νῦν μὲν ἀνώγοιμι πτολεμίζεμεν υἷας Ἀχαιῶν
> νήστιας ἀκμήνους, ἅμα δ' ἠελίῳ καταδύντι
> τεύξεσθαι μέγα δόρπον...

But in the first passage there is every reason to treat τεύξεσθαι as future of τυγχάνω. The meaning of the sentence will be 'I say that death will befall thee at my hands', and the construction is quite normal (cf. *Iliad* XI. 684, οὕνεκά μοι τύχε πολλὰ νέῳ πόλεμόνδε κιόντι). And in the second sentence τεύξασθαι, the aorist, should probably be read; for ἄνωγα usually takes a present or aorist infinitive, and indeed on a cursory inspection of Homeric passages I did not light upon a future infinitive following it.

I have therefore no evidence of the existence of τεύξομαι as a future of τεύχω, but, if it do exist, I am still quite certain that Aeschylus did not deliberately mystify his audience here by so using it and then adding κακῇ τύχῃ as if it bore its normal sense.

What then is wrong with the text? Apart from quite minor errors of copying, two things only: the misplacement of the line ἄτης...τύχῃ, which should follow νεῶν τ'...ἀναστάτης, and the telescoping of three separate short sentences which have no connecting particles such as would have indicated that they are separate. The required adjustments being made, we have:

> νεῶν τ' ἔπαρχος Ἰλίου τ' ἀναστάτης
> ἄτης λαθραίου τεύξεται κακῇ τύχῃ.
> οὐκ οἶδεν οἷα γλῶσσα μισητῆς κυνός·
> λέξασα.........φαιδρόνους δίκην
> τοιάνδε τολμᾷ...

where I assume ἔπαρχος (Canter) for ἄπαρχος, οἷα (Herwerden) for οἷα, and τοιάνδε (my own) for τοιάδε, as minor changes not needing defence.

What is to fill the gap after λέξασα in place of καὶ κτείνασα? The word δίκην in its new setting is the substantive 'justice', not the adverbial 'like'. 'That treacherous woman', says Cassandra, 'after talking of and ...ing Justice in gladness of heart dares justice of this sort: she murders her own husband.' The suggestion ἐκτείνασα will not serve now. Greek said ἐκτείνειν λόγους freely, but not ἐκτείνειν δίκην in the sense of talking at length about justice. But there is a rare word which will give the exact meaning wanted—ἀκτήνασα. The verb ἀκταίνω (or ἀκταινόω, for the grammarians recognise both forms) meant literally 'to raise up'; cf. *Eumen.* 36, ὡς μήτε σωκεῖν μήτε μ' ἀκταίνειν βάσιν. But it apparently had a metaphorical sense too; for though the explanation of the grammarians, ἀκταινῶσαι: τὸ ὑψῶσαι καὶ ἐξᾶραι καὶ μετεωρίσαι (see Bergk, *Lyrici Graeci*, *Anacr. fr.* 137, and L. and S. *s.v.* ἀκταίνω), might have reference to the literal use only, Plato (*Laws* II. 672 c) uses the word otherwise: ἐν τούτῳ δὴ τῷ χρόνῳ ἐν ᾧ μήπω κέκτηται τὴν οἰκείαν φρόνησιν, πᾶν μαίνεταί τε καὶ βοᾷ ἀτάκτως καί, ὅταν ἀκταινώσῃ ἑαυτὸ τάχιστα, ἀτάκτως αὖ πηδᾷ—where ἀκταινώσῃ ἑαυτὸ might well be paraphrased, I think, by ἐπάρῃ ἑαυτὸ or ἐπαρθῇ. I conclude then that ἀκταίνω could probably be used in the sense of 'to exalt' or 'to extol', and I complete my conjectural restoration of the passage by reading

λέξασα κἀκτήνασα φαιδρόνους δίκην.

Cassandra's reference to Clytemnestra's speech of welcome will be obvious; no hearer could have forgotten her concluding lines (910–11)

εὐθὺς γενέσθω πορφυρόστρωτος πόρος
ἐς δῶμ' ἄελπτον ὡς ἂν ἡγῆται Δίκη.

1235. θύουσαν ᾅδου μητέρ'...: My interpretation of this phrase is determined by the leading word θύουσαν, which is normally applied to a rushing or raging wind. Such a wind may easily be called a 'mother of destruction'; for μήτηρ is applied very freely to any source or cause, and ᾅδης no less freely to destruction in the abstract. With this interpretation the second half of the phrase harmonises: πνέουσαν carries on the imagery of θύουσαν, and ἄρη, like ᾅδου, is used in the abstract and not the personal sense. I cannot accept Headlam's contention that ῎Αιδου μητέρα means a 'hellish mother'. If 'hellish' be a proper epithet for Clytemnestra, it was *qua* wife and not *qua* mother that she earned it.

1249. οὔκ, εἰ παρέστη γ': Cassandra in the previous line has implied that Apollo is present (τῷδ' ἐπιστατεῖ λόγῳ) but not as 'Healer'; and the Chorus' right answer then is 'No indeed—if he really is (or was) here'. I read therefore παρέστη γ' for the MS. παρέσται γ'. Karsten's πάρεστιν gives equally good sense, but would have been less liable to such miscopying.

1252. I accept Hartung's παρεκόπης, and I insert σὺ before it. For the inferential use of παρεκόπης ἄν, see my note on *v.* 933.

1253. τοῦ τελοῦντος: The participle is to be read as future in tense.

1256. παπαῖ, οἷον τὸ πῦρ: I believe this to be a half line, exactly like ἰοὺ ἰού, ὢ ὢ κακά, at *v.* 1214, which introduced Cassandra's previous speech. The phrase ἐπέρχεται δέ μοι, which follows it in the MSS., looks like an indifferent attempt by some copyist or annotator to complete an iambic line. An exact correspondence with *v.* 1214 might be produced by doubling the παπαῖ.

1261. κἀμοῦ μισθὸν ἐνθήσει κότῳ: So the MSS., save that *f*, the most trustworthy, has μνείαν suprascript over μισθὸν. Now μνείαν is itself excluded by metre, and the obvious explanation of its presence is that it was a gloss on the more poetical word μνῆστιν. Should we then read μισθὸν or μνῆστιν? Clearly the abstract μνῆστιν harmonises far better with κότῳ. 'The draught of vengeance', says Cassandra, 'which Clytemnestra is compounding out of her anger against Agamemnon for his treatment of Iphigeneia will have her remembrance of me too as an ingredient'; and the truth of what Cassandra says is confirmed by Clytemnestra's own words at *vv.* 1444–7, where παροψώνημα introduces very similar imagery. The word μισθὸν is too concrete in meaning; it denotes only the actual wages, not the desire for retaliation. It was probably this difficulty which led Auratus to suggest, and not a few editors to adopt, ποτῷ in place of κότῳ. Given μνῆστιν, κότῳ will obviously stand.

1262–3. I regard the two lines, 1262–3, which I have omitted,

ἐπεύχεται θήγουσα φωτὶ φάσγανον
ἐμῆς ἀγωγῆς ἀντιτίσασθαι φόνον,

as a variant reading for vv. 1260–1, κτενεῖ...κότῳ, which I have retained. We have had a previous case of an alternative reading (though not there incorporated in the MS. text) at v. 301, and other examples, as I judge the text, are to be found at v. 1275 and v. 1306. If I am right here, there will be no question which pair of lines should be rejected; the pair which I have retained are supremely Aeschylean; the other pair might have been written by anyone. Incidentally, if genuinely Aeschylean, they would probably have had nọt ἀντιτίσασθαι but ἀντιτίσεσθαι (cf. Sept. 276.)

1267. The MSS. give ἴτ' ἐς φθόρον πεσόντ'· ἀγαθὰ δ' ἀμείψομαι, the only variation therefrom being ἀμείβομαι, which was written by the first hand in f. This present tense, in place of the future, is accepted by Wilamowitz-Moellendorff, and, I think, rightly. In the previous line διαφθερῶ may be spoken before Cassandra actually snaps the σκῆπτρον in two (for such, I assume, is the action implied), and the future tense is in point; but here ἴτ' ἐς φθόρον πεσόντα must surely accompany the gesture of dashing the στέφη on the ground, and the present tense ἀμείβομαι therefore becomes appropriate.

Of the suggested corrections of the corrupt ἀγαθὰ δ' none satisfies me. Hermann's ἐγὼ δ' ἅμ' ἕψομαι fails for two reasons, (1) because it ousts ἀμείψομαι, which might be called the keynote of the passage, and (2) because ἅμ' ἕψομαι, meaning necessarily 'I will accompany now' and not 'I will follow later', would imply that Cassandra was contemplating immediate suicide. Verrall's ἴτ' ἐς φθόρον· πεσόντα θ' ὧδ' fails likewise in my judgement in that it detaches πεσόντα from the preceding phrase to which, pace Wilamowitz-Moellendorff, it rightly belongs, and because, after the violence of ἴτ' ἐς φθόρον, such an addition as 'and now that you are on the ground I will requite you thus' sounds tame and frigid.

The problem, as I see it, is to restore the text in such a way that the line may begin with ἴτ' ἐς φθόρον πεσόντα· and end with ἀμείβομαι, and I suggest that the missing word between them is τῆδ'. This would imply that there have been at least two or more stages in the corruption which produced ἀγαθὰ δ'. First, I suppose, τῆδε was explained by ὧδε (cf. Hesychius τῆδε = ὧδε, ἐνταῦθα), and at some period ὧδε became incorporated in the line, with hiatus preceding it. Next there were two attempts made to obviate the hiatus, (1) by the insertion of γε, so as to read πεσόντα γ'· ὧδ', and (2) by the insertion of τε, so as to read (like Verrall) ·πεσόντα θ' ὧδ'—

the correction a θ' being probably suprascript over the correction a γ', with the result that they were amalgamated into ἀγαθ'.

In point of usage τῇδε, I think, was never quite synonymous with ὧδε, though it approached the meaning of ὧδε very closely. It meant rather 'herein', 'in this aspect', 'in this particular', and the like. Here the sense of τῇδ' ἀμείβομαι would be simply 'here is my retribution', but a commentator who, like Hesychius, should have explained the τῇδε by ὧδε would not have been seriously wide of the mark.

1271–2. The MSS. here give

κἀν τοῖσδε κόσμοις καταγελωμένην μετὰ
φίλων ὑπ' ἐχθρῶν οὐ διχορρόπως μάτην.

Headlam retains this and argues that μετὰ φίλων ὑπ' ἐχθρῶν οὐ διχορρόπως can mean 'by friends and foes alike', whereas, if the text means anything, it should surely be 'being mocked along with my friends by my enemies', a meaning which does not fit this context. Other editors, adopting Hermann's μέγα for μετὰ, would take φίλων ὑπ' ἐχθρῶν to mean 'by friends who behaved as foes', but the accumulation of adverbs, μέγα, οὐ διχορρόπως, μάτην, all associated with καταγελωμένην, becomes with this reading very cumbrous.

I accept Hermann's conjecture μέγα, but believe that there is corruption of the text in the second line also. What is Cassandra saying? She is complaining that at Troy, before Apollo brought her to her death at Argos, he allowed her to be mocked by her own people. The tenses ἐποπτεύσας... καταγελωμένην...ἀπήγαγε indicate this. The word φίλων then is appropriate; the word ἐχθρῶν may be suspected. I suggest therefore ὅτ' ἔχρων in place of ὑπ' ἐχθρῶν, and take μάτην not as an adverb but in its original usage as accusative of μάτη—with the resulting sense 'laughed to scorn when I steadfastly foretold the vanity of my friends' hopes'. It will be noticed incidentally that after the occurrence of ἔχρων the sentence καλουμένη δὲ...ἠνεσχόμην runs the more smoothly as carrying on the same subject.

The lengthening of the first syllable of ἔχρων, judged by general analogy, might be deemed exceptional enough to render my emendation suspect; but actual usage is in its favour. The imperfect of the simple verb occurs in Tyrtaeus II. 4, Pindar Ol. VII. 92, Hermesianax 89, Apoll. Rhod. I. 302 and II. 456, and in all of these the first syllable is necessarily long. I have not actually found an example of the imperfect in which it is short. Moreover even general analogy admits of many exceptions; Aeschylus himself lengthens a vowel so placed in ἔθρισεν (Agam. 536), νεκρῶν (Pers. 272 and 421), ἀκραῖς (P.V. 368), πατρί (Choeph. 14), μέλαθρα (Agam. 957), and ἐπέκρανεν (Suppl. 624).

1273–4. I find that in the conjecture of φοιβὰς instead of φοιτὰς, which I had made, I have been anticipated by Spanheim and by Enger. The

latter however wanted to read φοιβὰς οὖσ', which would give a wrong turn
to the sense of the passage as implying that ἀγύρτρια, πτωχός, τάλαινα, and
λιμοθνής were all to be associated with καλουμένη, and represented a series
of abusive names by which Cassandra was called. But that is not so: only
ἀγύρτρια could be deemed a term of abuse. The participle καλουμένη goes
with φοιβὰς—'I entitled to the name of Phoebus' own prophetess', that is
her boast; her pride in her office is prominent in her character (cf. vv. 1195
and 1202); and then the sentence runs on 'I endured it—their scorn—
like some poor starving ἀγύρτρια',—the words φοιβὰς and ἀγύρτρια being
thrown into juxtaposition to mark the extreme of contrast between Apollo's
own prophetess and some strolling priestess begging for alms.

1275. καὶ νῦν ὁ μάντις μάντιν ἐκπράξας ἐμέ: This has been interpreted in
two ways: (1) 'after having made me his prophet', (2) 'having made an end
of me as seer'. The former, which Paley and Headlam favour, is not, I
believe, Greek; at any rate they do not cite, and I cannot find, any example
of the usage. The latter, which Verrall favours, is Greek, but not sense
here; the aorist tense must imply that Apollo had ended Cassandra's seer-
ship before he brought her from her father's altar to her death in Argos.
But indeed he had not; we have heard her prophesying as steadfastly as
ever.

Neither of these interpretations then can stand; and if there were no
other aspect of the line which provoked criticism, the problem might appear
insoluble. But obviously, I think, the whole line can be dispensed
with. The sentence which began at ἐποπτεύσας δέ με has been interrupted
by a parenthesis (καλουμένη...ἠνεσχόμην), but there is no reason why it
should be broken off finally; ἀπήγαγε in itself recalls us to the main
sentence.

We have then two *data*: ἐκπράξας gives no satisfactory meaning here,
and the whole line is superfluous here. These constitute as it were cross-
bearings which should enable us to fix the true position of the line. Substitute it for v. 1269 (ἰδοὺ δ' Ἀπόλλων...), and the resulting
phrase,

καὶ νῦν ὁ μάντις μάντιν ἐκπράξας ἐμὲ
χρηστηρίαν ἐσθῆτα...,

is at any rate good Greek; ἐκπράσσειν τινά τι, 'to exact something of
someone', is a well-known prose usage. The interchangeability of the two
lines can hardly, I feel, be a mere coincidence. I suggest therefore that
here again we have a variant reading incorporated in the text (cf. 1260-3),
and that again we have to make our choice on literary grounds—between
ἰδοὺ δ' Ἀπόλλων... and καὶ νῦν ὁ μάντις.... Given that choice, no one, I
think, will hesitate; *stet* the former, *dele* the latter.

1277. I accept Headlam's κοπέντος for κοπείσης. He explains the change
of gender in the MSS. as having been 'a deliberate alteration made by a half-

intelligent corrector, who took the participle as referring to Cassandra, and therefore made it feminine'. He mentions *à propos* two similar alterations in this play: in v. 263, where two MSS. give σιγῶντι for σιγώσῃ, and in v. 271, where they give φρονούσης for φρονοῦντος. It will be noted that the plural immediately following in τεθνήξομεν and in ἡμῶν confirms the propriety of a reference here to Agamemnon's death as well as to Cassandra's. The acceptance of Headlam's κοπέντος involves the acceptance of Schütz' θερμὸν for θερμῷ.

1286. I accept, in lieu of the MS. κάτοικος, Wieseler's emendation κάκοιτος, which had occurred to me independently. The word is not known elsewhere, but is abundantly justified by Homer's fondness for κακὸν οἶτον. The emphasis thus given by Cassandra to her own sufferings leads naturally to her mention of the sufferings of others in the next two lines; but I recognise that Wakefield's κάτοκνος too would be quite appropriate as looking forward to ἰοῦσα πράξω....

1299. The correct reading here in place of the MS. χρόνῳ πλέω is hard to determine. I incline to accept Weil's χρόνοι πλέῳ, but, instead of breaking the line by a colon after ξένοι as he does, to read οὗ for the second οὔ, and let the line run on. 'There is no escaping for one whose hour is ripe.' The personal οὗ prepares well for ὁ δ᾽ ὕστατός γε.

1306. After Cassandra's ἰὼ πάτερ... the MSS. give to the Chorus the line: τί δ᾽ ἐστὶ χρῆμα; τίς σ᾽ ἀποστρέφει φόβος; which implies that Cassandra has already recoiled in horror from the door of the palace. But φεῦ φεῦ is in effect the stage direction; that exclamation should, I argue, accompany her recoil. And seeing that the Chorus, after the φεῦ φεῦ, ask precisely the same question in more Aeschylean language, I treat τί δ᾽ ἐστὶ χρῆμα... as an inferior variant, and omit it. Cf. my notes on 1260–3, and 1275.

1312 ff. I am surprised that editors in general should have tolerated so long the sequence of lines which the MSS. give:

> Χο. οὐ Σύριον ἀγλάισμα δώμασιν λέγεις

followed by

> Κα. ἀλλ᾽ εἶμι κἀν δόμοισι κωκύσουσ᾽ ἐμὴν
> Ἀγαμέμνονός τε μοῖραν.

i.e. Chorus: The house on your showing does not smell sweet.
  Cassandra: Still I will go and make my lament in the house too....

Karsten indeed was conscious of this incongruity; for he proposed θανοῦσι in place of δόμοισι; and this Mazon adopts. But there is no great likelihood that two common words as dissimilar as δόμοισι and θανοῦσι should have been confused, and some other remedy for the passage should be sought.

What is the situation?

The Chorus have been trying to allay Cassandra's fears—her fancied fears, as they think; and it is those well-meant but unintelligent efforts that Cassandra cuts short with her ἰὼ ξένοι, οὔτοι δυσοίζω... ἄλλως, 'Forbear, good sirs; these are no idle suspicions...'. The two lines ἀλλ᾽ εἰμι...βίος interrupt this necessary sequence, and incidentally create a sequence which savours of comedy. They cannot remain here: even though they should be emended, they would still interrupt the true sequence.

Where then do they belong? They are, I suggest, Cassandra's last words, and follow the line δούλης...χειρώματος. Consider the effect of transposing them to that place: (1) she quits the stage with the words ἀρκείτω βίος, and (2) in the words ἐμὴν Ἀγαμέμνονός τε μοῖραν she has led directly up to the comment of the Chorus which immediately follows,—their comparison of Agamemnon's and Cassandra's destinies.

I deal with a correction of the two transposed lines in a later note.

1315. I am tempted to suggest ἴτ᾽ ὦ ξένοι, used appealingly like ἴθ᾽ ὦναξ in a similar broken line in Soph. O.T. 1468, but I cannot show an interjection like ἰὼ to be wrong in usage here, and therefore leave it.

1316–7. I accept without hesitation Hermann's ἄλλως· for the MS. ἀλλ᾽ ὡς, but θανούσῃ μαρτυρεῖτέ μοι τόδε needs correction too. Instead of θανούσῃ the balance of thought requires a verb contrasting with δυσοίζω. Now δυσοίζω is a rare word, but on the evidence of Hesychius and of the Rhesus (724 and 805) its meaning is quite clear—'to suspect' (not, as L. and S. give, 'to be distressed'). 'It is no vain timorous suspicion', says Cassandra, 'which I entertain'; and what is the necessary antithesis? Simply 'I know'. Schütz therefore was on the right track when he suggested μαθούσῃ in place of θανούσῃ, but I should prefer a present tense, and suggest therefore νοούσῃ: νοεῖν is the true antithesis to δυσοίζειν, and if once νοούσῃ had been written instead of νοούσῃ, any scribe might have been tempted to write θανούσῃ by way of correction. With this we must read τότε for τόδε (an emendation in which Rauchenstein has anticipated me), and complete sense emerges: 'I do not merely suspect: I have knowledge; bear me witness thereof in that day when...'.

1322–3. ἅπαξ ἔτ᾽ εἰπεῖν ῥῆσιν ἢ θρῆνον θέλω | ἐμὸν τὸν αὐτῆς: So the MSS.; but Cassandra does not wish to make either a ῥῆσιν or a θρῆνον, but merely a short prayer. The word ῥῆσις meant in Greek a set and formal oration, and θρῆνος is of course a dirge; neither had anything in common with εὐχή, a prayer. We cannot have Cassandra at this point hesitating over the choice of a word, when she knows so well what she wants. Both words must go; and, if θρῆνον goes, ἐμὸν τὸν αὐτῆς is necessarily affected. But, be it noted too, ἐμὸν τὸν αὐτῆς is in itself not above suspicion; in such cases of the usage as I can readily find in Attic (e.g. Soph. El. 252, Arist. Plut. 33) the order is τὸν ἐμὸν αὐτῆς, and the same holds where some genitive other than αὐτῆs is added (e.g. Soph. Trach. 775, τὸ σὸν μόνηs δώρημα, Arist. Ach. 93, τὸν σὸν τοῦ πρέσβεωs (ὀφθαλμόν), Soph. O.C. 344, τἀμὰ δυστήνου κακά).

These are the difficulties, and here for once there is no kind of clue to the original text. But I hold that a guess which provides good sense is preferable to so unsatisfactory a reading as the MSS. offer. I read therefore boldly

$$\text{ἅπαξ ἔτ' εἰπεῖν καὶ πορευθῆναι θέλω}$$
$$\text{οἶμον τὸν αὐτῆs,}$$

urging in its favour the following considerations:

(1) That if εἰπεῖν were not absolute, but had been followed by a substantive such as ῥῆσιν, the line would probably have begun: καὶ τήνδ' ἔτ' εἰπεῖν ῥῆσιν (cf. v. 1431).

(2) That the phrase τὸν αὐτὸν οἶμον πορεύεσθαι was used by Plato (Rep. 420 b) and was probably borrowed by him from some poet; for οἶμος is not a prose word.

(3) That our text is derived from a MS. which was probably badly blurred or damaged at this point, as v. 1325 almost immediately following indicates. In such a case ῥῆσιν ἢ θρῆνον might represent two guesses at some visible portions of πορευθῆναι.

(4) The word οἶμον would be happily picked up by our transposed lines ἀλλ' εἶμι..., which now form the conclusion of this speech.

1323–6. The MSS. give:

$$\text{ἡλίῳ δ' ἐπεύχομαι}$$
$$\text{πρὸς ὕστατον φῶς, τοῖς ἐμοῖς τιμαόροιs}$$
$$\text{ἐχθροῖς φονεῦσι τοῖς ἐμοῖς τίνειν ὁμοῦ,}$$
$$\text{δούληs θανούσηs, εὐμαροῦs χειρώματος.}$$

In addressing myself to the correction of this passage I proceed on the assumption that Cassandra's last prayer has in it more vigour than a mere petition that the enemies who slay her may be punished. This she has already foretold at v. 1280—ἥξει γὰρ ἡμῶν ἄλλος αὖ τιμάορος, and indeed the very phrase τοῖς ἐμοῖς τιμαόροις here assumes that vengeance will be taken. The corrupt line ἐχθροῖς...ὁμοῦ must therefore, I argue, contain the main point of the prayer, and—for this seems to follow—furnish an effective contrast to δούληs θανούσηs....

Now in this line we need first a subject for τίνειν, for I take τίνειν to be correct as fitting in with τοῖς ἐμοῖς τιμαόροιs—'pay to my avengers'. What then if ἐλευθέρους be substituted for ἐχθροῖς? The subject is found, the contrast with δούληs provided, and (assuming a blurred or damaged MS. as suggested in the previous note) the two words are not too dissimilar.

Next we want an object for τίνειν. What can we get out of the corrupt φονεῦσι τοῖς ἐμοῖς? My answer is φόνευτρ' ἐμοῦ. True, the word φόνευτρα, 'the wages of killing', does not elsewhere occur : but we have λύτρα, σῶστρα, κόμιστρα and the like, and no word could be more apposite.

What then of ὁμοῦ? It is all that remained, I answer, in the damaged MS., of δόμους or of πρόμους. I prefer the latter; for it is a fuller reminder of Cassandra's former estate, and the ἐλευθέρους...πρόμους offers a fuller contrast to

δούλης θανούσης, εὐμαροῦς χειρώματος.

1313–4. ἀλλ᾿ εἶμι...ἀρκείτω βίος : These two transposed lines are satisfactory, as I have said, in their new position (1) as preparing for the comment of the Chorus which follows, and (2) as making ἀρκείτω βίος Cassandra's last words. But the MS. reading κἂν δόμοισι κωκύσουσ᾿ still leaves much to be desired. The phrase indeed is no longer grotesque, as it would be if it followed v. 1312, but it is obviously misleading. Cassandra does not expect to repeat her lamentations in the palace. She has already recognised the palace-gates as the gates of death (v. 1291). She knows that her hour is come (vv. 1299–1301, and v. 1320). She has declared that this is her last utterance (v. 1322). She has no desire, and knows that she will have no opportunity, to make lament in the palace too. The words κἂν δόμοισι κωκύσουσα would be false in this last scene, and Cassandra's last words must not be false. What then are we to read? I suggest τὰν δόμοισιν ὠκύνουσ᾿,—ἐμὴν Ἀγαμέμνονός τε μοῖραν. That will be truth, and poignant in its simplicity.

The rarity of the verb ὠκύνειν, which however Hesychius records as existing, may in itself account for the corruption.

1327–30. Weil was clearly right in assigning these lines to the Chorus; their whole tone is characteristic of the sympathetic onlooker.

1328. I accept Boissonade's ἂν πρέψειεν in place of the MS. ἀντρέψειεν. The σκιά, as Headlam well points out, suggests a ' pencilled shadow' as in σκιαγραφία, and anticipates in that way the clearer imagery of the succeeding line.

1330. καὶ ταῦτ᾿ ἐκείνων μᾶλλον οἰκτείρω πολύ : So the MSS., and I am not surprised that editors have disagreed over the pronouns. Paley makes ταῦτα refer to Agamemnon's case (τὰ εὐτυχοῦντα) and ἐκείνων to the misery of Cassandra; Verrall and Headlam vice versa. But is either sentiment appropriate? The Chorus are callous and almost brutal if they watch Cassandra depart after this last scene and dismiss her with the words 'I'm sorry for her, but Agamemnon has most of my pity'. And on the other hand, if they say that they pity Cassandra far more than Agamemnon, they have ill prepared for the ode on Agamemnon's fortunes which immediately follows. This is a dilemma; and I see only one means of escaping it, namely to read οὐ for καί. An οὐ may easily be misread as an abbreviated καί, and the same two syllables have, I believe, been confused in v. 1658, where see my note. The sentiment is then appropriate: 'all human affairs are pitiable,—misery hardly more so than prosperity'.

1339. Instead of the MS. reading τοῖσι θανοῦσι, it has been felt that we require a dative governed by ἐπικράνη as in vv. 1545-6. Obviously τοῖς θείνουσι, 'the strikers', gives the proper sense, and I prefer the present to Musgrave's θενοῦσι because of the irony involved in the present, which may mean either 'the strikers' (just as e.g. ἡ τίκτουσα may mean 'the mother') or 'those who are now striking'.

1347. I have given αὐτοῖς for the MS. reading ἄν πως. A correction is needed; and the simpler the line, the better.

1348-69. Why did Aeschylus revert from the trochaic to the iambic rhythm after only three lines? Was it for the sake of the ἐγὼ μὲν...ἐμοὶ δέ...κἀγὼ... which the natural emphasis of discussion required at the opening of each short speech? If so, I am right in retaining the trochaic rhythm in my translation to secure the same emphatic 'I...I...I...'.

The characterisation of the several speakers is very noticeable, varying in range from the cold incisive tone of No. 5 to the bluster of Nos. 8 and 9.

1359. I am astonished to find how many scholars from Conington to Mazon have concurred, either explicitly or by their punctuation of this line, in reading it as if τὸ βουλεῦσαι were the subject of ἐστι, and as if τοῦ δρωμένου could be supplied with πέρι. There should be a comma (for safety at any rate) after ἐστι, for τὸ βουλεῦσαι is the subject of πέρι used in the sense of περίεστι. The next speaker, who agrees, surely makes this clear. πέρι as an abbreviated form of περίεστι may not be common, but Hesychius (s.v.) definitely notes that it occurred.

1388. τὸν αὐτοῦ θυμόν: αὐτοῦ is emphatic; otherwise τὸν θυμόν alone would suffice. 'It was his own soul he sped this time,' she means,—'not that of some victim like Iphigeneia'. In v. 1385 above αὐτοῦ is of course the adverb, 'then and there'.

1391-2. ἧσσον ἢ διὸς νότῳ | γᾶν εἰ σπορητὸς : Thus the MS. reading, in which Porson substituted διοσδότῳ γάνει for διὸς ν'τῳ γᾶν εἰ. That emendation has been so universally accepted that there is some temerity in calling it in question. But if a critic should attempt to approach the MS. reading de novo, as if Porson's suggestion had never been made, might he not feel that the one word in the text with which it would be dangerous to interfere was νότῳ? It was this South Wind, Νότος, which gave its very name to the spring rains, the νοτίαι εἰαριναί of which Homer speaks (Il. VIII. 307); it was Νότος which might be said, in the words of this passage, βάλλειν ψακάδι, to shed his gentle rain on the growing corn in spring-time, before June, as in those climes, brought harvest. May not νότῳ therefore be

NOTES   159

deemed the pivotal word on which the emendation should turn? If νότῳ be
corrupt, if Porson's διοσδότῳ be what Aeschylus wrote, is it not an amazing
accident that by mistaking a Δ for a N the copyist should have introduced
into the text a word so singularly appropriate to it, a *mot juste*? The mathe-
matical odds against so felicitous an error must be enormous. Yet if it
happened, it can have been nothing but a casual error ; it can hardly have
been a deliberate attempt at correction if the same scribe wrote γᾶν εἰ immediately after it and thereby demonstrated that he did not understand
what he was copying.

Admirable therefore as Porson's emendation may be, I believe νότῳ to
be sound, and, if νότῳ, then Διὸς νότῳ, which is as natural an expression as
Διὸς ὄμβρος in Homer (*e.g. Il.* v. 91). I believe that the corruption of the
text is confined to γᾶν εἰ. What kind of word then do the structure and
meaning of the sentence require or admit at this point? Obviously a verb,
and a verb repeating the meaning of χαίρουσαν. And the verb γαίει, 're-
joices', exists. L. and S. quote it indeed as found only in the participial
form γαίων,—in Homer several times in the phrase κύδεΐ γαίων, and
once in Empedocles. But Hesychius shows clearly that there was no
such restriction on the verb's usage; he quotes it in the forms γαίειν,
γαίεσκον, γαίουσα, and γαίων. I read therefore Διὸς νότῳ γαίει σπορητὸς, a
phrase which recalls the not dissimilar ἀμφὶ δὲ λειμὼν ἐρσήεις γάνυται of
Apollonius Rhodius (ι. 880). Indeed the corruption γᾶν εἰ might quite
well be due to a superscript or marginal γάνυται explaining γαίει, though
perhaps the very rarity of γαίει accounts adequately in itself for the copyist's
perplexity.

1394–8. The construction of ἦν...ὥστ᾽ ἐπισπένδειν is an example of the
same idiom as occurred earlier in *vv.* 378–9, on which see my note. The
genitive πρεπόντων is a partitive genitive forming the object of ἐπισπένδειν
and placed early, before the ὥστε, exactly like ἀπήμαντον in 378–9, for
emphasis. The dative νεκρῷ belongs jointly to πρεπόντων and ἐπισπένδειν,
and means not 'a corpse' but 'this corpse'. The line therefore means, 'If
one might pour upon his dead body such libations as really befit it'.

Thus far Headlam, following van Heusde, explains the passage correctly;
but, judging by his translation rather than his notes, I should say that he
just missed the meaning of the next line. Aeschylus has given all possible
emphasis to τάδε. The ἄν—strictly speaking an unnecessary ἄν, for im-
personal imperfects such as ἐξῆν do not require it—the ἄν follows and
stresses τάδε. And when τάδε is spoken, the whole significance of it was
left to the actor to interpret; by some gesture Clytemnestra had to show
that in 'pouring the fitting libations' she would be emptying the vials
of her wrath on the dead man; the libations proper to him are her curses ;
in the next sentence ἀραίων by its very position explains her meaning—'he
has filled our cup with evil, and now let him drain it himself along with the

curses those evils bring'; but superb acting was demanded so that that
τάδε should be understood as it was spoken.

And if this be the true interpretation, does it not follow that an optative
ἐκπίνοι is wanted in place of ἐκπίνει? Clytemnestra's revenge is not
achieved in full, her hatred is not allayed, by Agamemnon's death; her
curses are still justly, she claims, poured out like wine on the dead body;
'even though he be gone from this world', she prays, 'may he still drink
to the very dregs the cup of damnation'—ἐκπίνοι μολών. The very contrast
of μολών with ἐν δόμοις calls for this final imprecation. For the full purport
of such a curse see my Introduction (ad fin.).

1426-9. I adopt Hermann's ἐμπρέπειν for εὖ πρέπει, and punctuate
(with Paley) so as to make ὥσπερ...ἐπιμαίνεται parenthetic, and λίπος...
ἀτίετον dependent on ἔλακες. The word ἀτίετον in the sense of 'unpunished'
occurs in Eum. 839. The Chorus are referring to Clytemnestra's words,
βάλλει μ' ἐρεμνῇ ψακάδι φοινίας δρόσου (v. 1390).

1431. An imperative is far more satisfactory to my thinking than an
indicative, and I have given ἀκούεθ' in place of ἀκούεις. Clytemnestra has
addressed the Chorus previously in the plural at v. 1394 and again at
v. 1401.

1434. οὔ μοι φόβου μέλαθρον ἐλπὶς ἐμπατεῖ: Various renderings have
been proposed. Paley (accepting ἐμπατεῖν) translates: 'I have no expectation
of fear (for it) to tread in the palace'—a somewhat timid oath—while Verrall
and Headlam agree in rendering, 'my hope' (or 'my confident spirit') 'sets
no foot in the halls of Fear'. I cannot accept either, and I believe the
line to be corrupt, for the following reasons: (1) we want a future rather
than a present; (2) ἐμπατεῖν is not known to mean 'to enter'; its natural
sense is 'to trample upon' and it is so used in the late authors when
it occurs; (3) a tenuous reason perhaps to advance—my ear dislikes the
jingling rhythm of a line which should be majestic. No one of the reasons
alone is final, but cumulatively they persuade me that ἐλπὶς ἐμπατεῖ is
corrupt. Consider the effect of the massive and simple ἐμπελάσσεται in
its place; a future is provided; a word well proven in usage fits the
construction (cf. Soph. Tr. 17, πρὶν τῆσδε κοίτης ἐμπελασθῆναί ποτε); and
dignity of rhythm is achieved. Nor is it hard to see how the corruption
occurred: assume that a scribe once omitted two syllables and wrote ἐμπεται
and then corrected his error by means of a superscript ελασσ somewhat
cramped perhaps, and in the next stage our present MS. reading might well
have resulted.

1446. Hermann, accepting the scholiast's explanation of φιλήτωρ—viz.
ἐκ ψυχῆς φιλουμένη—which implies that the word is a compound of φίλος
and ἦτορ (cf. μεγαλήτωρ), gave τῷδ' in place of the MS. τοῦδ'.

NOTES 161

1447. I find no difficulty in the two genitives depending on παρο-ψώνημα—'the spice which her εὐνή gives to my χλιδή'. The word εὐνῆς picks up κεῖται φιλήτωρ τῷδε so clearly as to remove any possible ambiguity. Headlam's interpretation seems to me far-fetched.

1450. τὸν ἀεὶ φέρουσ' ἐν ἡμῖν | Μοῖρ' ἀτέλευτον ὕπνον: so the MSS. The words ἐν ἡμῖν are to my mind obviously corrupt, though, as so often in like cases, the traditional text has found scholars to defend it. My inclination is to look for another epithet of ὕπνον here; τὸν ἀεὶ...ἀτέλευτον is not a pleasing pleonasm; and ἄμηνιν suggests itself as the word I want. In L. and S. it is cited as occurring in Josephus only; but it is an obviously permissible alternative to ἀμήνιτος. The epithet is clearly appropriate; the Chorus seeks rest from μῆνις and all the manifestations of μῆνις which surround them.

1458–61. In view of the uncertainty which exists concerning the metre of this passage, no attempted restoration can be considered more than plausible. I believe the sense to be, 'Oh misguided Helen, all the destruction you caused at Troy has as its crown this calamity'. Taking ἀνδρὸς οἰζύς therefore, 'the calamity that has befallen Agamemnon', as the subject, I would substitute for ἐπηνθίσω (which is almost certainly corrupt) ἐπήκρισεν. The construction in simplified form would then be νῦν δὲ τελείαν πολύμναστον ἐπήκρισεν δι' αἷμ' ἄνιπτον τὴν τότε ἐν δόμοις οὖσαν ἔριν ἐρίδματον ἀνδρὸς οἰζύς. It was ἐρίδματος (which pace Hermann and others I take in its natural sense of 'firm-built') which suggested to me ἐπήκρισεν as the main verb. Hesychius and Eustathius say that ἐπακρίζω = θριγκόω, and I believe them to be right; for in Aesch. *Choeph.* 932, where alone the word occurs,

ἐπεὶ δὲ πολλῶν αἱμάτων ἐπήκρισε
τλήμων 'Ορέστης,...

the scholiast's interpretation ἐπ' ἄκρον ἦλθε is probably a mere guess based on a corrupt text. By all analogy ἐπακρίζω should be a transitive verb, and I believe that we should there read θημῶνα in preference to τλήμων. The two passages would then be closely akin in expression.

1470. I accept Pearson's δ', in preference to Hermann's τ', to mark what I believe to be the beginning of the main sentence.

1474. I have added δίκας to fill a gap in the text; 'she boasts that her lawless (or discordant) song is in honour of Justice'. Cf. vv. 1405–6 and 1432–3. The exact reading which the scholiast had before him is hard to determine, but it apparently had something to do with δίκη.

1479. The MSS. give νείρει, for which I have substituted νείκει (Scaliger). Casaubon's νείρᾳ (based on Hesychius, νείρη· κοιλία ἐσχάτη) does not appeal to me. A technical anatomical term seems out of place here.

LAA   11

1480. The line ends according to the MSS. with νέος ἰχώρ. Headlam's νέος ἴχαρ is ingenious, but ἴχαρ is neither known nor in my judgement likely to exist. I place a colon at τρέφεται, and read νεόχμ' ὦρτο. It has the merit of simplicity.

1492-3. κεῖσαι δ'...ἐκπνέων: In this refrain the Chorus picture themselves as standing by the dying Agamemnon; hence the tense of ἐκπνέων. As onlookers they address him—'in this tangled web hast thou been laid low to breathe thy last...'.
Since κοίταν appears to be a cognate accusative following κεῖσαι, I have given a comma only at ἐκπνέων.

1495. Enger's insertion of δάμαρτος after δαμεὶς here (and in v. 1519) merely in order to lead up to v. 1497 is not justified: ἐκ χερὸς alone, 'at close quarters', affords a good sense.

1497-8. αὐχεῖς εἶναι τόδε τοὔργον ἐμόν, whether read as a statement or as a question, does not fit well on to what has gone before; for the Chorus have made no strong assertion to that effect. Nor again do the following lines μηδ'...ἄλοχον fit on well to the Chorus' opening line; the μηδὲ would have to mean 'do not even...'; whereas, if the previous line had begun with μή, μηδὲ would mean simply 'nor'. Both difficulties disappear at once if we read μὴ δῆτ' αὔχει τόδε τοὔργον ἐμόν, and suppose that the insertion of an unnecessary εἶναι has led to the exclusion of μὴ δῆτ'.

1498. Hermann rightly suspected ἐπιλεχθῇς. Herodotus used the *middle* in a sense similar to that required here, but there is no parallel for this passive usage. My suggestion ἐνιδεχθῇς provides a word of similar appearance and well-attested usage.

1499. Maehly's conjecture κτεῖναί σφ' in place of εἶναί μ' would make the expression of thought more logical; but perhaps a little confusion of thought is not inappropriate here.

1507-8. The turn of expression is interesting. An ἀλάστωρ might be either some murdered man returning to this world to exact his own vengeance or some δαίμων acting on his behalf. The vague πατρόθεν may be understood in either sense. See my Introduction (*ad fin.*).

1509. βιάζεται...: This sentence provides almost a definition of an ἀλάστωρ (see Introd. *ad fin.*): 'there is a power of destruction (Ἄρης) from the nether world (μέλας) pressing on in pursuit of vengeance'.

1523-7.
> οὐδὲ γὰρ οὗτος δολίαν ἄτην
> οἴκοισιν ἔθηκ';
> ἀλλ' ἐμὸν ἐκ τοῦδ' ἔρνος ἀερθέν,
> τὴν πολύκλαυτόν τ' Ἰφιγένειαν
> ἀνάξια δράσας ἄξια πάσχων....

Thus the MSS.; and I am at a loss to understand how the first three lines have so long escaped criticism. There are four several counts on which I ask for judgement against them:

(1) οὐδὲ γὰρ οὗτος would mean 'Then did not he *either* commit treachery', and not as the context requires, 'Then did not he *too...*'. Verrall admits this in his note, but ignores the point in his translation.

(2) If οὗτος is the subject of the whole sentence, ἐκ τοῦδε is impossible Greek; it should be ἐξ αὑτοῦ or (where there is no great emphasis on the pronoun) ἐξ αὐτοῦ.

(3) No evidence is offered that ἀερθέν ever meant 'conceived' or 'begotten'. Headlam's rendering, 'that branch that grew from me, that he made grow', has a certain verbal plausibility in that αἴρεσθαι can be used of a certain kind of 'growth' (cf. Thuc. II. 75 ᾔρετο δὲ τὸ ὕψος τοῦ τείχους μέγα), but there is no parallel for the use of it in such a context as the present. Pearson's attempt (*Class. Review* XLIV. 55) to base an explanation on the Latin usage of *suscipere* (cf. Plaut. *Epid.* 561 *filiam quam ex te suscepi*) carries us no further; it is true, as he says, that 'ἀναιρεῖν and ἀναιρεῖσθαι are used either of the father or of an outside agent' who 'undertakes the charge of' a child; he might have added that ἀναιρεῖσθαι can be used too of a woman who conceives a child (cf. Herod. VI. 69); in fact ἀναιρεῖσθαι provides a complete parallel to the usages of *tollere* and *suscipere* in relation to children. But the usage of a compound of αἱρέω has no bearing on the use of αἴρω or ἀείρω.

(4) The τ' in the fourth line, which metre requires, has to be struck out, and πολύκλαυτον altered to πολυκλαύτην (a desperate remedy even though prescribed by Porson), if τὴν...Ἰφιγένειαν is to be in apposition to ἔρνος.

All these difficulties are swept away if the passage open in the most natural way with ὧδε γὰρ αὕτως and the ἀλλ' before ἐμὸν be omitted, as well as the mark of interrogation at ἔθηκ'. The participle ἀερθέν will then have a known meaning; the simple αἴρω (as well as the compound ἀπαίρω) bears sometimes the meaning of the Latin *tollo*—to 'remove' or 'do away with', and Hesychius expressly quotes ἀρθῆναι=ἀπολέσθαι; while the order of the pronouns ἐμὸν ἐκ τοῦδ' (which more than any other factor, I imagine, has led to the mistranslation of ἀερθέν) is now found to give the precise emphasis which the sentence requires. The Chorus have spoken of δολίῳ μόρῳ, and Clytemnestra defends the treachery as being part of her retaliation: 'Treacherous, you say? Yes, for there was equal treachery in the blow dealt to this house by *his* slaying of *my* child'. The subject of ἔθηκε is the whole composite phrase ἐμὸν ἐκ τοῦδ' ἔρνος ἀερθέν.

So then, as a result of this emendation, the MS. reading τὴν πολύκλαυτόν τ' Ἰφιγένειαν can stand,—provided, that is, that in the following line we do not accept Hermann's amazing suggestion of ἄξια for ἀνάξια. The latter

may not scan, but it does make sense: Hermann's ἄξια upsets the scansion
of the previous line, and requires a most artificial rendering (as = ἄξια ὧν
πάσχει) to produce sense. Surely the case is clear as regards ἀνάξια: it is
a perfectly good gloss on a word which it has itself ousted. What was that
word? All that we know is that, since Ἰφιγένειαν has the final syllable
short, the missing word began with a consonant, and that it bore the
meaning of ἀνάξια. After thinking over many possibilities, I select as most
probable ξένα δή.

1535–6. The MSS. in v. 1535 give δίκη and βλάβης instead of δίκα and
βλάβας, except that g has δίκα with η suprascript. The error in the case of
βλάβης has remained hitherto uncorrected, with the result that interpretation has been handicapped by the assumption that the word is in the genitive
singular, whereas the true form βλάβας may equally well be accusative plural
and furnish the object of the verb θηγάνει. If this view be adopted, it
remains only to choose between δίκα and μοῖρα as subject of the verb. I
think it *prima facie* probable that Δίκα should be the subject; Justice conceived as a ruling power is so prominent throughout the play; but further
the whole balance of the sentence appears to require Δίκα as subject, whereas
Μοῖρα can easily be altered to Μοίρας and read as dependent on θηγάναισι.

1539. ἀργυροτοίχου δροίτας: The epithet which the MSS. give appears to
me out of tone with the context; ἀγκυλοτοίχου is an easy alternative; it
will suggest that Agamemnon's body lies huddled within narrow limits
instead of lying in state on some princely couch.

1553. κάππεσε, κάτθανε, καὶ καταθάψομεν: So the MSS., but Paley in my
judgement was clearly right in ejecting κάτθανε as a gloss on κάππεσε,
and in filling its place with the indispensable ἡμεῖς.

1554. It may be true, as Hermann believed, that two lines have fallen
out after οἴκων, but there is no certainty that Clytemnestra's anapaestic
utterances were balanced as strophe with antistrophe.

1595. If Aeschylus is following the common version of the story, namely
that Atreus put the hands and feet of the dead children on one side in
order to confront Thyestes with them after he had eaten less recognisable
parts of their flesh (ἄσημα), the text with the substitution of Casaubon's
ἔκρυπτ᾽ for ἔθρυπτ᾽ is satisfactory so far as the contrast of the two clauses
τὰ μὲν... and ἄσημα δὲ... is concerned. But ἄνωθεν ἀνδρακὰς καθήμενος can
hardly be correct; for ἀνδρακὰς = *viritim* and ought to be used only to
qualify a plural. I suggest therefore ἄνευθεν (or ἄπωθεν) ἀνδρακὰς καθημένους, a second accusative after ἔκρυπτε. The change of subject in the
second clause, without specific mention of Thyestes, who obviously is
included in those described as ἄνευθεν καθημένους, does not seem to me

difficult in rapid narrative. There is a similar omission soon afterwards at 1606: the subject of συνεξελαύνει is left to the hearers' intelligence.

The substitution of ἔκρυπτε for ἔθρυπτε hardly needs defence; the tense settles the matter: ἔθρυπτε would mean 'he kept on chopping up', whereas ἔκρυπτε means 'he was keeping hidden'; for κρύπτω in the present means either 'to hide' or 'to keep hidden'.

1597. ἄσωτον, ὡς ὁρᾷς, γένει: This grim jest, accompanied by a gesture at ὡς ὁρᾷς, indicating Agamemnon, is necessarily expanded in my translation. It is in the same vein as προθύμως μᾶλλον ἢ φίλως, to which some editors have taken exception, in v. 1591.

1605. τρίτον γὰρ ὄντα μ' ἐπὶ δέκ' ἀθλίῳ πατρὶ, 'I was my wretched father's thirteenth child',—so runs the text of the MSS., and seldom has a scribe perpetrated a more humorous error. Instead of ὄντα μ' ἐπὶ δέκ' I have given ὄντ' ἐπίδικον,—'third in heirship'. Verrall, I observe, suggested ἐπίδικα...πατρὶ as meaning 'in satisfaction of my father's claim'—a piece of mockery put, as it were, into Atreus' mouth. But ἐπίδικον used quite naturally by Thyestes to lead up to τραφέντα δ' αὖθις ἡ δίκη κατήγαγεν offers, I think, a simpler restoration of the passage. As I read the passage, συνεξελαύνει in point of time refers back to v. 1585. Aeschylus' version of the story, I assume, is that, when Atreus first drove Thyestes out, he allowed him to take with him his third and youngest child, Aegisthus, then an infant in arms, but detained the two elder children, to serve perhaps as hostages; and that when Thyestes returned as a suppliant, hoping it may be to recover those two children, Atreus slew them and served them up at table. The phrase τρίτον γὰρ ὄντ' ἐπίδικον can properly refer back only to the time when the two elder children were still alive. Verrall certainly (see his Introduction p. xxxv and his note *ad loc.*) and perhaps others have read συνεξελαύνει as referring to events subsequent to the banquet.

1612 ff. The sequence of thought is clearly, 'Aegisthus, I will not condescend to abuse...but this much I say: due punishment will overtake you'. The more logical correction therefore of the MS. τόνδ' ἔφης in v. 1613 is not Pauw's τόνδε φὴς but τόνδ' εἰ φῂς, the portion of the sentence preceding οὔ φημι being preferably subordinate.

1625-48. After μὴ παίσας μογῇς (v. 1624), the MSS. give to the Chorus the speech beginning γύναι, σὺ τοὺς ἥκοντας...in the following form:

γύναι, σὺ τοὺς ἥκοντας ἐκ μάχης νέον
οἰκουρὸς εὐνὴν ἀνδρὸς αἰσχύνουσ' ἅμα
ἀνδρὶ στρατηγῷ τόνδ' ἐβούλευσας μόρον;

In this text αἰσχύνουσα is generally and rightly agreed to be the unintelligent correction of a scribe who believed that the Chorus were now addressing

166 NOTES

Clytemnestra, whereas γύναι is really a term of abuse applied to Aegisthus. We should read therefore (with Keck) αἰσχύνων,—not αἰσχύνας as several editors (following Wieseler) give. There is no reason for supposing that the scribe in changing the gender of the participle thought fit also to change the tense.

With the further treatment of these lines and of the whole altercation between Aegisthus and the Chorus I have already dealt in my Introduction (p. xxv). The remedy which I have there advocated in respect of these three lines is amended punctuation and transposition, so that after Aegisthus has said (at v. 1639)

τὸν δὲ μὴ πειθάνορα
ζεύξω βαρείαις...

the Chorus may retort

γύναι, σὺ τοὺς ἥκοντας ἐκ μάχης νέον;

and then continue with a statement (not a question),

οἰκουρὸς εὐνὴν ἀνδρὸς αἰσχύνων ἅμα
ἀνδρὶ στρατηγῷ τόνδ' ἐβούλευσας μόρον.

'It was only by staying at home and seducing Clytemnestra that you con-trived to kill their leader.'

For a full discussion of the other points involved in this transposition, see the Introduction.

1644. (=1626, as transposed.) There is no adequate reason for ejecting the σὺν of the MSS. and adopting Spanheim's νιν. If σὺν is retained, αὐτὸς means (as often) 'by thyself' (i.e. = μόνος), and ἔκτεινε will need to be read as imperfect, carrying on the tense of ἠνάριζες in the same sense.

I am tempted to wonder whether in choosing the word ἠνάριζες Aeschylus was associating it in any way with ἠνορέη as opposed to the word γυνή which follows. My translation is just coloured by that possibility.

1649–51. These lines have been distributed in various ways between Aegisthus and the Chorus, and lacunae also have been suspected. The rather pointless phrase ἔρδειν καὶ λέγειν has also been challenged, and Auratus' ἔρδειν κοὺ λέγειν has been incorporated in several suggested set-tings of the passage. I believe that correction to be right; but it will follow, I think, that the line containing ἔρδειν κοὺ λέγειν should follow, and not precede, that which contains τοὔργον οὐχ ἑκὰς τόδε. I therefore take εἶα δή, φίλοι λοχῖται... as Aegisthus' active response—rather than verbal reply—to the final insult of the Chorus, γύναι...μόρον. Then I assign to the Chorus ἀλλ' ἐπεὶ δοκεῖς τάδ' ἔρδειν κοὺ λέγειν, γνώσει τάχα, followed at once by their counter-summons to action εἶα δή, ξίφος πρόκωπον....

I understand δοκεῖς to be used as equivalent to ἀξιοῖς, as above at v. 16, like the English 'if you think to take action and not reply...'.

1653. The plurals δεχομένοις and αἱρούμεθα probably indicate that this last line in the crisis of the quarrel is to be spoken clamorously by the whole Chorus.

1656. The MSS. have πημονῆς δ᾽ ἅλις γ᾽ ὕπαρχε μηδὲν ἡματώμεθα. I am surprised that editors should have been content to accept Scaliger's ὑπάρχει· and continue with μηδὲν αἱματώμεθα (Jacob) or μηδὲν ἡματωμένοις (Hermann). Clytemnestra, I think, could not have said 'without any bloodshed'; she must have said 'without any *more* bloodshed'. But Scaliger was at fault too in converting the comparatively rare second person imperative of ὑπάρχω into the commonplace third person present indicative. The corrupt word in the line is, I suggest, ἅλις γ᾽. I would read

πημονῆς δ᾽ ἄλλης ὕπαρχε μηδέν· ἡματώμεθα.

There is dignity in that final perfect which denotes the irrevocable past.

1657-8. H. L. Ahrens' στείχετ᾽ αἰδοῖοι for the MS. στείχετε δ᾽ οἱ is a clever and safe correction. This phrase of the sentence ends obviously at δόμους. The following words of the MSS., πεπρωμένους τούσδε πρὶν παθεῖν ἔρξαντες (or ἔρξαντα) καιρὸν, need attention. Auratus first condemned τούσδε, which is *extra metrum*, and by common consent it is ejected. Next ἔρξαντα looks like an attempted correction of ἔρξαντες designed to restore correct scansion; it too may be disregarded. Then, passing to constructive proposals, I observe that πεπρωμένους is the leading word of the phrase; that again in the next short sentence χρῆν is the leading word; and finally that in the sentence after that there is a reference to δαίμων in the sense of 'fate' or 'destiny'. This suggests to me that we should read, say, Πεπρω-μένης if the remainder of the phrase will support that genitive. Now the only recommendation Clytemnestra can make to the Chorus, as regards fate, is that they shall yield to it—πρὶν παθεῖν, as she says. So then ἔρξαντες probably conceals εἴξαντες or στέρξαντες; both words have been tried by would-be correctors. The former would need a dative to follow it, the latter an accusative. Well, καιρὸν is an accusative, and, though we need a word beginning with a vowel, καιρὸν need not be altogether corrupt. What of οὖρον? Pindar, *Olymp.* XIII. 38, has the phrase δαίμονος οὖρον, and the whole phrase Πεπρωμένης, πρὶν παθεῖν, στέρξαντες οὖρον seems to me thoroughly Aeschylean.

If my emendation be right, the omission of the article with Πεπρωμένης implies the complete personification of Destiny under that name. Such personification was apparently unknown to Homer and Hesiod, and on the other hand was familiar to late writers like Lucian, who uses the name Εἱμαρμένη with or without the article freely (*e.g.* XLIII. *passim*, and LXXIV. 13). The earliest evidence which I can find bearing on the matter is supplied by two passages of Plato. In the *Gorgias* (512 E) he quotes τὴν εἱμαρμένην οὐδ᾽ ἂν εἷς ἐκφύγοι (for which cf. Aesch. *P. V.* 518) as a proverbial adage

favoured by women; and in the *Phaedo* (115 A) we have Socrates saying ἐμὲ
δὲ νῦν ἤδη καλεῖ, φαίη ἂν ἀνὴρ τραγικός, ἡ Εἱμαρμένη, where the phraseology
implies the tragic personification of Destiny. It is fitting then that Πεπρωμένη should be personified for the first time, if this be the first time, by a
woman and in tragedy; for what is true of εἱμαρμένη may be assumed true
of πεπρωμένη.

1673. The last word of each of the last two lines of the play is missing
in the MSS. The first of them could be nothing but ἐγώ, but editors have
not been well-advised in accepting καλῶς to end the play (on Canter's and
Auratus' suggestion) merely because the scholiast has the paraphrase: ἐγώ,
φησί, καὶ σὺ κρατοῦντες τῶνδε τῶν δωμάτων διαθησόμεθα τὰ καθ᾽ αὑτοὺς καλῶς.
That may indicate that the scholiast had καλῶς in his text, or it may not;
but one thing is certain, that θήσομεν καλῶς, without an accusative such as
the scholiast supplies, is not Greek.

Further the order of the words is to be noticed: the whole cadence of
the sentence indicates that τῶνδε δωμάτων depends on the final missing
word; for otherwise Aeschylus would have written ἐγὼ | καὶ σὺ δωμάτων
κρατοῦντε τῶνδε—πράξομεν καλῶς or whatever the ending might be. Karsten,
when he suggested τῶνδε πημάτων τέλος, appreciated what the order of
words implies—namely that κρατοῦντε is used absolutely, in contrast
merely with ματαίων,—'their yelpings are ineffectual, we have power'. But
Karsten's remedy is not justified unless there be no word in the Greek
language which will combine with θήσομεν to produce a phrase in which
δωμάτων may be retained. I have tried many words: I find one that satisfies me,—σέβας, with δωμάτων as objective genitive depending on it. Just
as κρατοῦντε balances ματαίων, so will σέβας provide an effective antithesis
to ὑλαγμάτων, and there is dignity in Clytemnestra's final words: 'Thou
and I, assured of power, will cause our house to be held in awe'.

For EU product safety concerns, contact us at Calle de José Abascal, 56–1°,
28003 Madrid, Spain or eugpsr@cambridge.org.

www.ingramcontent.com/pod-product-compliance
Ingram Content Group UK Ltd.
Pitfield, Milton Keynes, MK11 3LW, UK
UKHW012347130625
459647UK00009B/597